PROFESSIONAL
CAKE DECORATING

Photography by

STEVEN MARK NEEDHAM

Illustrations by

CHRISTINE MATHEWS

BICENTENNIAL
1807
WILEY
2007
BICENTENNIAL

JOHN WILEY & SONS, INC.

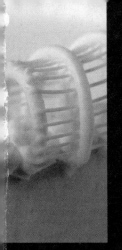

PROFESSIONAL
CAKE DECORATING

TOBA GARRETT

Published by John Wiley & Sons, Inc., Hoboken, New Jersey
Published simultaneously in Canada

Design by Mauna Eichner and Lee Fukui

For general information on our other products and services or for technical support, please contact our Customer Care Department within the United States at (800) 762-2974, outside the United States at (317) 572-3993 or fax (317) 572-4002.

Wiley also publishes its books in a variety of electronic formats. Some content that appears in print may not be available in electronic books. For more information about Wiley products, visit our web site at www.wiley.com.

Library of Congress Cataloging-in-Publication Data:

Garrett, Toba.
  Professional cake decorating / Toba Garrett ; photography by Steven Mark Needham ; Illustrations by Christine Mathews.
    p. cm.
  Includes bibliographical references.
  ISBN-13: 978-0-471-70136-1 (cloth)
  ISBN-10: 0-471-70136-X (cloth)
  1. Cake decorating.   I. Title.
TX771.2.G36 2006
641.8'6539--dc22

2005035002

Printed in the United States of America

10 9 8 7 6 5 4 3

To Phoenix, our love

Contents

Introduction

Professional Cake Decorating was developed as a book on the subject that is standardized, thorough in scope and technique, and a highly professional study guide that addresses the needs of a reemerging and growing industry. Over the past two decades, many of my professional and vocational students have expressed an interest in one book that teaches, explains, and guides them through the difficult and specialized techniques used in the cake decorating industry. I am happy to say that *Professional Cake Decorating* is such a book.

Drawing on thirty years of training, traveling, teaching, and running an independent cake decorating business, I unfold the secrets of cake decorating and teach this intricate art using more than 200 step-by-step and portrait photographs, more than 125 drawings and patterns, more than 35 tested recipes, a gallery of the most spectacular cake and confectionery art imaginable, and a plethora of personal hints and proven techniques.

This textbook is designed for the serious study and mastery of cake decorating. The student can expect a guiding hand to take them from the most basic techniques of piping cake borders and roses to designing a tiered cake featuring advanced embroidery piping, Australian string and bridgework, overpiped and cushion lattice techniques, a three-dimensional pastillage structure, hand-sculpted sugar roses, full-size fruits and vegetables made from marzipan, beautiful handpainted flowers, or a life-size water pitcher decorated with stunning piping and embroidery work that is filled with exquisite and exotic gumpaste flowers.

Each lesson ends with a review that reinforces the concepts and techniques presented and helps prepare the student for the upcoming lesson. Students can study in a classroom, kitchen environment, or independently at their own pace, as the book helps develop their professional habits and skills. Each chapter's practical review provides students the opportunity to continue practicing the skills and steps necessary to master the techniques.

An *Instructor's Manual* (0-471-78197-5) for *Professional Cake Decorating* is available to qualified adopters. This manual is designed to aid the instructor in delivering instructions in a clear and easy manner. It assists in designing lessons to fit students' needs, presents helpful hints and exercises for struggling students, and provides an answer key to each End-of-Lesson Review. The *Instructor's Manual* also provides steps and techniques for organizing and designing a curriculum for the length of time allocated to the cake decorating portion of students' training. *Professional Cake Decorating* is also designed for use by industry professionals such as bakers, cake decorators in small communities and large store chains, specialty shop owners, and independent cake designers.

For the small bakery, this book can be an invaluable resource for rejuvenating cake decorating skills. There is always a market for cakes that are professionally designed and executed. A professional training guide such as this book empowers bakers and gives them the confidence and the ability to try new techniques. *Professional Cake Decorating* can be useful in dramatically improving the overall look and design of cakes.

In larger establishments such as supermarket chains, *Professional Cake Decorating* can be a valuable training guide and an excellent resource for the baker and decorator. Supermarket training is relatively short and specific to the types of cakes produced. The supermarket artist is often limited in the designs used at the facility. However, customers often want a variation on a theme or something slightly different that may require a technique the decorator does not possess. This is a perfect opportunity to reach for a book that provides immediate assistance and quickly conveys the skills necessary to produce cakes to fulfill the customer's request. The improved cakes can increase sales and offer the customer more choices.

Professional Cake Decorating is also an invaluable guide to the established professional who is skilled in a wide range of techniques. I refer to other texts when custom designing for a client, thinking of new designs or options for a photo shoot, or reviewing an unusual technique. A book such as this is helpful when a technique is unfamiliar or when a project requires unusual skills, such as painting on a cake and knowing to mix gel or paste colors with liquid whitener to bring out the pastel shade of the food color. The icing on the cake is thus a canvas on which the artist can express ideas, no matter his or her skill level.

Professional Cake Decorating is also a baking text with a wide range of cake, sugarcraft, and icing formulas designed for small and large kitchens. Cake decorating books often lack recipes because the focus of the book is on how things *look* rather than how they *taste*. This book emphasizes the importance of good recipes, their functionality, and their scope. The reader has many recipes to choose from to apply their decorating skills.

Cake decorating is an art and requires consistent practice, just like learning a language. Skills must be studied and practiced to master them. *Professional Cake Decorating* is the perfect start. I hope this textbook is the one decorators, from students to professionals, reach for to learn, practice, and master cake decorating skills.

ACKNOWLEDGMENTS

Without the generous help and support of the following people, this book could not have been written. I owe them all a great deal of thanks and sincere gratitude. They are Nigar Hale; Julie Kerr; Scott Amerman; Amy Zarkos; Steven Mark Needham, my photographer; Christine Mathews, my illustrator; and Tina Cinelli, my chief assistant.

I would also like to thank Rick Smilow, president of the Institute of Culinary Education, for providing kitchen space; Mary Bartolini, for scheduling my space and offering a true helping hand; and my pastry colleagues, including

Nick, Andrea, Michelle (thanks for the chocolate recipe), Cara, Faith, Jeff, Gerri, Rebecca, Margaret, Scott, Reeni, Kathryn, Melanie, Chad, and Barbara from Florida. I also wish to thank the officers of the Institute of Culinary Education, including Steve Tave, Richard Simpson, and Ed Varites, and all the staff of the school for their constant support.

Thanks to my organizational families, including the Confectionery Arts Guild of New Jersey and the International Cake Exploration Société, for their continued support and love. To Maria McEvoy, Rosemary, Wally, Colette, Francisco, Janet, Toni, Marilyn (Mo), Jeanette, Jeannine, Stephanie, and to my many, many friends and colleagues in the cake and confectionery art community—too many to name and list—thank you all.

Special thanks to my husband, James Garrett, my lifelong partner; our beloved son, Phoenix; to my dad, George Edward; my beloved mother, Sarah Elizabeth; my sisters, Chicquetta and Valerie; and my brother, Kartrell; to my in-laws, James and Jean Garrett; and to Laurie, George, Sharon, Candy, my aunt Estelle; Jackie and family; and Jean and family.

And many, many thanks to the individuals instrumental in my development. These teachers come from many parts of the world. They are Elaine MacGregor, Eleanor Rielander, Geraldine Randlesome, Marite de Alvarado, Julie from Deco Cake & Candy School, Joan Mansour, Marie Sykes, Pat Simmons, Tombi Peck, and Pat Ashby.

I would also like to acknowledge the chef instructors who reviewed the proposal and manuscript for *Professional Cake Decorating*. They are Mark Cross, Capital Culinary Institute of Keiser College; Alison Dolder, Clark College; Lynne A. Johnson, Connecticut Culinary Institute; and Cheryl Miranda, Milwaukee Area Technical College.

Finally, thanks to my agent, Wendy Lipkind.

History of Cake Decorating

THE DEVELOPMENT OF THE CAKE

Cakes were very different during the time of the Roman Empire than they are today. Those cakes were actually very thin bread. For wedding nuptials, honey cakes or sweet breads made from rich fruit and nuts were used as sacred objects. These sweet elements were offered up to the gods and crumbled over the bride's head by her groom so she would be blessed with abundance and fertility.

Wedding guests picked up pieces of the broken cake to keep for good luck. Besides being seen as a charm of good fortune, the cake was also a symbol of fruitfulness. The Romans carried this tradition to Great Britain in 54 B.C., and it became part of local custom. Eventually, the crumbling of cake turned into the crumbling of, specifically, sweet wheat cakes. After the crumbled sweet wheat cakes were gone, the guests were supplied with sweetmeats, a mixture of nuts, dried fruits, and almonds. This was called *confetto*, and the tradition continued for hundreds of years. Eventually, the tradition was replaced with rice, colored paper, flower petals, and birdseed as new types of confetti.

In medieval England, the earliest form of a wedding cake was small spiced sticky buns stacked in a towering pile. Folklore has it that if the bride and groom could kiss over the pile, it brought a lifetime of health and prosperity.

Decorated cakes made their first appearance during the reign of Great Britain's Elizabeth I. They did not debut as wedding cakes, however, but as extraordinary centerpieces at banquets. Many were adorned with almond paste, which was known as *marchpanes* and dates back to 1494.

Bride's pie was popular at weddings. Elaborate ones were savories and contained fillings of oysters, pine kernels, lambstones, sweetbreads, and spices. Some contained minced meat or just mutton. The crust of the pie, however, was elaborately decorated. By the seventeenth century, bride's pie was replaced with the bridal cake made from flour, fat, yeast, dried fruits, almonds, and spices.

Cakes became popular in London society at this time, especially Oxfordshire and Banbury cakes, which have a high proportion of flour to fat and sugar.

Ale yeast was used as a rising agent. These cakes contained ingredients similar to those of their predecessors, such as dried fruits and spices, but the new recipes yielded a more breadlike mixture. By 1733, the Christmas cake or rich fruitcake was actually called plum cake. This cake quickly became a standard item. One early recipe called for currants, flour, cloves, cinnamon, mace, nutmeg, blanched and ground almonds, citron, lemon and orange peel, rosewater, ale, yeast, cream, and butter. Modern fruitcake recipes have not changed drastically. Some recipes omit the yeast and incorporate beaten egg whites. Some incorporate raisins and additional nuts.

In America, during the eighteenth century, rich or dark fruitcakes were not as popular. Pound cake and plain white cake were the staples of American cake making. White cakes were generally prepared as thin layers with a soft white frosting. The white cake represented purity and an affinity with the bride. A black cake was a fruitcake, iced in a hard icing (such as royal icing), and more likely to be called a wedding cake. Both white and black cakes were elaborately decorated in the English style to disguise the type of cake inside.

By the late 1890s both white and black cakes were commercially successful, with the white cake becoming the typical bridal cake and the black cake was the groom's cake. This was the American tradition, which still pertains in some parts of the country, but it did not carry back to England. The bridal cake today can be a white, pound, carrot, spice, German chocolate, or cheesecake, but the groom's cake is almost always chocolate, with a red velvet cake currently the most popular.

THE DEVELOPMENT OF ICING

More than two centuries ago, icing evolved from simple glazes. Usually the foundation of the glaze was rosewater syrup. This syrup was brushed on either a cooled cake or on a cake that just came out of the oven. The cake was then returned to the oven on low temperature and allowed to dry. As the cake dried, an opaque sheeting of white icing formed over it.

White icing was a lavish display in itself, and its whiteness was a direct indicator of the quality and expense of the sugar from which it was produced. White icing on a wedding cake two hundred years ago symbolized purity, virginity, and extreme wealth.

England has imported sugar since the Middle Ages. By the middle of the sixteenth century, sugar was readily available in a variety of qualities. By the mid-seventeenth century, double-refined sugar was available for purchase. Confectioner's sugar did not appear until the latter part of the nineteenth century.

From the seventeenth to the nineteenth centuries, the term *icing* usually meant that the cake was marzipan. Marzipan was chiefly a celebration food, considered both a substance and a delicious confection. As a substance, it was paired with sugar paste (also known as rolled fondant), and it could be shaped, sculpted, or molded into beautiful centerpieces. It could be rolled, cut, stamped out, or dried, and candied fruits or spices could be added to it. It could also be iced with glaze and dried in a warm oven before further garnishing. Icing continued to evolve until the mid- to late nineteenth century, when royal icing was accepted and the art of piping began.

The early stages of sugar paste (rolled fondant) developed as early as 1558. The recipe included rosewater, sugar, lemon juice, egg white, and gum tragacanth, then called *gum dragon*. This vegetable compound is still used in commercial rolled fondant today.

The term *double icing* was used in the mid-eighteenth century for covering a cake with almond-flavored icing (not marzipan) followed by a coating of sugar icing (an early royal icing). By the mid-nineteenth century, double icing had gained prominence, with marzipan used as the first icing followed by coats of royal icing.

THE DEVELOPMENT OF PIPING AND DECORATING

Piping was developed in the Bordeaux region of France, perhaps by accident, in the middle part of the nineteenth century. A French confectioner cut off the point of a paper cornet (then called a *poke*) and filled it with leftover meringue icing. He used it to write his name on his workbench. While the shop owner was displeased, he quickly realized the potential. The poke was later filled with royal icing, and the development of piping began. Soon after, the technology was refined, and small metal funnels with various shapes were developed by the French and made to fit into the bottom of the piping bag.

A typical wedding cake in the mid- to late nineteenth century in Great Britain was a neat and simple cake. It was covered with smooth white icing and white sugar paste roses around the top edge. The side of the cake might feature a band of large red roses with green leaves. The top of the cake was flat and plain, with a small vase of roses repeating the decoration of the sides. This was the direct forerunner of today's wedding cakes, and it made the development of the distinctive wedding cake style of elaborate, highly repetitive, and formal iced decoration possible.

In late nineteenth century Great Britain, the chief purpose of piping was for elaborate wedding cakes, often for the royal family. Heavy and elaborate encrustation developed and other techniques were established. Schülbé, a famous confectioner of the period, developed net and stringwork and lacy latticework, all piped separately and then attached to an iced cake. In 1882, heavily encrusted piped tops could be purchased for placement on an iced or non-iced cake. Piping continued to develop and rapidly became the norm for cake decorating.

During the Victorian era, royal weddings were the few occasions on which grand piping and sugar paste architecture was seen or displayed. In 1858, the cake for the Princess Royal and Prince Frederick William of Prussia wedding was between six and seven feet high and was divided into three compartments (now known as *tiers*), which were all in white. The first tier was heavily encrusted work on which stood a crown. Eight columns on a circular board supported an altar on which stood two cupids holding a medallion with the likeness of the Princess Royal on one side and the Prussian prince on the other. The middle tier contained niches with four statues depicting innocence and wisdom. The top tier was decorated with a plethora of orange blossoms and silver leaves. The sides of the cake displayed the coats of arms of Great Britain and Prussia, placed alternatively on panels of white satin. Between each coat of arms was a medallion of the bride and groom, encircled by orange blossoms and an imperial crown. When the cake was served, each slice was decorated with a medallion of the bride and bridegroom.

Most of this cake was not cake at all but icing architecture made from sugar paste and royal icing. When Prince Leopold was married in 1882, there were three tiers, and they were all cake.

CAKES AND CAKE DECORATING TODAY

In Great Britain today, rich fruitcakes are still used for a variety of celebrations, including christenings, birthdays, anniversaries, and weddings. These cakes are generally covered in marzipan and iced in royal icing. The designs are not nearly as elaborate as those of 150 years ago. The work today is simpler, yet exquisitely elegant and precise. Many cakes in Great Britain are also iced in rolled fondant. This medium gives the confectioner greater options in design and application. Icing a cake in sugar paste is far easier and faster than icing a cake in traditional royal icing.

The Australians have adapted the English style of cake making, but they use royal icing for piping and design work only, not as a cake covering. Sugar paste was adopted decades ago, as it cuts better and remains soft for a longer period. The cakes are first covered in marzipan and then in a layer of plastic icing (sugar paste and rolled fondant). Bernice Vercoe, author of *The Australian Book of Cake Decorating* (1973), says that royal icing is hard and brittle as a cake covering, and it tends to crack and separate from the cake when cut. She also talks about the time is takes to ice a cake in royal icing versus sugar paste, which can be rolled out and is extremely adaptable to cakes of any shape.

In South Africa, royal icing and sugar paste are both used as cake icing. This gives the cake artist flexibility and speed as well as the option for tradition. In the Philippines, Argentina, and Mexico, rolled icing is used both to ice the cake and to accent it. These cakes usually have three-dimensional sugar paste sculptures or exquisite floral designs on top to complete the confection. In the Caribbean Islands, rum and black cakes have a long tradition, and recipes are guarded and handed down from generation to generation. These cakes can be iced or not, but if iced, they are first covered with a layer of marzipan, then a coating of royal icing.

While royal icing dries hard, this is a positive feature for wedding cakes whose heavy upper tiers need to be supported. This approach was taken before doweling became popular. Also, adding a little glycerin to beaten royal icing helps it stay hard on the outside but soft inside. In addition, the invention of meringue powder—an egg white product with flavoring, salt, powder vanilla, and a preserve—made a royal icing that does not dry quite as hard as traditional royal icing.

PROFESSIONAL
CAKE DECORATING

Lesson

1

BASIC PIPING SKILLS

Basic Border and Floral Skills

You will need the following equipment and recipes to complete this lesson:

Swiss Meringue Buttercream Icing
(page 262)

Small paper cones

12-in. (30 cm) flex or
lightweight pastry bag

coupler

piping tips: #18 star, #2 round,
#67 leaf, and #352 leaf

gel food colors

toothpicks

full-sheet parchment paper

masking tape

scissors

rubber spatulas

small offset metal spatulas

small metal bowls

plastic wrap

Equipment

Before practicing cake decorating, it is important to be familiar with the equipment used by cake decorators. The right equipment is crucial to getting the best results; you need the right-size cake pan for baking the cake, the right parchment paper for lining the cake pan, and the right metal tip for each type of piped decoration. Having the right tools at the right time pays off both in the early stages of your training and as you move on to more difficult tasks.

The equipment in Illustrations 1.1–1.4 is grouped into four sections. These items are by no means all of the equipment you could use in professional cake decorating. Many other tools are shown throughout the book.

Illustration 1.1
Cake decorating equipment (counterclockwise from left): 28-gauge white florist wires, 24-gauge green florist wires, pack of white plastic stamens, two sable paintbrushes, cone and serrated tool, dogbone tool, Xacto knife, modeling stick, Chinese paintbrush, quilting tool, angled tweezers, metal ball tool, scissors, small offset metal spatula, large offset metal spatula, yellow cell pad, wire cutters, white plastic smoothers, nonstick rolling pin, ruler, electronic scale, and large plastic disposable pastry bag.

Illlustration 1.2
Cake decorating equipment (counterclockwise from left): PME 0 tip, clay gun with changeable disks, assorted crimpers, florist tape, icing nail, couplers, and assorted metal tips. The items are sitting on a ½-in. (1.3 cm) foil-covered corkboard.

Illustration 1.3
Cake decorating equipment (counterclockwise from right): white plastic rose leaf cutters, white plastic rose petal cutters, extra-large rose calyx cutter, small rose calyx cutter, large plastic rose leaf cutter, assorted flower formers, assorted plunger flower set, embossed leaf cutter, white plastic plunger blossom cutter and small leaf cutter, large silicone leaf press, small silicone leaf press, assorted metal cutters (for petit fours or cookies), tiger lily cutter, calla lily cutter, and medium-size metal calyx cutter.

Illustration 1.4
Cake decorating equipment (counterclockwise from left): squeezer bottles, color wheel, assorted ribbons, assorted petal dusts, adding machine paper, and assorted gel food colors. The items are sitting on a ½-in. (1.3 cm) foil-covered corkboard.

Introduction to Basic Border and Floral Skills

Welcome to your first lesson on basic border and floral skills. These essential skills are the bread and butter of our industry. The importance of learning them well can't be stressed enough. The more you practice these skills, the easier it will be for you to learn advanced skills. This book is designed to take you step by step, lesson by lesson, through learning this extraordinary art. Patience and practice must become your way of life if this is your passion.

New Skill: Paper Cones (Cornets)

Quick Prep

> Small triangle-cut parchment paper
> Small offset metal spatula
> Masking tape

Before you can begin piping, you must learn how to create paper cones, or cornets, which are essential to the decorator and pastry chef. These quick piping bags allow you to decorate cakes, plaques, cookies, petit fours, or any other medium that calls for piping. Paper cones provide control when piping; the smaller the bag, the greater the control. These cones are also quick to clean up because you just throw them out when the project is complete. Let's begin.

STANDARD CONE

The standard cone is used when a metal tip is to be placed inside the cone. This allows for accuracy and control when piping all sorts of icings. To begin, cut parchment paper into an equilateral triangle—that is, with the three sides of the triangle of equal length. Alternatively, fold a large piece of parchment paper in half lengthwise and then fold one end of the folded paper to the opposite corner, forming a triangle. Crease the paper with an offset metal spatula. Turn the paper over and fold the triangle shape upward to double the number of shapes. Continue turning the paper over and folding until you have used all of the parchment. Carefully cut each triangle with a pair of scissors or use an offset metal spatula. To cut with an offset spatula, place the spatula at the center crease of the folded triangular parchment. The spatula should be angled at 45 degrees with your opposite hand as a weight on the triangles. Move the spatula in a sawing motion—keeping your opposite hand firmly on the triangle until the triangles are separated. A full sheet of parchment paper measures 24 × 16 in. (60 × 40.6 cm). You can get 12 small paper cones from one full sheet of parchment paper. Let's make the cone.

If you are right-handed, mark the letter *A* at the left corner of the triangle, *B* at the top, and *C* on the right side. If you are left-handed, reverse the letters *A* and *C* only. The location of the *B* remains the same.

In your writing hand, hold the triangle-cut paper like a pyramid, supported by four fingers under the paper and your thumb on top. With your other hand, move angle *A* to angle *B* (see Illustration 1.5a). Once *A* reaches *B*, turn angle *A* around so it is in front of angle *B*. The angles should meet at the center without overlapping (see Illustration 1.5b).

Illustration 1.5
Making a standard paper cone.

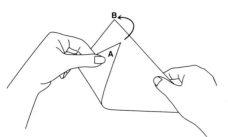

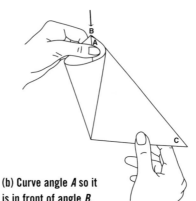

(a) Move angle *A* to angle *B*.

(b) Curve angle *A* so it is in front of angle *B*.

(c) Move angle *C* around and up the back of angle *B*.

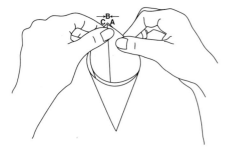

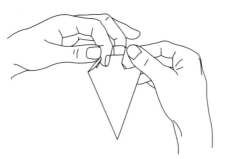

(d) Angles *A*, *B*, and *C* should not overlap.

(e) Turning the cone so the seam faces you, fold the flap and seal the edge.

Hold the top of *A* and *B* in your writing hand and use the other hand to move angle *C* around and up the back of angle *B* (see Illustration 1.5c). Adjust the cone so angles *A*, *B*, and *C* are dead center and not overlapping (see Illustration 1.5d). Turn the cone around so the seam faces you. Carefully fold about 1 in. (2.54 cm) of flap inside the cone and seal the edge of the cone with your fingernails (see Illustration 1.5e). The standard cone is complete.

When you are ready to use the cone, cut off about ½ in. (1.3 cm) of the point and drop a standard metal tip inside the cone. Add your piping medium and fold the left side of the cone toward the seam. Overlap the seam with the right side of the cone and then fold the top of the cone once or twice to secure the medium inside.

THE TAPERED CONE OR FRENCH CONE

The tapered cone is invaluable to the pastry student or decorator. This cone is tightly wrapped and more pointed and angular, so a metal tip is not required. This allows the decorator to pipe extremely fine lines.

To begin, mark the corners of an equilateral triangle as you did for the standard paper cone. Continue exactly as you did for the standard cone, with *A* on the inside, *B* in the middle, and *C* on the outside (see Illustrations 1.6a and b).

Turn the cone around so the seam faces you. Place your thumbs on the outside of the seam and your middle fingers on the inside seam. Begin to overlap seams *A* and *C* only. As you overlap seams *A* and *C*, pull up on the angles to

Decorator's Hint

Secure the seam of the paper cone with masking tape on both the inside and outside seams. Then, fold the top edge about 1 in. (2.54 cm) inside the cone.

Illustration 1.6
Making a French cone.

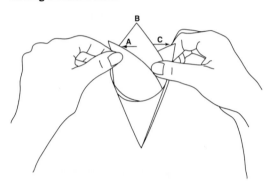

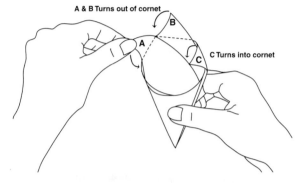

(a) Overlap angles *A* and *C* until angle *A* locks.

(b) Fold angles *A*, *B*, and *C* to complete the French cone.

shape the point at the bottom of the cone. Angle *B* remains still. Continue to pull up on angles *A* and *C* until angle *A* locks and you can't adjust it any more (see Illustration 1.6a).

Fold angle *A* outside the cone and seal it by pressing the fold with your fingernail. Fold angle *B*, which is on the inside, to the outside and seal with your fingernail. Then fold angle *C*, which is on the outside, to the inside and seal with your fingernail. The cone is complete (see Illustration 1.6b).

When you are ready to use the cone, place your piping medium inside the cone and fold the top to secure it. Cut the tip as small or as large as you wish and begin piping.

Icing Facts

For this lesson, you will prepare Swiss Meringue Buttercream (page 262). This classic icing is rich in texture and taste. It requires a great deal of butter and thus is considered a true buttercream. This icing is perhaps the most frequently used by pastry chefs, with Italian Meringue Buttercream as a close second. The flexibility and stability of both Swiss Meringue and Italian Meringue buttercreams mean you can use them to ice cakes and pipe borders with relative ease. In addition, you can use these icings as the base for other icings, including white and dark chocolate buttercreams, amaretto mocha, and praline mocha, to name a few.

The ingredients of Swiss Meringue Buttercream are butter, granulated sugar, egg whites, and flavoring. This is a cooked icing and must be carefully prepared. The egg whites and sugar are heated to 140°F. Heating them accom-

Special Note

In the commercial cake industry, this icing is rarely used, or it is prepared with a combination of butter and solid vegetable shortening. All-purpose vegetable shortening contains little or no water and leaves an aftertaste on the back of your palate. While this is acceptable in the baking industry, other types of solid vegetable shortenings can be used that do not have an aftertaste. High-ratio shortenings are used in the baking industry to replace butter or margarine. High-ratio shortening is considered an emulsifier and can be substituted for butter in recipes that call for butter or margarine. That is because it contains the same amount of water as butter and margarine. Additionally, it does not leave an aftertaste. You must add water to the regular solid vegetable shortening sold in supermarkets to make it a substitute for butter or margarine. Remember, however, high-ratio shortening is no substitute for actual butter or margarine.

Different types of high-ratio shortenings are covered in Lesson 3 (page 36): Buttercreams made largely with vegetable shortening are generally used in the commercial baking and cake decorating industry. This is discussed further in Lesson 2 (page 26), which introduces Decorator's Buttercream Icing.

plishes two goals. It allows the egg whites and the heat of the stove to dissolve the sugar granules. If they are not dissolved, the buttercream will taste crunchy and look unattractive. The second reason for heating the egg whites and sugar is that you will get more volume when you whip the mixture. The result is light and creamy icing that melts in your mouth. With it, you can

Color Facts

When coloring icings, remember that people eat with their eyes as well as their mouths. A soft pastel icing with accents of stronger colors is more eye-appealing than a cake iced entirely in electric blue or Christmas green. When coloring icing, remove a tiny amount of color using a toothpick. Add just a portion of the color on the toothpick to the icing and stir until you begin to see signs of the color. If a deeper shade is desired, add more color to the icing bowl. If you need a lot more color, use a clean toothpick to remove additional color, as fat or oil from the icing can contaminate the food colors. Remember, it is easier to add color than to take it away. If the color is stronger than you want, add uncolored icing to soften the deeper color.

ice a cake extremely well, pipe borders, and even write on the cake's top.

Prepare the icing for this lesson. If working in teams of two, prepare a medium batch. If working alone, prepare half of the small batch. Once the icing is prepared, remove 16 oz (454 g) from the batch. Color it a soft pastel tone if you like. Remove an additional 2 oz (57 g) from the batch and color it moss green or mint green. Place the rest of the icing in a plastic container with a lid or in a zippered bag and refrigerate until the next session.

In the pastry industry, for both baking and cake decorating, professional-strength food colors are used. These colors come in gel, paste, and powder. Gel colors blend easily but may require a little more color. Paste colors take a longer time to blend but require a little less food color. Powder food colors require a lot of color, as they are not as concentrated.

The different forms may yield different results. For example, a truer red is obtained from gel than from paste.

Prepare your pastry bag and load the coupler into the bag. Attach a #18 star tip to the end of the coupler. Place the cap over the tip. Your pastry bag is now ready. Prepare a small paper cone. Cut ½ in. (1.3 mm) from the tip and drop a #2 round metal tip into the bag. Load the cone with ½ oz (14 g) moss green icing and seal the paper cone. Both bags are now ready for this lesson.

Decorator's Hint

If you don't have moss green food color, use leaf green food color with a hint of chocolate brown to achieve a moss green.

Warm-up Exercises

Be sure to relax before you begin. Remember, learning a fascinating art takes a great deal of time and practice.

You will now be introduced to the pastry bag and the art of pressure control piping. You will find that by applying steady pressure, you can pipe amazing designs. Steady pressure improves your results for all piping tasks.

Anyone can squeeze a bag and watch icing squirt out all over the place. However, when you learn to control the squeeze, your icing will flow out of the bag with ease and will hold the shape of the bag's tip.

Next, determine your position in relation to the table or surface you are going to practice on. In a professional environment—bakery, restaurant, hotel, or specialty shop—space is limited, and you will almost certainly have to stand. In a classroom environment, where space permits, it is best to sit while practicing basic skills. Sitting helps you relax and develop control as you learn these crucial first stages of cake decorating. Later, after you have mastered basic skills and techniques, you should practice standing and piping, which is the norm in a busy kitchen.

Cake decorating contains many aspects of fine art, and standing is not appropriate for many of the tasks and techniques in this book. A cake decorator or designer in his or her own shop almost always sits while working. This is rarely possible in other professional environments, however, no matter how complicated the task. Of course, every kitchen is a different case. But you would be hard-pressed to find a pastry chef sitting in a busy restaurant or bakery!

Spread out a full sheet of parchment paper and tape the corners with masking tape. If your space is too small for the full sheet, cut it in half.

Now you need to figure out what position to start piping from and in which direction to move. Cake decorators generally pipe at a 90-degree angle or a 45-degree angle from the forward position. Variations on these two angles are occasionally needed for fullness or shape. These variations are discussed with the associated border piping techniques.

The type of border determines the direction in which to begin. If you are piping shells, ovals, reverse shells, rope, garlands, or any other borders that decorate the top or bottom edge of a cake, then you should start at the 9 o'clock position if you are right-handed and 3 o'clock if you are left-handed. As you begin to pipe, rotate the cake in the opposite direction. That is, if you start at the 9 o'clock position and begin piping counterclockwise, turn the cake clockwise as you make your way around it. You will start and end at the 9 o'clock position. Now, let's begin.

Pick up your pastry bag and position the star tip at a 45-degree angle to the surface. If you're not sure what a 45-degree angle is, place the tip perpendicular to your work surface, with the pastry bag straight up and down and the tip touching the surface. This is a 90-degree angle. A 45-degree angle is half the distance from 90 degrees to the surface. Move your hand and bag toward you, half the distance from 90 degrees. You are now at a 45-degree angle (see Illustration 1.7).

Illustration 1.7

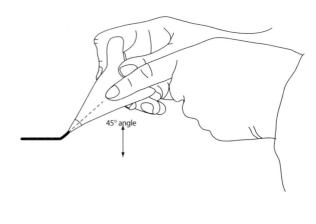

(a) A paper bag at a 90-degree angle.   (b) A paper cone at a 45-degree angle.

Hold the pastry bag in your writing hand and use your opposite hand for control. This is crucial to good decorating. With one or two fingers of the opposite hand, touch the pastry bag or tip for control. Apply an even amount of pressure and allow some of the icing to expel from the bag. Gently lift the bag about 1 to 2 in. (2.5 cm to 5 cm) as you continue to apply pressure. Allow the icing to flow through the tip to form a line (see Illustration 1.8). Gently pull the bag to-

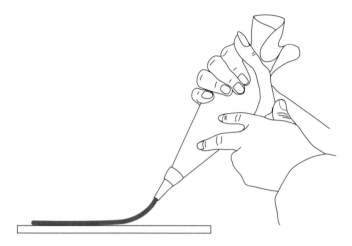

Illustration 1.8
A straight line is piped by lifting the icing tip from the surface and applying even pressure.

ward you as you continue to squeeze. By lifting and squeezing with even pressure, you can pipe a straight line. When you want to end the line, gently lower the tip toward the surface and start easing off the pressure. Touch the surface and stop the pressure. Drag the tip toward you. If the piped line is bent or shows no control, keep practicing.

Next, practice piping a curved line using the same technique. The higher you lift the tip, the better you can see the line or curve as it is piped (see Illustration 1.9). As long as you continue to squeeze, the line of icing will not break. If the line breaks, you know you stopped squeezing without noticing it. Continue practicing until you can pipe straight and curved lines perfectly.

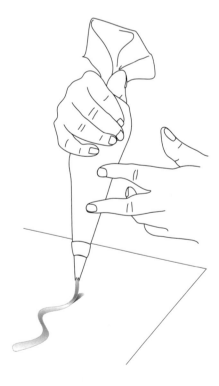

Illustration 1.9
Piping a curved line.

Now, let's practice the circle. Draw some circles on your parchment paper. Using the same technique as for straight lines and curves, touch the surface at either the 9 o'clock or 3 o'clock position. Raise the tip as you squeeze with even pressure. The higher you raise the tip, the better you can see the circle (see Illustration 1.10). When you are ready to close the circle, gently lower the tip and bag as you ease off the pressure. Try this a few more times until you can pipe perfect circles. (See examples of a piped circle, curved line, and straight line in Illustration 1.11.) You are now ready to begin border skills.

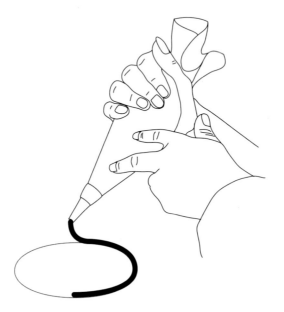

Illustration 1.10
Piping a circle.

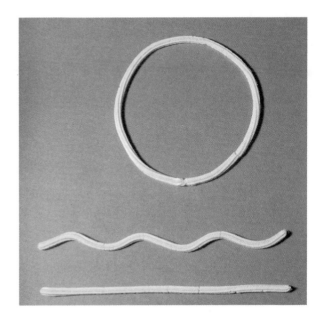

Illustration 1.11
A piped circle, curved line, and straight line.

Practicing Border Skills

New Skill: Star Flower

The star flower is the most basic piped flower. While it is extremely easy to do, it can be done poorly and look awful. Repeated star flowers form a border when piped along the top edge of a round or rectangular cake. However, this flower looks best piped in clusters of three and with tiny leaves between each seam. You will learn to pipe leaves toward the end of Lesson 1.

To begin a star flower, position the #18 star tip and pastry bag at a 90-degree angle to the surface. The tip should touch the surface and should not be lifted until the flower is formed. If you are piping on a buttercream-iced cake, refrigerate the cake first to harden the surface. Apply a burst of pressure, allowing the icing to protrude about ¼ in. (6 mm) from the tip. Stop the pressure immediately and ease the tip straight up. This forms an attractive flower with an open center. If you jerk the tip up too quickly, it will injure some of the petals as you exit. Continue to pipe this flower in clusters of three. Alternatively, pipe lines of this flower, allowing ¼ to ½ in. (6 mm to 1.3 cm) between each.

To complete the flower, add a center in a contrasting tone with a #2 round tip in a small paper cone. To do this, position the tip at the flower's center, between a 45-degree and 90-degree angle, barely above the surface. Apply a small amount of pressure and stop. Move the tip to the left or right to exit the piping. Stop and ease the tip from the center of the flower.

VARIATIONS

You can also pipe the star flower without a center. To achieve this, position the #18 star tip at a 90-degree angle to the surface of the cake or practice surface. Apply a burst of pressure and allow the icing to extend about ¼ in. (6 mm) from the tip. Before you stop the pressure, gently raise the tip about ¹⁄₁₆ in. (1 mm). Next, stop the pressure and pull the tip straight up to exit the flower. The center of the flower is now closed and requires no center.

Another variation is the commercial star flower seen in many bakeries. This type is achieved by raising the tip about ¼ in. (6 mm) from the surface at a 90-degree angle. Squeeze the pastry bag and allow the icing to touch the surface. Stop the pressure and pull the tip straight up. The flower has a puffy look and is acceptable when doing fast decorating in a busy environment.

Last, try piping a star flower with a slight twist. Position the tip at a 90-degree angle with the tip touching the surface. Apply a burst of pressure as you form the flower, but before you stop the pressure, lightly twist your wrist to the left or right. Stop the pressure and ease the tip up. You now have a star flower with a twist (see Illustration 1.12).

Decorator's Hint

1. If the icing is too soft, it is difficult, but not impossible, to give the star flower an open center. Simply stop the pressure when the flower is made and gently ease the bag straight up. Centers are easier using Swiss and Italian Meringue Buttercreams than other buttercreams.

2. If you are right-handed, move the tip to the right to complete the flower's center. If you are left-handed, move the tip to the left.

Decorator's Hint

If the icing is too soft, the center automatically closes when you exit the flower. To stiffen Swiss Meringue Buttercream, refrigerate the buttercream or place it over a bucket of ice. To stiffen other buttercreams, add 10x confectioners' sugar to the individual bowl. This should correct the problem.

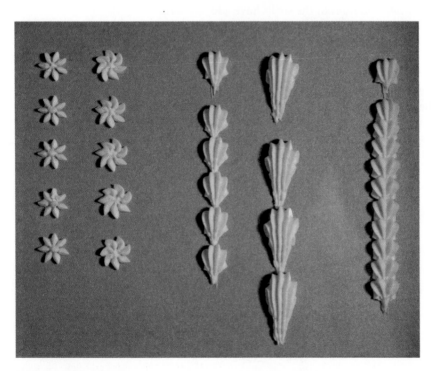

Illustration 1.12
From left to right: star flower variations, small and large shells, and ballooning.

New Skill: Small Classic Shells

Shells are the bread and butter of cake decorating. You cannot pass a bakery without seeing shell borders on the top or bottom of a cake. It is simply the most widely used border. Unfortunately, it is often not done well, so practice and patience will put you in front of your competitors.

Small shells or classic shells can look striking and tailored. Use these shells on cakes ranging from 4 to 7 in. in diameter (10 to 17.8 cm). Use a #18 star tip for small shells.

To begin a classic shell, position your star tip at a 45-degree angle and touching the surface. (Be sure to refrigerate iced cakes first to firm the surface before using this technique. A firm surface is essential to achieving the desired results.) Apply a burst of pressure, allowing a small amount of icing to protrude from the tip. Push the tip forward slightly and apply more pressure, building up the head of the shell. Then, slightly pull the tip toward you, easing off the pressure. Stop the pressure and pull toward yourself to exit the shell.

To connect the next shell to the first, place the tip about ¼ in. (6 mm) behind the previous shell. Repeat the instructions for the classic shell. When you move forward, touch only the tail of the previous shell and continue to pull the tip toward yourself. Practice this until you have perfected the technique (see Illustration 1.13).

New Skill: Large Shells

Large and sumptuous shells are magical. Although making them is a basic skill, doing it well can be one of your strongest assets in the cake decorating industry. These shells take on a form of their own. They are wide at the top and narrow at the bottom. The sides of the shells have a lovely scroll.

To begin, position your tip and pastry bag at an angle between 45 degrees and 90 degrees. If you want the sides of the shell to look scrolled, the angle should be closer to 90 degrees. Raise the tip slightly from the surface. Apply a burst of pressure and allow a small amount of icing to protrude from the tip. Move the tip slightly forward and continue with pressure as you build up the head of the shell. Then, gradually pull the tip toward you and lower the tip to scratch the surface. Ease off the pressure and stop. This isn't easy! Learning to pipe large shells takes a lot of practice and a looser grip on the pastry bag (see Illustration 1.13). Continue practicing for a good 15 minutes and then go on to the next border—but come back later and practice this again.

Decorator's Hint

If condensation builds up on an iced cake after it is removed from the refrigerator, the only thing to do is to let the cake sweat. Eventually, the moisture will be reabsorbed by the icing. However, if a lot of fine pipe work in royal icing was on the cake when it was refrigerated, some of it may collapse. You can purchase special refrigerators that zero out the humidity, but they are expensive. Cakes iced with buttercream should not sweat. If they do, the only solution is to let them rest at room temperature and allow the icing to reabsorb the moisture.

Decorator's Hint

The type of icing used for piping large shells will vary in the way the shells look. For instance, if you pipe these shells using Swiss Meringue Buttercream, you need less pressure to form them than if you use the Decorator's Buttercream Icing, which is firmer. Firmer icing allows more control as you build your skills and accomplish beautiful large shells.

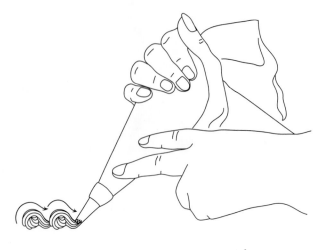

Illustration 1.13
Shells can be piped one after the other for a seamless effect.

New Skill: Ballooning

Ballooning is the technique of piping small classic shells without tails and then piping the next shell directly in back of it. These shells look like herringbone. This is a nice technique that can be used to adorn the top edge of a cake. If you are careful, they can be used at the bottom edge too.

Position the tip and pastry bag at a 45-degree angle. Apply a burst of pressure, allowing some of the icing to expel from the tip. Slightly push the tip forward to build the head of the shell and then pull toward you. Stop the pressure. Immediately repeat this step, pushing the head of the shell into the back of the previous shell so they are piggybacked. Repeat to form a beautiful pattern that resembles herringbone (see Illustration 1.12).

New Skill: Zigzag

The zigzag is perhaps one of the easiest bottom borders to create. A zigzag border gives the illusion that the cake is larger than it really is. That is because only one side of the border actually touches the cake, while the bulk of the icing decorates the cake board.

To begin a zigzag border, position the tip and pastry bag at a 45-degree angle. Apply a burst of pressure as you drag the tip to the left or right side about ½ in. (1.3 cm). Then move the tip slightly down and drag it in the opposite direction (see Illustration 1.14). Continue piping and dragging the tip back and forth until you complete the border. For a larger or thicker border, slightly raise the tip from the surface as you move it back and forth.

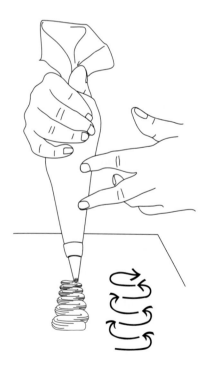

Illustration 1.14
The piping tip is moved in one direction and then in the opposite direction for a zigzag effect.

VARIATIONS

For a lavish, formal look, pipe shells directly on top of the zigzag. To do this, first pipe the zigzag. Then position the tip at the rightmost edge of the zigzag. Pipe the large shells directly on top, but be careful not to injure the zigzag (see Illustration 1.15.)

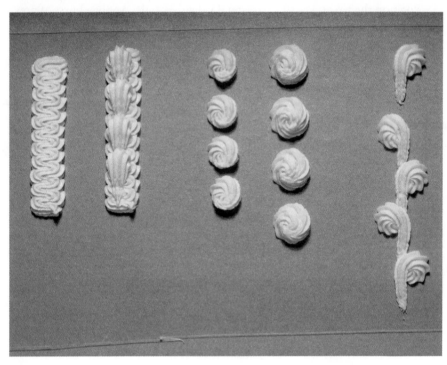

Illustration 1.15
From left to right: zigzag variations, small and large rosettes, and reverse shells.

New Skill: Rosettes

Rosettes are a staple in the world of cake decorating. They are typically piped from whipped ganache but can be made from buttercreams or whipped sweetened cream. Twelve very large rosettes adorn a 10-in. (25.4 cm) round cake. These often have cocoa powder sifted over them and a coffee bean or a candied violet placed on top. Like star flowers, rosettes look best in clusters of three with small leaves between each seam. You will learn to pipe leaves at the end of this lesson.

To pipe a small rosette, position the #18 star tip and pastry bag at a 90-degree angle. Remember, a right-handed person will start at the 9 o'clock position and a left-handed person at the 3 o'clock position. Raise the tip slightly from the surface. Pipe a tight circle without any space in the center. Once you pipe this one circle, stop the pressure but continue to move the tip in a continuous motion. Ease the tip away from the rosette.

To pipe a large rosette, you can use the same tip that you used for small rosettes but apply greater pressure, or you can use a #22 star tip or any giant star tip. Position the tip exactly, as if you were piping a small rosette. When you pipe the first circle, leave a space in the center. Once you complete the circle, move the tip in a continuous circular motion inside the center of the rosette. Ease off the pressure and gently move the tip away from the rosette (see Illustration 1.15).

New Skill: Reverse Shells

When piped on a round or rectangular cake board, reverse shells give the appearance of beautiful sculpted scrolls. While they are invaluable as a quick technique to dress up a cake, they do require strict attention to make them lush and uniform.

For practice, draw a line down the middle of your work surface with a nontoxic pen or pencil. Position the #18 star tip and pastry bag at an angle between 45 degrees and 90 degrees to the left of the line. Raise the tip slightly from the surface and apply a burst of pressure. Move the tip in a clockwise direction. When you reach the 11 o'clock position, apply more pressure and swing the tip around and down to the 6 o'clock position. The tail end of the reverse shell should be about ½ in. (1.3 cm) long.

Next, position the tip to the right of the just completed reverse shell, with the tip again at an angle between 45 degrees and 90 degrees. The tip should be close to the tail end of the shell but slightly to the right of it. Raise the tip slightly from the surface and apply a burst of pressure. Move the tip in a counterclockwise direction. When you reach the 1 o'clock position, apply more pressure and swing the tip around and down to the 6 o'clock position, overlapping the previous tail. Extend the tail to ½ in. (1.3 cm). Repeat in the opposite direction to continue the reverse shells (see Illustration 1.16).

Decorator's Hint

The purpose of piping reverse shells in a straight line is to emphasize the elegant length of the tail. This detail is often missing when reverse shells are piped in a curve on a round cake. A short tail end is overwhelmed by the top portion of the shell.

When you pipe reverse shells on a round cake, swing the tail end toward the center of the round to form the left side of the shell. When piping the right side of the reverse shell, end the tail about ¼ in. (6 mm) from the circle's edge.

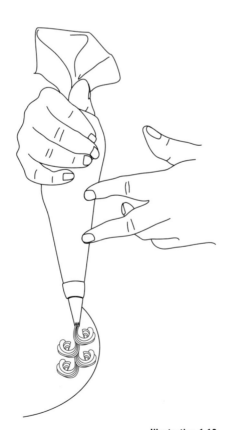

Illustration 1.16
Piping reverse shells.

New Skill: Fleur-de-Lis

This beautiful border flower is not used in the same way as the star flower or rosette. It is typically formed at the top edge of the cake and extends down the sides. A fleur-de-lis is simply a large centered shell with two reverse shells—a perfect wedding cake border design.

If piping on a flat surface, first position the #18 star tip at an angle of 45 to 90 degrees. If applying this technique to an iced cake, position the tip at a 90-degree angle at the top edge of the cake (see Illustration 1.17). Raise the tip slightly from the surface and apply a burst of pressure, allowing some of the icing to extend from the tip. Move the tip forward slightly. Continue with pressure as you build up the head of the shell, then gradually pull the tip toward you. Extend the tail of the shell about ¾ in. (1.9 cm) or ¼ in. (6 mm) longer than a regular large shell. Ease off the pressure as you scratch the surface.

Decorator's Hint

The fleur-de-lis is usually accompanied by drop strings that connect one fleur-de-lis to another. This technique is covered in Lesson 4.

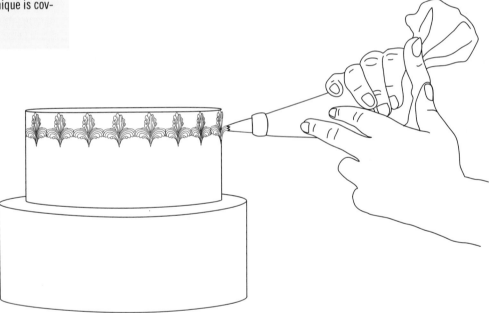

Illustration 1.17
When piping along a cake edge, hold the piping tip at a 90-degree angle.

Next, position the tip at the bottom of the shell. Move the tip ¼ to ½ in. (6 mm to 1.3 cm) to the left of the shell. Then move the tip upward ¼ to ½ in. (6 mm to 1.3 cm). Position the tip and pastry bag at an angle between 45 and 90 degrees. Raise the tip slightly from the surface and apply a burst of pressure. Move the tip in a clockwise direction. When you reach the 11 o'clock position, apply a burst of pressure and swing the tip around and down to the 6 o'clock position. The tail end of the reverse shell should overlap the centered shell. Stop the pressure and ease away. Move the tip to the right ¼ to ½ in. (6 mm to 1.3

cm) and then upward ¼ to ½ in. (6 mm to 1.3 cm). Raise the tip slightly from the surface and apply a burst of pressure. Move the tip in a counterclockwise direction. When you reach the 1 o'clock position, apply a burst of pressure and swing the tip around and down to the 6 o'clock position. The tail should overlap the left and centered shell. Stop the pressure and ease away (see Illustration 1.18).

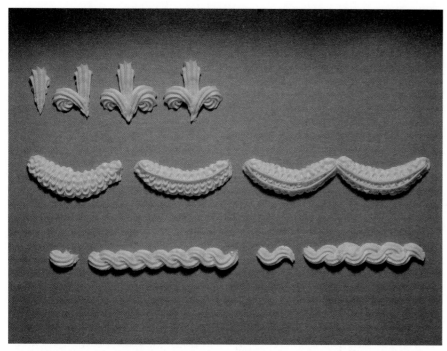

Illustration 1.18
From top to bottom: the steps to create fleurs-de-lis, steps to create connecting garlands, and *C*-shape and *S*-shape rope variations.

New Skill: Garlands

While the most common name is garlands, in the United States they are sometimes called scallops, and in Great Britain they are called crescents. By any name, the look is lush and lavish if carefully done. This cake decorating technique perhaps works best on the side of the cake, near the top edge. It can also be used near the bottom of the cake just above the bottom border. The technique is similar to the zigzag bottom border, but tighter. Variations can make this border spectacular!

To practice, measure equal distances on your work surface. For example, use a graphite #2 pencil to draw the shapes on parchment paper. Each part of the garland should be shaped in a half-circle about 2 in. (5 cm) long. Mark five connected half-circle or scallop shapes for practice.

When ready, position the #18 star tip and pastry bag at an angle of 45 degrees. For right-handers, position your body at the 9 o'clock position. For left-handers, position your body at the 3 o'clock position. Apply a burst of pressure as you drag the tip to the surface in a tight zigzag motion. Start out with light pressure, increase as you reach the center of the scallop, and decrease as you approach the end of the scallop. Repeat this technique to form the pattern (see Illustration 1.19).

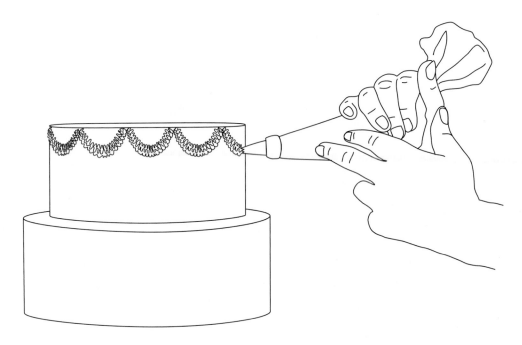

Illustration 1.19
Piping garlands on a cake adds a beautiful effect.

VARIATION

For a more ornate look, use a #2 round metal tip and a contrasting icing color to pipe lines on top of the completed garlands. This striking addition upscales a plain garland to a real beauty. To begin, load the pastry bag or a small paper cone with a #2 round metal tip and the contrasting icing. Position the tip at the top edge of the first finished garland at a 45-degree angle. Apply pressure to the bag as you slowly raise the tip about ½ in. (1.3 cm) above the garland. Allow the icing to form a scalloped shape as it lies across the center of the garland. Lower the tip and reduce the pressure as you reach the end of the scallop. Repeat for additional garlands. For a double string line, repeat this procedure, starting with the first garland, but let the second line drop below the centered line. Taper the end of the string to the garland (see Illustration 1.18).

New Skill: Rope

The rope border is a perfect finish for an iced cake. It is often seen as a top border on a basket weave cake. It is also sometimes seen as a top and bottom border, although piping it at the bottom is a little sticky. There are two ways of piping this border: the half-*C*, or open quotation mark, and the *S* shape.

C shape: For a right-handed person, position the tip and bag at a 45-degree angle. Slightly raise the tip from the surface. Pipe a small curve that looks like an open quotation mark or a half-*C*. For a left-handed person, pipe a closed quotation mark, or a backward half-*C*. Next, hold the tip perpendicular to the surface in the center of the curve. Apply steady pressure as you raise the tip and end the stroke slightly in front of the first curve. The pipe stroke should look like a backward *S*. Position the tip in the center of the next curve and make another backward *S* (see Illustration 1.20).

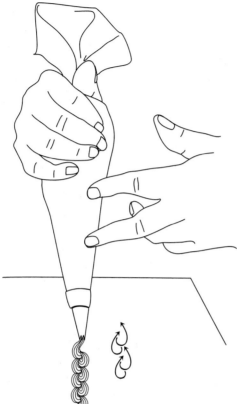

Illustration 1.20
Backward and forward half-*C*s are used to create this rope effect.

S shape: For a right-handed person, pipe a small elongated *S* at a 45-degree angle. For a left-handed person, pipe an elongated backward *S*. Position the tip perpendicular to the center of the bottom curve. Apply pressure as you raise the tip slightly and pipe an *S* shape. Repeat this pattern until you have piped the rope (see Illustration 1.18).

New Skill: Leaves

Leaves complete a floral spray by adding fullness and lushness. They can also be used alone as a decorating motif for a fall cake, and they are especially impressive when used with grapes and sweet pea clusters (see Lesson 3).

Several tips are used for leaf piping. The most common are the #67 (small leaf) tip and the #352 leaf tip. Both tips produce realistic-looking leaves; however, the #352 is the favorite of most decorators and designers because it pipes a quick and easy leaf without any fuss. The #67 tip requires extra-soft icing or royal icing, and the leaves tend to split unless your pressure control is precise. In this exercise, you will practice with both tips (see Illustration 1.21).

Load a small paper cone with a #67 tip and second small paper cone with a #352 leaf tip. Add 1 tsp of moss green buttercream icing to each cone and carefully fold them closed. Practice using the #67 tip first.

Illustration 1.21
From left to right: leaves piped with a #352 leaf tip and a #67 small leaf tip.

To begin, position the #67 tip and small paper cone at a 45-degree angle. Position the pointed side of the tip at a 45-degree angle. You should be able to see the open side of the tip through the sides. Because the cone is quite small, place your thumb on one side of it and your fingers on the other. Touch the surface and apply a burst of pressure. Build-up the top of the leaf and gently ease-off the pressure. When you stop, the end of the leaf should come to a point. If it doesn't, the point of the leaf splits apart. Should the point of the leaf come apart, use a toothpick to push it together. The icing is too stiff and needs more liquid in the icing. The leaf should be ½ to 1 in. (1.3 to 2.54 cm) in length. Swiss Meringue Buttercream should be soft enough to do this with good results. Buttercream that is too soft (or too stiff) will result in a distorted leaf shape. If you are using a stiffer buttercream, add ½ tsp (2.5 ml) of liquid to 4 oz (114 g) of buttercream for a softer consistency.

With the #352 leaf tip, piping leaves is much easier, even with stiff icing. Position the open side of this tip at a 45-degree angle. Apply a burst of pressure and leave the tip in place for a few seconds to build up the head of the shell, then pull the tip toward you. Stop the pressure. The leaf ends in a pointed tip, which is what you want. Leaves made with a #352 tip should be ¼ to ½ in. (6 mm to 1.3 cm) in length.

END-OF-LESSON REVIEW

Pipe the following exercises on a rectangular cardboard or a parchment half-sheet. The presentation of these borders is extremely important.

1. Pipe two rows each of classic and large shells (20 shells each).

2. Pipe 20 rosettes (10 small and 10 large).

3. Pipe a line of reverse shells (a total of 8 left and 8 right shells).

4. Pipe 6 fleurs-de-lis.

5. Pipe 6 garlands with strings.

6. Pipe a rope line using the *C* and *S* shape techniques.

PERFORMANCE TEST

Choose two of the three following items:

1. Pipe small or large shells around a 10-in. (25.4 cm) cake circle.

2. Pipe reverse shells around a 10-in. (25.4 cm) cake circle.

3. Pipe a rope border around a 10-in. (25.4 cm) cake circle using the *C* or *S* technique.

FLORAL PIPING SKILLS

Rosebud, Half-rose, and Full-blown Rose

You will need the following equipment and recipes to successfully complete this lesson:

Decorator's Buttercream Icing (page 260)

Buttercream Icing for Piped Roses (page 266)

small paper cones

12-in. (30 cm) flex or lightweight pastry bag

couplers

piping tips: #103 or #104 petal-shape tip, #2 round tip, #67 or #352 leaf tip

#6 or #7 icing nail

2 × 2 in. (5 cm) pieces of parchment paper

gel food colors

toothpicks

full-sheet parchment paper

masking tape

scissors

offset metal spatulas

rubber spatulas

small metal bowls

plastic wrap

Lesson 2 focuses on developing strong basic piping skills. In this lesson, you will make rosebuds, half-roses, and full-blown roses. These flowers are formal in appearance and provide immediate gratification. They are useful in the following ways: on iced cakes, as part of a formal floral spray, or individually on cookies or cupcakes.

Special attention is required, as these flowers look odd when they are piped too quickly. Often, in the industry, you have little time to pipe a perfect flower. In a busy bakery or restaurant, time is money. Thus, one often sees fragmented elements of a rose rather than a beautifully piped flower.

Decorator's Buttercream Icing is the primary medium for producing these flowers in this lesson, as it is most suitable and stable. You will use Buttercream Icing for Piped Roses, a stiffer version of Decorator's Buttercream Icing, when you learn to pipe full-blown roses. Flowers made of Royal Icing (page 273) are introduced in a later lesson.

Skills Check

Before starting this lesson, it is important to have a full understanding and practical knowledge of basic borders covered in Lesson 1. Because these new skills are based on old skills, a thorough and careful review of top and bottom borders is essential.

The makeup of both Decorator's Buttercream Icing and Buttercream Icing for Piped Roses is the opposite of the Swiss Meringue Buttercream. Buttercream Icing for Piped Roses is based on the Decorator's Buttercream. The icing for piped roses is stiffer and does not break down nearly as quickly as the Decorator's Buttercream Icing. These buttercreams have a higher ratio of sugar to fat, whereas Swiss Meringue Buttercream has a higher fat-to-sugar ratio. (This is why using an emulsified shortening is important.) Adding meringue powder (dried egg white) to Decorator's Buttercream causes the icing to dry with a crust on the outside while remaining soft inside. It also allows the buttercream to last longer and is preferable when piping or icing cakes in warm weather.

Icing Facts: Decorator's Buttercream Icing and Buttercream Icing for Piped Roses

THESE BUTTERCREAMS DO NOT REQUIRE COOKING

Both icings uses some butter and some solid vegetable shortening (although in large baking establishments, this icing is usually made with all emulsified vegetable shortening).

Confectioner's sugar

Meringue powder and salt

Milk and/or liqueur and extracts

This icing is extremely sweet and is often used on cakes for children, on cupcakes, and on birthday cakes. It is creamy and must be covered to prevent drying. However, if neither butter nor any other milk product is used, this icing does not need to be refrigerated.

Decorator's Hint

When working in a busy environment, you may not have the option of using different buttercreams for different roses. In this case, Decorator's Buttercream Icing is your best bet. The problem is the icing becomes limp after one or two full-blown roses are piped. As a temporary solution, good for a few roses, add 1 to 2 oz (28 to 57 g) confectioner's sugar to 8 oz (228 g) Decorator's Buttercream Icing.

Icing

Prepare Decorator's Buttercream Icing and Buttercream Icing for Piped Roses using the recipes on pages 260 and 266, respectively. If practicing alone, prepare ½ recipe of the smaller quantity. Color each icing with your choice of paste or gel food colors. Load a pastry bag with pastel icing and a #103 or #104 petal-shaped metal tip. Make a small quantity of moss green icing for the sepal and calyx, seen on rosebuds and half-roses. For this, you will use the #2 round tip.

Color Facts

Decorator's Buttercream Icing and Icing for Piped Roses can be colored or not. Moss green, ideally made from a small portion of Decorator's Buttercream, is the recommended foliage color to complement the rosebud and half-roses. The stiffness of the Icing for Piped Roses makes it inappropriate for the green leaves. A pastel tone for the Decorator's Buttercream Icing and a pastel tone for the Icing for Piped Roses are desired. Only a small portion of the Decorator's Buttercream Icing is used for foliage. To make moss green, use leaf green with a touch of chocolate brown.

New Skill: Rosebud

A rosebud is not difficult to pipe. Actually, the rosebud is a backward *S* piped with a petal-shaped tip. The flower isn't completed and doesn't look like a rosebud until the greenery is added, which gives it dimension. Rosebuds can be done rather quickly; this does not mean they should have flaws. They are generally piped directly on an iced cake, but you can pipe them onto parchment or wax paper, refrigerate them, and carefully remove them and stick them on iced cakes or cupcakes with a dot of buttercream icing.

To begin making a rosebud, position a #103 or #104 petal-shaped metal piping tip at a 45-degree angle. Touch the wide end of the tip to the surface. Slightly pivot the tip to the left (if you're right-handed, to the right if left-handed). Squeeze the pastry bag as you pivot the tip, forming a small curve. This is Step 1 (see the top row of Illustration 2.1).

Decorator's Hint

To save time, substitute for the sepal and calyx by piping a leaf directly under the flower. Place 1 tsp (7 g) moss-green icing in a small paper cone with a #67 or #352 leaf tip. Position the tip at a 45-degree angle to the bottom of the flower. With a controlled burst of pressure, squeeze the bag, allowing the head of the leaf to appear, and then pull the tip toward you, easing off the pressure. Stop the pressure and exit the leaf.

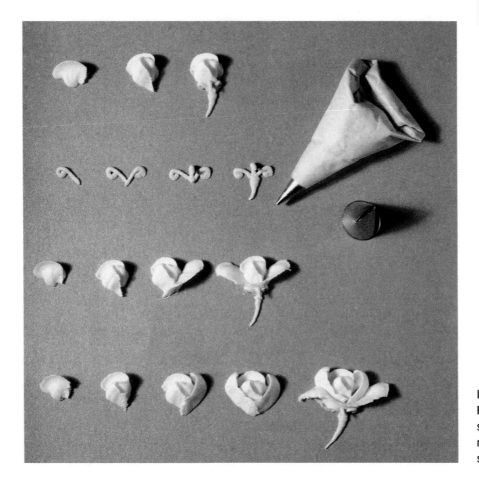

Illustration 2.1
First row: the steps to creating a rosebud; second row: creating the sepal and calyx; third row: the creation of a half-rose; fourth row: the steps to creating an alternative half rose.

While the tip is still attached to the icing, raise it slightly and move it to the left (or right, if you are left-handed), about two-thirds the distance of the curve for the petal. Continue to squeeze as you lower the tip and touch the surface at the 6 o'clock position. Stop the pressure and exit the flower by moving the tip to the right in an upward motion. This is Step 2.

Finish the flower by piping the sepal and calyx at the bottom of the flower. The sepals are the leaves that surround the flower, and the calyx is the base from which the flower grows. To proceed with the sepal and calyx, position the #2 round tip with moss-green icing at the bottom of the rosebud (6 o'clock position). Move the tip slightly to the left, pipe a small upward curve, and return to the center. The curve is piped clockwise (see the second row of Illustration 2.1). Do the same on the reverse side, except for piping the curve counterclockwise. For the center curve, position the tip where both curves end. Squeeze the bag and pull the tip in an upward curve. Stop the pressure and pull the tip toward you, leaving the center sepal suspended. Now, position the tip at the bottom of the flower for the calyx. Apply a burst of pressure at the 6 o'clock position and drag the tip about ¾ in. (1.9 cm). Ease off the pressure as you drag the tail of the calyx. (See the four steps to create the sepal and calyx in Illustration 2.1.)

New Skill: Half-Rose

Half-roses are an extension of the rosebud with two or three additional petals. These do appear as abstract as the rosebud; however, care must be taken to learn and perfect them. You can use half-roses on your favorite cake, cupcake, or cookie for a perfect finish.

First, pipe a rosebud (without the sepal and calyx) as illustrated in this lesson. This is Step 1. Next, position a #103 or #104 petal-shaped piping tip at a 45-degree angle at the upper right-hand corner of the rosebud. Tilt the tip to the right, making sure the wide end is touching the surface of the cake. Apply steady pressure as you drag the tip toward the front of the flower. Start tilting the tip to the left as you overlap the front of the flower. Stop the pressure at the end of the petal. This is Step 2. Repeat this procedure for the petal's left side. Remember to tilt the tip to the left before you start to pipe the petal and tilt the tip to the right as you drag it to complete the petal. The second petal should overlap the first.

Complete the half-rose by piping the sepals and calyx exactly as for the rosebud. This is Step 3. (See row 3 of Illustration 2.1 for the progression of creating a half-rose.) Remember, in a busy environment, you can pipe a leaf instead of the sepal and calyx to complete the rose.

VARIATION

This variation of the half-rose is perhaps the most beautiful. It is a close rose, meaning that the petals curve "inward," except for the last petal, which starts at one end of the flower and extends to the opposite end.

Begin by piping a rosebud (without the sepal and calyx). The first two of the three petals are closed petals. Position the #103 or #104 petal-shape tip and pastry bag at the upper right side of the rosebud. At a 45-degree angle, drag the tip to the surface as you make a backward C as close to the rosebud as possible. Slightly overlap the petal in front the rosebud. For the second petal, position the tip at the upper left-hand side of the rosebud, again at a 45-degree angle.

Decorator's Hint

For a more open look to the overlapping petals of a half rose, press the tip of both petals with a rounded toothpick for a prettier look.

(Remember to touch the wide end of the tip to the surface). Drag the tip to the surface as you pipe a tight C and overlap the first petal in front of the rosebud.

For the third and final petal, position the tip at the upper right-hand corner of the half-rose and tilt it as far to the right as you can. Your angle should be slightly above the work surface. Drag the tip toward the front of the flower and slowly turn it to the left. When you reach the front of the flower, your tip should be at almost a 45-degree angle. Continue to drag the tip to the upper left-hand side of the half-rose. Continue to turn the tip to the left as far as you can. Slowly ease off the pressure to complete the petal. Add the calyx to the front of the flower to complete this variation.

New Skill: Full-blown Roses (Traditional Technique)

The full-blown rose is perhaps the flower most widely used on cakes. These piped roses are as American as apple pie. A bakery cake isn't complete until full-blown roses adorn it.

The traditional way to pipe a full-blown rose is to pipe its base out of the same type of buttercream you will use to pipe the petals—all 16 of them. Load a pastry bag with 8 oz (228 g) Buttercream Icing for Piped Roses or the variation given at the beginning of this lesson. This is a stiffer buttercream icing than the traditional Decorator's Buttercream Icing. Buttercream Icing for Piped Roses is simply Decorator's Buttercream Icing without all of the liquid, a little less shortening, and a little more butter. Because of the stiffness of the icing, you will also be able to pipe a rose base and rose petals.

Put a coupler inside the pastry bag. Use a dab of buttercream icing to stick a piece of parchment paper approximately 2 × 2 in. (5 × 5 cm) on a #6 or #7 icing nail. Position the pastry bag perpendicular to the center of the icing nail with the coupler touching the nail. (Remember, the pastry bag has no tip at the moment. You will pipe the base using the coupler only—or a #15 round tip if you prefer.)

Apply a burst of pressure as you squeeze the pastry bag. Gently pull up on the bag as you start to ease the pressure. Stop when you have piped about 1 to 1¼ in. (2.5 to 3.2 cm) in height. As you pull up and away, the cone should come to a point. If it does not, dip your fingers in a little cornstarch and press the tip together with your thumb and index finger to form a point on top of the cone. This is Step 1 (see Illustration 2.2).

Place the icing nail with the cone on a piece of Styrofoam to hold it in place while you add a #103 or #104 petal-shaped tip to the coupler. Position the tip at an angle to the cone between 45 and 90 degrees. Be sure to touch the wide end of the tip to the right side of the cone (at the 3 o'clock or 9 o'clock position) and about ½ in. (1.3 cm) down from the tip of the cone.

Squeeze the pastry bag and raise the piping tip steadily about ½ in. (1.3 cm) above the tip of the cone. Begin to turn the icing nail counterclockwise as you wrap a layer of icing over the tip of the cone. Gradually ease off the pressure and pull the tip down, touching the sides of the cone. This is the first petal and Step 2 (see Illustration 2.2).

For the next three petals, position the piping tip at the overlapped seam. This time, hold the tip at a 45-degree angle with the tip's wide end touching the seam. Position the tip about ½ in. (1.3 cm) from the tip of the cone at the 3 o'clock position. Slightly tilt the tip to the right. Apply even pressure to the pastry bag as you turn the icing nail counterclockwise and move the tip up and

Illustration 2.2
A traditional full-blown rose (from left to right): the piping tip and icing nail, the base of the rose, and the first petal, the rose with 4 petals, completed half-rose (9 petals), completed 16-petal full-blown rose.

down to form the next petal. Stop the pressure. Continue with the next petal, starting where you left off, using the same technique of moving the tip up and down as you turn the icing nail. Pipe the fourth and last petal and end where the first petal began. You now have a rosebud. This is Step 3.

For the next five petals, position the tip at any seam or at the center point of one of the last three petals piped. Hold it slightly lower than the previous petals. At a 45-degree angle, tilt the tip slightly to the right. Squeeze the pastry bag as you pipe the next petal up to the midpoint of the previous petal, then down. Remember to turn the icing nail counterclockwise. Position the tip slightly in back of the petal you just piped (to overlap) or start where you just left-off. Repeat the technique to pipe the next petal. Continue until you have piped five overlapping petals. This is a half-rose and Step 4.

For the last seven petals, tilt the rose to the left as you tilt the piping tip to the right (to get under the petals). Position the tip at the center of one of the petals. Remember, you are slightly under the previous petals. With the tip's wide end touching, pipe seven overlapping petals. The rose is now complete, with a total of 16 petals. If you didn't use up the space on the cone, don't worry. You can cut that off when the rose is dry or leave it on and pipe leaves between a cluster of roses to hide the bases. This is Step 5. (See Illustration 2.2 for the five steps of the rose.)

New Skill: Full-blown Roses (Nontraditional Technique)

This technique is useful for the busy decorator with little time to make bases. The rose base is made of any edible material that will enhance the taste of the rose such as rolled fondant, marzipan, or chocolate plastic.

Shape ½ oz (14 g) of your favorite modeling paste into a ball by placing the paste in your nonwriting hand, setting your writing hand on top and rotating both hands until the ball forms. This is Step 1 (see Illustration 2.3).

Reposition your writing hand on the ball with your index and middle fingers on the left side. Rotate the ball back and forth, applying pressure to shape the ball into a cone. Pinch to a point. This is Step 2. Use the rose base pattern (see Appendix 1) to measure bases made out of rolled icings.

Illustration 2.3
A nontraditional full-blown rose (from left to right): the paste base as a ball, the base in cone form, the first rose petal, the rose with 4 petals, and the completed nontraditional full-blown rose.

Decorator's Hint

The need to be prepared when working in a production environment cannot be stressed enough. In a classroom environment, you are learning to develop your skills, your quickness, and, most important, your neatness. These all become very important when working in the industry. In a busy professional environment, nontraditional techniques can be invaluable. Having bases or completed roses done ahead of time, especially in a bakery, can mean success and steady employment for the decorator. If there isn't time to make bases, the decorator can also use commercial candies, such as Hershey's Kisses, to pipe roses on. With a chocolate, marzipan, or fondant center, the bakery can charge more for piped roses and thus generate more revenue and increase customer satisfaction.

Place a dab of buttercream icing on a #6 or #7 icing nail and set a piece of 2 × 2 in. (5 × 5 cm) parchment paper on top of the nail. Place another dab of buttercream on top of the parchment paper and secure the cone on the nail. This is Step 3.

Pipe petals using the traditional method for full-blown roses (see Illustration 2.4).

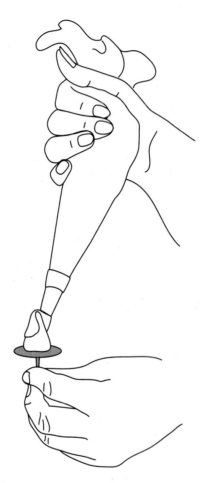

Illustration 2.4
Hold the pastry bag in one hand and begin piping petals onto the rose base. Use your other hand to rotate the icing nail while holding the rose base.

END-OF-LESSON REVIEW

1. How many petals are piped on a rose base to complete a full-blown rose?

2. Tips of what shape are used to pipe roses, rosebuds, and half-roses?

3. What is the green part of a rosebud or half-rose called?

4. When piping a half-rose, does it matter if you start at the upper right-hand corner or upper left-hand corner to start the overlapping petal? Why?

5. At what position is the metal tip when piping a rosebud or a half-rose?

6. Why is the Decorator's Buttercream Icing a good choice in warm weather?

7. True or False: The classic recipe for Swiss Meringue Buttercream calls for a lot of solid vegetable shortening and butter.

8. True or False: When piping a nontraditional full-blown rose, use rolled fondant only to make the icing base.

9. How many additional petals are needed to pipe a half-rose variation after the rosebud is piped?

10. If you don't have moss-green food color in your food color kit, how would you make it?

PERFORMANCE TEST

Pipe the following:

| 8 rosebuds | 5 half-roses | 2 traditional roses | 2 nontraditional full-blown roses |

INTERMEDIATE PIPING SKILLS

Cake and Border Designs

You will need the following equipment and recipes to successfully complete this lesson:

Practice Buttercream Icing (page 266)

medium-size paper cones

two 12-in. (30 cm) flex or lightweight pastry bag

couplers

piping tips: #10 round tip, #67 leaf tip, or #352 leaf tip; #47 or #48 basketweave tip; #18 shell tip; #103 or 104 petal-shaped tip; #88 combination tip (shell and petal shape)

gel food colors

toothpicks

full-sheet parchment paper

masking tape

scissors

offset metal spatulas

rubber spatulas

small metal bowls

plastic wrap

Lesson 3 teaches beautiful cake finishing skills that can be quickly learned and easily applied. The techniques learned and mastered will provide you with enough confidence to tackle more advanced cake decorating projects. Another goal is to learn how to work neatly, cleanly, and precisely. This is extremely important, as Lesson 4 requires great accuracy.

The new icing in this lesson is Practice Buttercream Icing. It is based on the Decorator's Buttercream Icing, but the difference between the two is extremely important: This icing does not need to be refrigerated because it contains no milk or butter. In fact, this icing can be used for many of the piped exercises in this book. Leftover buttercream icing can be stored in a plastic container with a lid and placed on a baker's rack until the next class session.

Icing Components

> 10x confectioner's sugar
> Solid vegetable shortening or high-ratio shortening
> Meringue powder
> Water

Because we are not going to eat this icing, we can use the simplest ingredients. This icing is designed to perform well. While it can be eaten, it does not taste particularly good.

New Skill: Grape Clusters

Grape clusters add a beautiful dimension to any iced cake. They can be piped in buttercream or royal icing or hand-shaped in rolled fondant, marzipan, or white or dark chocolate plastic. Either way, you can make them white or pale green for a formal cake, such as a wedding cake, or purple for a dramatic birthday or anniversary cake.

To apply grape clusters to an iced cake, first measure the cake into equal sections. Although grapes can be piped anywhere on a cake, they look especially nice when piped off the top edge of the cake and extended down the side.

The consistency of the icing for piped grapes is crucial. Prepare Practice Buttercream Icing (page 266), then measure out 8 oz (228 g) for this exercise. Add 1 to 1½ tsp (5 to 7.5 ml) water to slightly soften the icing. Next, measure out 6 oz (170 g) of the 8 oz (228 g) and color it a deep violet or a pale green; alternatively, leave it white. Color the remaining 2 oz (57 g) moss green for natural-looking leaves. Beat the icing well in a small bowl to incorporate the color and load a pastry bag with the icing and any round metal tip. In Illustration 3.1, a #10 round tip is used for the grapes. For the leaves, load a medium-size paper cone with a #67 or a #352 leaf tip and place the moss-green icing inside the paper cone.

Grapes must be piped upside down on an iced cake so only the rounded edges show. Give them a natural look by starting at the side of the cake and moving up to the top edge—that is, start at the middle of the cake and pipe the grapes toward the top edge. This may seem awkward at first, but you will understand as you are piping the grapes. Use a tilting turntable, if you have access to one, as the angle makes it easier to pipe grapes. In lieu of a tilting turntable, you can place almost any object under the cake board to tilt the cake—a piece of Styrofoam, a small jewelry case, a small stapler, a brand-new plastic container, or even a remote control. (I have used all of these.) (See Illustration 3.1.)

Use a cardboard round or square when piping grapes on a flat surface. You can rotate the cardboard as the grapes are finished.

Decorator's Hint

High-ratio shortening is an emulsifier designed specifically for high-volume baking and decorating. It contains water, is temperature stable, and controls air well when whipped. It is much more stable than supermarket vegetable shortening and is not as heavy or noticeable on the back of one's pallet. This is a staple in most bakeries and hotels. The most popular brands are Sweetex, Alpine, and BakeMark.

High-ratio shortening, also known as *emulsified shortening*, is essentially liquid oil or fat made solid by hydrogenization. At a certain point, emulsifiers are added to the shortening, improving its chemical properties with respect to holding sugar, water, and fat as well as distributing these ingredients to make a good emulsion—in other words, an icing with a fluid smoothness and consistency when piped.

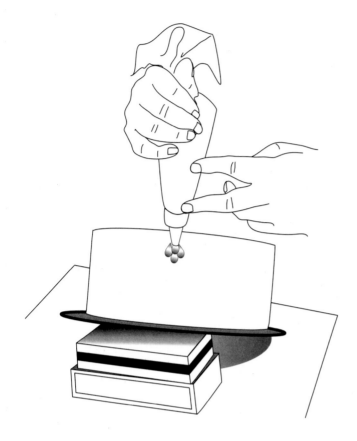

Illustration 3.1
To pipe grape clusters, tilt the cake toward you and begin piping the grapes along the side of the cake, moving up toward the top edge.

First, position the tip and pastry bag at a 45-degree angle. Apply a burst of pressure as you allow some of the icing to protrude from the icing tip, then slightly push the tip forward and pull the tip toward yourself, as if you were piping a small classic shell. Ease the pressure and drag the tip to end the first grape. Then pipe grapes on each side of the first grape. The first grape should protrude from the others. Continue to pipe grapes on the side, aiming for a triangle-shaped group. Next, pipe grapes on top of each other for a full and luscious look.

To complete the grape cluster, position a #67 or #352 leaf tip at a 45-degree angle in back of the grapes. Angle the tip slightly. Apply a burst of pressure, build up the head of the leaf, and then gently pull away to exit. Repeat this on the opposite side to complete the grape cluster (see Illustration 3.2).

Illustration 3.2
Piping grape clusters (from left to right): grapes are piped by first pushing the piping tip forward and then pulling the tip back toward you; pipe grapes on each side of the first grape, creating a triangle look; pipe grapes on top of the other grapes and complete the cluster with piped leaves.

New Skill: Sweet Pea Clusters

This striking border gives a lot of dimension to any cake. It is simply a series of petals or flutes compactly piped. Like the grape cluster border, this border is piped upside down from the side to the top edge of an iced cake. Again, you are aiming for a triangle shape (see Illustration 3.3).

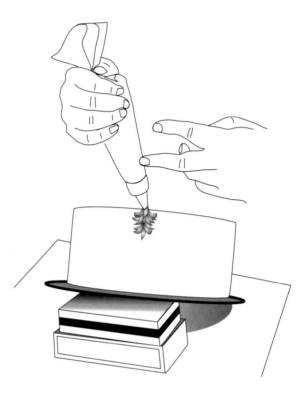

Illustration 3.3
Just like grape clusters, sweet pea clusters are piped along the side of a cake toward the top edge.

For this exercise, you want the regular consistency of the Practice Buttercream Icing rather than the softer consistency you used for the grapes.

Use a cardboard round or square so you can rotate it. Load a pastry bag with lavender, pink, or yellow buttercream icing. Attach the #103 or #104 petal-shaped tip to your pastry bag.

Hold the tip and pastry bag at a 45-degree angle to the surface, with the wide end touching. Apply a burst of pressure, allowing some icing to flow through the tip. Drag the tip to the surface as you pull the tip toward yourself. Angle the back of the tip up as you ease the pressure and stop. This is called a flute. Now position the tip at the upper left- or right-hand side of the flute, wide end of the tip touching the surface. Slightly angle the tip to a 45-degree angle. Apply a burst of pressure as you drag the tip to the tail end of the flute. Stop the pressure and pull the tip toward you. Now position the tip at the opposite side of the flute and repeat the squeeze-and-pull technique. You now have a small sweet pea cluster (see the middle of Illustration 3.4). To build on this, position the tip at the left- or right-hand side of the small cluster and repeat the squeeze-and-pull technique. As you continue to build the sweet pea cluster, develop a triangle shape—that is, make the cluster narrow at the bottom and wide at the top. Once the triangle is formed, the cluster is done.

Next, position a #352 or #67 leaf tip at the center point of the wide end of the triangle. Angle the tip slightly as you apply a burst of pressure. Pull the tip toward you as you end the leaf, then position the tip at the opposite side of the leaf you just formed and repeat the squeeze-and-pull technique. (See Illustration 3.4.)

Illustration 3.4
Piping sweet pea clusters (from left to right): pipe the first flute by dragging the piping tip along the surface toward you; add sweet pea leaves along the sides of the flute, forming a small cluster; complete the sweet pea cluster by piping leaves at the top of the triangle shape.

New Skill: *E* Shells

E shells are a simple way to make a uniform top border to an iced cake. They can be piped with any star tip but perhaps look best when piped with either a #16, #18, or #21 icing tip.

First, position the pastry bag with the tip at a 45-degree angle to the top edge of the cake. Right-handed pipers should start piping at the 6 o'clock position. Slightly raise the tip and begin to pipe a counterclockwise rosette. When the tip reaches the 9 o'clock position, drag the tip to the surface of the cake and extend the tail of the rosette about ¼ in. (6 mm). Stop the pressure and ease the pastry bag and tip toward you. When piping the next *E* shell, position the tip where the last *E* shell was left off and repeat the technique. Repeat this step as many times as needed to produce a beautiful border (see Illustration 3.5).

New Skill: Curved Shells with Shell Accents

Curved shells with shell accents make a dramatic border on the top edge of a round or rectangular cake. Because of its layered look, this border resembles a short fleur-de-lis.

To begin, attach a #18 star tip to the pastry bag and position the tip and pastry bag at a 45-degree angle. Start with a left reverse shell: Raise the tip slightly from the surface and position the tip and pastry bag at the 6 o'clock position. Apply a burst of pressure and move the tip in a clockwise direction, forming a small rosette. When the tip reaches the 12 o'clock position, continue to apply pressure as you move the tip to the 5 o'clock position. Ease the pressure and

> ### Decorator's Hint
>
> Left-handers start piping *E* shells at the 6 o'clock position but pipe in a clockwise direction.

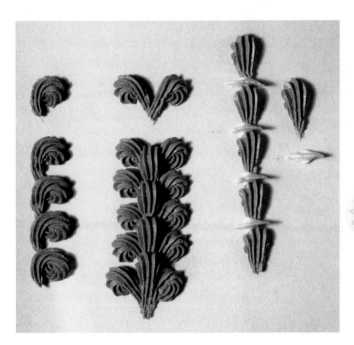

Illustration 3.5
From left to right: *E* shells, curved shells with accents, and shells with flutes.

touch the tip to the surface. Repeat this procedure for the opposite reverse shell, ending at the 7 o'clock position. Both left and right reverse shells should end in a V shape (see Illustration 3.5). Pipe the next set of left and right reverse shells directly under the previous reverse shells, forming a pattern.

For the centered shell, position the tip and pastry bag at an angle between 45 and 90 degrees. Raise the tip slightly from the surface and pipe large shells in the center of the reverse shells. (See Illustration 3-5.)

New Skill: Shells with Flute

Shells with flutes are an unusual top and bottom border design. The flute between the shells dresses up the border. You need a #18 star tip attached to the pastry bag for the shells and a #103 or #104 petal-shaped tip in a small paper cone for the flutes.

Begin by using the #18 star tip to pipe small or large shells around the top or bottom edge of a round or rectangular cake. Now switch to the #103 or #104 petal-shaped tip, positioning the wide end between two of the connecting shells. Touch the surface and apply a burst of pressure, allowing the flute to move forward slightly. Then pull the tip toward you and ease the pressure. Angle the bag and tilt it up slightly as you drag the tip to the surface of the cake. Repeat this procedure until you have piped a flute between each set of shells (see Illustration 3.5).

New Skill: Ruffles

Traditionally, ruffles are piped on the sides of the cake, near the top. They are piped in a crescent shape and thus may look crowded or overdone. In my opinion, using ruffles as a bottom border gives the decorator another choice besides shells and bead borders.

To start, load a pastry bag with a #103 or #104 petal-shaped tip with icing. Turn your body slightly to the left (if you're right-handed) or right (if you're left-handed). You're ready to begin.

First, position the tip flat on your work surface with the narrow end pointing toward you. Angle the tip to 45 degrees. Apply a burst of pressure and allow some of the icing to protrude through the icing tip, then raise the tip slightly and then down to the surface. Continue this up-and-down motion as you continue to apply pressure. The ruffles should appear uniform and even (see Illustration 3.6).

For a double ruffle, position the tip on top of the previous ruffles. Apply pressure as you move the tip up and down; this time apply lighter pressure. (See Illustration 3.6.)

VARIATION

For a spectacular ruffle with a finished edge, try using the #88 combination tip. This specialized tip has a petal shape at one end and a star shape at the other. When you pipe ruffles with this tip, the top of the ruffles has a zigzag finish.

To begin, position the tip with the petal-shaped opening facing you at a 45-degree angle. Apply a burst of pressure as you move the tip up and down in a

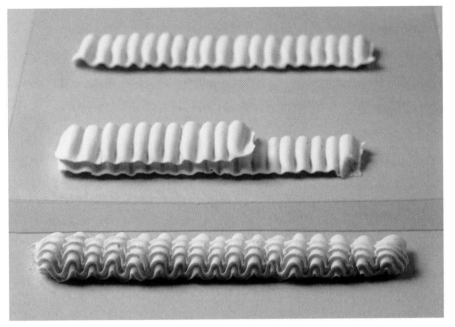

Illustration 3.6
Ruffles (top to bottom): a single piped ruffle; a double ruffle; and a spectacular ruffle with a zigzag finish, which is created wiht a #88 combination tip.

steady motion. Notice that the ruffles are heavier but prettier than traditional ruffles. Stop the pressure when complete and gently pull away (see Illustration 3.6). In fact, when piping a double ruffle using the #103 or #104 petal-shape tip—the #88 combination tip makes a prettier top ruffle.

New Skill: Swags

Like ruffles, swags were widely used on wedding or celebration cakes during the 1960s and early 1970s, but the look was heavy and overdone. Swags look more attractive if piped singly or doubled near the top edge of a cake, or, as a refreshing change, near the bottom.

Measure your work surface into 2-in. (5 cm) sections. Load a pastry bag with a #103 or #104 petal-shaped tip. Slightly turn your body to the left (if right-handed) or slightly to the right (if left-handed). Angle the tip so the wide end touches the surface. Apply a burst of pressure as you drag the wide end in a scalloped or crescent shape. As you reach the end of the swag, pivot the tip slightly clockwise (if right-handed) or counterclockwise (if left-handed) to taper off. Continue with the next swag. The swags should be piped in almost an uninterrupted motion for consistency (see Illustrations 3.7 and 3.8).

To make a double swag, position the tip slightly above the first set of swags and repeat the procedure, be sure to make contact with the surface by dragging the tip. When tapering off at the end, you may injure the bottom layer of swags. Don't worry, rosebuds, half-roses, or star flowers can be piped between the swags to disguise the injury.

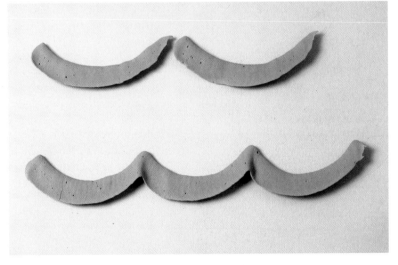

Illustration 3.7
Swags. Top row: single swags; Bottom row: swags should appear to have an uninterrupted flow.

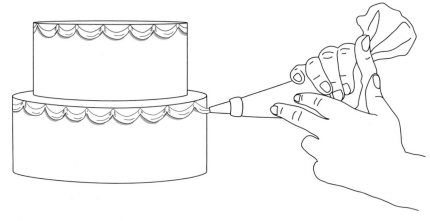

Illustration 3.8
Swags piped directly onto a cake should look continuous, with no breaks.

New Skill: Bows

Bows make a nice finish to a bouquet of piped flowers on a cake. They can also be piped on plastic wrap with a #101 petal-shaped tip (a very small tip). Once air-dried or refrigerated, the bows can be removed from the plastic wrap and set between garlands with a dot of buttercream icing.

Position a #103 or #104 petal-shaped tip in your pastry bag at a 45-degree angle. Position the wide end of the tip on the surface. Drag the tip as you apply steady pressure, making a figure 8. Starting with the left loop, drag the tip up and around. When you return to the center position, drag the tip up and around to the right. Once you are back again at the center position, drag the tip and taper the icing to form the left streamer. Finally, reposition the tip at the center position, drag the tip, and taper the icing to form the right streamer (see Illustration 3.9).

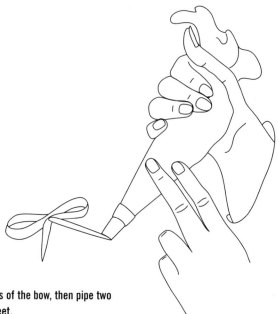

Illustration 3.9
Piping a bow: Make a figure 8 for the loops of the bow, then pipe two streamers at the point where the loops meet.

New Skill: Basket Weave

Although basket weaving is an old-world technique, it is still commonly used and produces a stunning cake without a lot of effort. Amateurs and pros alike can give a tailored look to a cake with basket weave. With a little effort, your basket weave cake can be a work of art.

Basket weaving can be accomplished with several types of icing tips. Although the #47 and #48 are popular tips and often used to create this look, you can use round tips (#7, 8, 9, 10, 12), star tips (#16, 18, 20, 21, 22), or even petal-shaped tips (#101, 102, 103, or 104).

To begin, load a #47 or #48 tip, or any of the others mentioned above, in your pastry bag. Position the icing tip and pastry bag at a 90-degree angle to the top edge of the cake. Apply a burst of pressure as you pipe a vertical line down the side of the cake. Make sure to keep the tip just above the surface of the cake. Once you reach the bottom, ease the pressure and stop. This is called the down-stroke (see top left of Illustration 3.10). Now, reposition the tip and pastry bag at the top of the cake. Begin piping the crossover strokes by starting about ½ in. (1.3 cm) before the downstroke. Pipe over the downstroke and extend the piping another ½ in. (1.3 cm) (see top of Illustration 3.10, second from left). For a right-handed person, begin piping at the left side of the downstroke. For a left-handed person, begin piping at the right side of the downstroke.

Pipe the next crossover stroke, but remember to leave a tip space to be filled in after the next downstroke. To achieve this, place the metal tip just under the first crossover stroke. Squeeze the pastry bag gently, leaving a small line of icing. Stop the pressure. This is just a marker for you to find the correct distance between each crossover stroke. Position the tip and pastry bag at the other end of the crossover stoke and leave another marker.

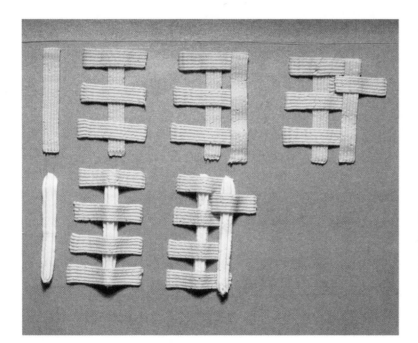

Illustration 3.10
Basket weave (top row, from left): the down-stroke, crossover strokes, another downstroke that covers the first round of crossover strokes, and a crossover stroke over the second downstroke. Bottom row: the steps to create basket weave, using different colors and a #18 star tip for the downstroke.

Next, position the tip under the marker and pipe another crossover stroke, making sure the tip is just above the surface of the cake. Repeat until you reach the bottom of the cake.

Finally, pipe the next downstroke. Start the downstroke just inside the crossover stroke. Remember to keep the tip just above the cake. Position the tip at each tip space and pipe a crossover stroke, extending the icing about ½ in. (1.3 cm) beyond the tip space. Repeat this until you have filled each tip space. Reposition the tip and pastry bag at the top of the cake and pipe another downstroke. Continue the pattern until you have completed a basket weave design around the entire cake (see Illustration 3.11).

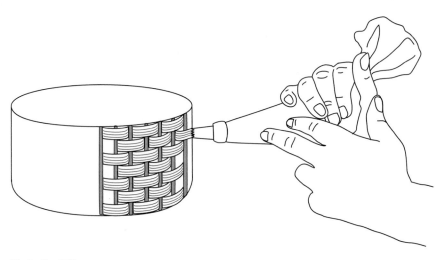

Illustration 3.11
Basket weave piped on a cake creates a dramatic effect.

END-OF-LESSON REVIEW

1. What shape are you aiming for when piping grapes or sweet pea clusters?

2. True or False: When piping grape clusters, to achieve the rounded edges of the grapes, it is best to pipe right-side up.

3. What types of icing tips are used to pipe sweet pea clusters? Give examples of icing tip numbers.

4. True or False: You can pipe grapes with #5, 6, or 7 round icing tips.

5. Where would you use a piped bow?

6. Where would you place a curved shell with shell accent border?

7. Where are flutes placed on a shell border?

8. True or False: You can use only #47 and #48 tips to pipe basket weave.

9. The first stroke in basket weaving is called a: (a) down weave (b) downstroke (c) down line

10. The empty spaces between crossover strokes are called: (a) an empty space (b) a zero space (c) a tip space

11. The length of a crossover stroke is approximately: (a) ½ in. (1.3 cm) (b) 1 in. (2.5 cm) (c) 1½ in. (3.8 cm)

PERFORMANCE TEST

Pipe the following exercises on a rectangular cardboard or a parchment half-sheet. The presentation of these borders is extremely important.

1. Pipe two sweet pea clusters on a Styrofoam.

2. Pipe two grape clusters on a Styrofoam.

3. On a round cardboard, pipe a shell with a flute, an *E* shell, and a curved shell with shell accents.

4. Pipe a 5-in. (11.5 cm) basket weave on a round or rectangular Styrofoam.

5. Finish the basket weave with a rope border.

ADVANCED PIPING SKILLS

Part I: Advanced Overpiped Top and Bottom Border Designs

You will need the following equipment and recipes to successfully complete this lesson:

Meringue Powder Royal Icing (page 273)

small and medium-size paper cones

piping tips: #0, #2, #3, and #5 round tips; #18 star tip; #101 and #103 petal-shaped tips; #88 combination tip (star and petal-shaped)

gel food colors

rounded toothpicks

small metal bowls

offset metal spatulas

rubber spatulas (brand-new)

rectangular Styrofoams

small and medium parchment cones

Welcome to Lesson 4. This is a big chapter, so it is divided into two parts: Advanced Overpiped Top and Bottom Border Designs and Advanced Top and Bottom Border Designs. Mastery of this lesson and all of the piping techniques will give you a thorough grounding in pressure control, precision, and overpiping development. Also in this lesson you will learn advanced top and bottom border designs appropriate for high-end wedding cakes and the basics for competition-style decorating. Strict attention to detail is most important here, as these piping skills will determine how well you progress beyond them.

Also new to this lesson is the introduction of Royal Icing. Up to this point, you have been using Swiss Meringue Buttercream, Decorator's Buttercream Icing, Buttercream Icing for Piped Roses, and Practice Buttercream Icings. With the exception of Practice Buttercream Icings, these icings are creamy and delicious to eat. Royal Icing serves a different purpose. It is a decorative icing rather than an eating icing. Although it is edible and often seen on decorated cookies, it is not as palatable as buttercream icings.

We discuss two types of Royal Icing in this textbook. The first is Egg White Royal Icing, which is usually used for fine stringwork, lace work, filigree work, and intricate embroidery work. (These techniques are covered in Lesson 7.) It is usually not flavored, except for a little lemon juice. Its basic components are 10x powdered sugar, room-temperature egg whites, and lemon juice. The second type is Meringue Powder Royal Icing. This is the icing used in this lesson. Meringue Powder Royal Icing is much lighter than the denser Egg White Royal Icing and is whiter in color. When less strenuous piping is needed on a rolled-iced cake, this is the icing to use. Meringue Powder Royal Icing can be used to pipe embroidery work, drop-string work, Swiss dots, cookie decorating, and as a glue in gingerbread houses.

Outside of the United States, royal icing is used as an eating icing. Although it dries quite hard, a little glycerine keeps it firm but soft inside. Glycerine is a product found in food colors that preserves them and keeps the colors flowing. You can also purchase glycerine separately, which is used in homemade rolled icing to keep the icing soft.

In this lesson, you will use a lot of paper cones—that is, paper cornets. Paper cones are recommended for fine or intricate piping. Because they are small and fit easily in your hands, they allow excellent control over your piping. The smaller the pastry bag (or paper cone), the more control you will have in piping detailed work. If you prefer, however, you can use a flex, canvas, or plastic disposable pastry bag to do these exercises.

Make a large batch of Meringue Powder Royal Icing. Although you won't get too much done in one session, the icing can be stored and rebeaten for future sessions. Meringue Powder Royal Icing can be left without refrigeration for several days in a well-ventilated and air-conditioned room, or refrigerated with plastic wrap on the surface of the icing and a tight-fitting lid on top of that.

Some decorators prefer paste colors to gel when coloring Royal Icing, as gels thin the icing. However, incorporating paste colors requires a lot of beating. Coloring large amounts of Royal Icing, whether with gel or paste, can be tricky.

Decorator's Hint

Practically all of the piping done in buttercream icings can also be done in both royal icings.

Decorator's Hint

When mixing food colors into royal icings, use a brand-new rubber spatula that hasn't touched any grease products. Any deposit of fat or oil on a rubber or offset metal spatula will break down the royal icing. Do not pipe royal icing on a buttercream-iced cake! For best results, use a rectangular Styrofoam for these exercises; you can pipe different designs on all sides. The Styrofoam need not be iced to pipe directly on it.

New Skill: Top Border—Overpiped Scallops

Quick Prep

5 medium-size paper cones
piping tips: #0, #2, #3, and #5 round tips
4 oz (114 g) Meringue Powder Royal Icing (page 273)
contrasting color for paper cone with #0 round tip

This skill is important to the decorator's development. It teaches concentration, precision, and how to align lines on top of each other. This is an important skill to have when learning Australian-style bridgework cake decorating in Lesson 11.

Before piping the first border, cut four paper cones ½ in. (1.3 cm) from the tip. Place the #0, #2, #3, and #5 round tips in the cones. Load each cone with 1 Tbsp (14 g) of icing. If you wish, you can color the icings with gel or paste food colors for contrast. Once the cones are loaded, place them in a bowl covered with plastic wrap or an airtight container. This is important, as Meringue Powder Royal Icing air dries quickly. You can also place the tip of each cone under a damp sponge to prevent them from clogging.

Divide one side of the Styrofoam into four equal parts. This can be achieved by using adding machine paper or a ruler. Measure from the left to the right side of the cake and divide the length by four. Mark the four sections on your cake dummy using a pencil. Mark the top edge and the bottom of the cake as well. When marking the bottom, measure about ½ in. (1.3 cm) from the bottom of the Styrofoam. This will allow you to pipe a border under your cake design, if you choose. Finally, stick your marked Styrofoam to a foiled-covered rectangular cake board with a little of the Meringue Powder Royal Icing. (See page 117 for instructions on covering a board with foil.)

(See page 117 for instructions on covering a board with foil.)

> ### Decorator's Hint
>
> If you don't have much time to do these lessons, work on both the top and bottom borders at the same time. This way, you can proceed with one section while the other is drying. Note that this lesson is executed in stages because of the drying time needed between exercises.

STAGE 1

Using a #5 round tip with a paper cone, position your hand at a 45-degree angle at the upper left-hand corner of the Styrofoam. Touch the surface at the marked point. Apply a burst of pressure, allowing some of the icing to flow from the icing tip. Then, squeeze and allow the icing to flow. Move the tip and icing to the next mark on the Styrofoam, allowing the icing to form a scalloped shape. Touch the surface and stop the pressure. Start the next scallop right next to where you left off. Complete the second, third, and fourth scallops. Allow these to dry for 15 to 20 minutes (see the top left of Illustration 4.1).

Position a #3 round tip approximately ¼ in. (6 mm) below the first scallop. Using the same technique, pipe four scallops under the first row of scallops. Allow these to dry 15 to 20 minutes.

Position a #2 round tip about ¼ in. (6 mm) below the second set of scallops. Pipe four more scallops (see the top middle of Illustration 4.1). Stage 1 is complete.

STAGE 2

Return to the first set of scallops—those piped with a #5 round tip. Position the #3 tip directly on top of the first scallops and apply a burst of pressure, allowing a thinner string to drape on top of the first scallop. When you reach the end of the scallop, drag the tip to the edge. (This allows less buildup between sections of scallops). Continue with the second, third, and fourth scallops. Allow this to dry for 15 to 20 minutes.

Position the #2 round tip at the second set of scallops (piped with the #3 tip). Apply pressure as you pipe a second line directly on top on the first. Continue until you have added a second line to the second row of scallops. Allow this to dry for 15 to 20 minutes.

Position a #0 tip at the third set of scallops (piped with a #2 round tip). Apply pressure as you pipe a second line directly on top on the first. Continue until you have added a second line to the third row of scallops. Allow this to dry for 15 to 20 minutes (see the top right of Illustration 4.1). Stage 2 is complete.

STAGE 3

Return to the first row of scallops. Pipe a third and fourth row of scallops with the #2 round tip and allow to dry for 15 to 20 minutes. You can pipe the next row right after the first row without letting the first row dry. Pipe one row of scallops with the #2 round tip over the second row of scallops and allow to dry for 15 to 20 minutes. Pipe nothing on the third row of scallops for the time being. Stage 3 is complete.

STAGE 4

This is the final stage of overpiping for all the scalloped borders. When piping the last row, it is best to use a contrasting color to emphasize the depth of each row. Starting with the first row, pipe a row of scallops with the #0 tip, followed by the second and third rows of scallops.

Pipe some fine embroidery under the third row of scallops to complete the look. Using the #0 round tip, pipe a continuous *M* that conforms to the shape of the scallops (see the bottom of Illustration 4.2). You should be about ¼ in. (6 mm) below the third row of scallops (see the top right of Illustration 4.1).

Your first exercise is complete! Remember, this isn't easy, but the discipline acquired is invaluable.

Decorator's Hint

When you pipe these scallop lines from one point to another, remember to pull away from the point of contact and allow gravity to lower the line to a crescent or scallop shape. Be sure to judge the distance from one point to another and slightly drag the tip to the end of the scallop.

Illustration 4.1
Top of the cake: creating overpiped scallops.
Bottom of the cake: the stages of creating overpiped garlands with scallops.

Illustration 4.2
Top: *U* embroidery. Bottom: *M* embroidery.

New Skill: Bottom Border—Overpiped Garlands (Crescents) with Scallops

Quick Prep

4 medium-size paper cones
1 large paper cone
piping tips: #0, #2, #3, and #5 round tips; #18 star tip
8 oz (228 g) Meringue Powder Royal Icing (page 273)

Piped garlands were discussed in Lesson 1. This lesson provides additional practice with this technique along with developing concentration and precision work. This is especially valuable in competitions.

The same technique used for the top overpiped scallops is used for the bottom borders. When the bottom borders are piped, you start from the lowest position and work toward the middle of the cake. Be sure the bottom of the Styrofoam is already measured.

STAGE 1

Starting near the bottom of the cake, position the #18 star tip at the left edge of the corner (if right-handed). Garlands are like zigzags, only tighter and using more pressure. Apply pressure as you drag the tip to the cake surface in a tight zigzag motion, starting with low pressure and building to high pressure at the midpoint of the garland. Reverse the procedure by applying heavy pressure and then easing it as you taper the first garland to the next marking. Repeat this for the next three markings for a total of four garlands. Allow to dry for 15 to 20 minutes. This is called reverse first row (see bottom left of Illustration 4.1).

In the meantime, make your next marking about ¼ in. (6 mm) above the drying garlands. This is the reverse of the top border. Position a #5 round tip at the marking and pipe a scallop shape from one marking to the next. Repeat this three more times for the reverse second row.

For the reverse third row, position a #3 round tip ¼ in. (6 mm) above the reverse second row. Pipe four scallops.

For the reverse fourth row, position a #2 round tip ¼ in. (6 mm) above the reverse third row. Pipe four scallops. This is the end of Stage 1. Let all this dry for at least 15 to 20 minutes before proceeding.

STAGE 2

Position a #5 round tip at the top edge of the reverse first row (the piped garlands). Pipe four scallops on the top edge of the garlands. Now, on the same reverse first row, pipe another four scallops at the bottom edge of the garlands.

For the reverse second row, use a #3 round tip to pipe four scallops directly on top of the scallops piped with a #5 round tip.

For the reverse third row, use a #2 round tip to pipe another four scallops on top of the scallops piped with a #3 round tip.

For the reverse fourth row, use the #0 tip to pipe four scallops on top of scallops piped with a #2 round tip. Allow all this to dry for 15 to 20 minutes. This is the end of Stage 2 (see the second from bottom left of Illustration 4.1).

STAGE 3

You may wish to try a contrasting color for these rows.

For the reverse first row, use a #3 round tip to pipe four scallops on top of the double scallops piped with a #5 round tip.

For the reverse second row, use a #2 round tip to pipe four scallops on top of the scallops piped with a #3 round tip.

For the reverse third row, use a #0 round tip to pipe four scallops on top of the scallops piped with a #2 round tip. Pipe nothing on the reverse fourth row. Let all this dry for 15 to 20 minutes. This is the end of Stage 3 (see the third scallop section from the bottom left of Illustration 4.1).

STAGE 4

This is the final stage for all reverse rows.

For all four reverse rows, use a #0 round tip to pipe scallops in a contrasting color for each of the four rows.

Using a #0 round tip and a contrasting color, pipe *U*-shaped embroidery ¼ in. (6 mm) above the reverse fourth row (see the top of Illustration 4.2). Position the tip against the cake when you pipe the *U* embroidery. Drag the tip to the cake as you pipe a continuous *U*, conforming to the scalloped shape (see the bottom right of Illustration 4.1). Your second exercise is complete!

New Skill: Top Border—Short Overpiped Scallops

Quick Prep

Medium-size paper cones
piping tips: #0 and #3 round tips
3 oz (85 g) Meringue Powder Royal Icing (page 273)

The skills used here develop concentration, which is important in Australian bridgework.

This top border is not as demanding as the overpiped scallop top border because there are only two rows to pipe. The photo shows the top border divided into nine sections, with the fifth scallop as the center point. For greater ease, divide the top border into eight equal sections. After completing this lesson, divide the bottom of the cake into four equal sections, as done in the previous exercise.

STAGE 1

Position your hand and the #3 round tip in the paper cone at a 45-degree angle at the upper left-hand corner of the Styrofoam. Touch the surface at the marked point on the Styrofoam. Apply a burst of pressure, allowing some of the icing to flow from the icing tip. Then, squeeze and allow the icing to flow. Move the tip to the next mark on the Styrofoam, allowing the icing to form a scalloped shape. Touch the surface and stop the pressure. Start the next scallop right next to where you left off. Complete the rest of the scallops. Allow these to dry for 15 to 20 minutes. Stage 1 is complete.

STAGE 2

Position the #0 round tip directly on top of the first set of scallops, piped with a #3 round tip. Apply a burst of pressure and allow a thinner string to drape on top of the first scallop. When you reach the end of the scallop, drag the tip to the edge. (This decreases buildup between sections of the scallops.) Continue with the rest of the scallops. Allow to dry for 15 to 20 minutes.

Decorator's Hint

You will need to rebeat the Meringue Powder Royal Icing, if you made a large recipe at the beginning of this lesson. Also, if you are using this icing over several days, you must rebeat it daily. You can rebeat small quantities by hand, but large quantities—say, 16 oz (454 g)—use a machine with a paddle attachment. Condensation may appear in the icing after it sits for any length of time. This makes it softer than originally. You may need to add 1 to 2 Tbsp (14 to 28 g) of confectioner's sugar per 16 oz (454 g) to get the icing back to medium-stiff consistency.

Illustration 4.3
Top: short overpiped scallops. Bottom: the stages of piping ruffles with overpiped scallops.

Position the #0 round tip approximately ¼ in. (6 mm) below the first scallop. Using the same technique, pipe eight scallops under the first row. Allow these to dry 15 to 20 minutes. The top border is completed (see Illustration 4.3).

New Skill: Bottom Border—Ruffles with Overpiped Scallops

Quick Prep

> 3 medium-size paper cones
> 1 large paper cone
> piping tips: #0, #3, and #5 round tips; #88 star/petal
>   combination tip
> 8 oz (228 g) Meringue Powder Royal Icing (page 273)

To prepare, place the round tips in the medium-size paper cones and the combination tip in the large cone. Load 2 Tbsp (28 g) icing in the combination tip. Load 1 Tbsp (14 g) icing in the #0 and #3 round tips, using a contrasting color in the #0.

The same technique is used for both the bottom borders and top overpiped scallops. Remember, when piping the bottom borders, start from the lowest position of the cake and work toward the middle. Be sure the bottom of the Styrofoam is measured before you begin.

STAGE 1

At the bottom of the cake, position the combination tip at the left edge of the corner (if right-handed). The star-shape end is placed against the cake with the petal shape toward you. Apply pressure in an up-and-down motion—keeping the scalloped (or crescent) shape. Remember to taper the end of the ruffles when you reach the next marking. Repeat this for the other three marked sections for a total of four ruffles. Allow this to dry for 15 to 20 minutes (see bottom left of Illustration 4.3).

The next marking is ¼ in. (6 mm) above the drying ruffles. This is the reverse of the top border. We call these reverse rows 1, 2, 3, etc. Position a #3

---

round tip at the marking and pipe a scallop shape from one marking to the next. Repeat this three more times for the reverse second row. Stage 1 is complete.

STAGE 2

Back at the reverse first row, position the #5 round tip at the front edge of the ruffle. Pipe a scallop border from one marking to the next. Repeat this for the next three ruffles for a total of four scallops. Pipe another series of scallops in the center of each ruffle with the same #5 round tip. Allow the shape to drape in the center. Pipe a total of four scallops (see the scallop section second from left in the bottom row of Illustration 4.3).

Still on the reverse first row, use the #3 round tip to pipe eight more scallops directly over the scallops piped with a #5 round tip. There should be four scallops for the ruffles' outside edge and four scallops for the center (see the third from the bottom left in Illustration 4.3). In this instance, you do not need to wait for the first set of scallops to dry.

For the reverse second row, use the #0 round tip and a contrasting color to pipe a scallop over the scallops piped with the #3 round tip. Repeat this three more times for a total of four scallops. The reverse second row is now complete.

STAGE 3

Return to the reverse first row. Using the #0 round tip and contrasting color, pipe scallops from left to right to the border that was previously piped with the #3 round tip. This applies to both the outside ruffles' edge and the inside ruffles' center. The reverse first row is complete.

To complete the design, position the #0 round tip in contrasting color ¼ in. (6 mm) above the reverse second row, touching the cake. Drag the tip as you pipe a continuous *U*, conforming to the scalloped shape.

You can place plunger flowers at each scallop section for a beautiful finish (see the bottom right of Illustration 4.3), but you need to let the scallops completely dry first. (See plunger flowers in Lesson 17.) This exercise is now complete!

New Skill: Top Border—Single Swags with Overpiped Scallops

Quick Prep

3 medium-size paper cones
1 large paper cone
piping tips: #0, #2, and #3 round tips; #102 petal-shaped tip
6 oz (170 g) Meringue Powder Royal Icing (page 273)

To prepare, place the round tips in the medium-size paper cones and the petal-shaped tip in the large cone. Load 1 Tbsp (14 g) icing in the round tips, using a contrasting color in the #0 and #2. Load 2 oz (57 g) icing in the petal-shaped tip.

This exercise continues to develop concentration and discipline.

STAGE 1

Position your hand and the petal-shaped tip at a 45-degree angle at the upper left-hand corner (if right-handed) of the Styrofoam. Remember, when piping swags, the wide end of the tip must touch the cake's surface. Touch the surface at the marked point on the Styrofoam and apply a burst of pressure. Drag the tip from one marked point to another, following a scalloped pattern. As you reach the next marked position, angle the tip slightly to the right to taper the end of the swag. Repeat the technique for the next three marked positions. Let dry for 5 minutes.

Position the #3 round tip at the top edge of the first swag. Overpipe the top edge of the swags with four scallops. Let dry for 15 to 20 minutes. Stage 1 is complete (see the top left of Illustration 4.4).

STAGE 2

Using the #2 round tip and a contrasting color, overpipe the first row of scallops that were previously piped with the #3 round tip (see the bottom right of Illustration 4.4). Let dry for 15 to 20 minutes. Stage 2 is complete.

STAGE 3

Using the #0 round tip and the same contrasting color, overpipe the first row of scallops piped with the #2 round tip.

Position the #0 round tip ¼ in. (6 mm) just below the swags and pipe four scallops. This exercise is complete.

Illustration 4.4
Top: the steps for piping single swags with over-piped scallops. Bottom: the steps for piping double swags with overpiped scallops.

New Skill: Bottom Border—Double Swags with Overpiped Scallops

Quick Prep

> 5 medium-size paper cones
> 1 large paper cone
> piping tips: #0, 2 #2s, #3, and #5 round tips; #103
>   petal-shaped tip
> 6 oz (170 g) Meringue Powder Royal Icing (page 273)

To prepare, place the round tips in the medium-size paper cones and the petal-shaped tip in the large cone. Load 1 Tbsp (14 g) icing in the round tips, using a contrasting color in the #0 and one of the #2s. Load 2 oz (57 g) icing in the petal-shaped tip.

STAGE 1

Position your hand and the petal-shaped tip with the paper cone at a 45-degree angle at the bottom left-hand corner of the Styrofoam. Remember, when piping swags, the wide end of the tip must touch the cake's surface. Touch the surface at the marked point on the Styrofoam and apply a burst of pressure. Drag the tip from one marked point to another, following a scalloped pattern. As you reach the second marked position, angle the tip slightly to the right to taper the end of the swag. Repeat for the next three marked positions. This is the reverse first row (see the bottom left of Illustration 4.4). Allow to dry for 15 minutes before piping an additional swag just above the reverse first row.

Position the same #103 tip about ¼ in. (6 mm) above the first swag. Drag the tip from one marked point to another, following a scalloped pattern. As you reach the second marked position, angle the tip slightly to the right to taper the end of the swag. Repeat for the next three marked positions. This is the reverse second row (see the middle section of the bottom row in Illustration 4.4).

For the reverse third row, position the #2 round tip about ¼ in. (6 mm) above the reverse second row using the icing that is a non-contrasting color. Pipe four scallops. Then, go back to the beginning of the reverse third row and pipe 4 additional scallops with the #2 round tip in contrasting color. The reverse third row is complete.

For the reverse fourth row, pipe four scallops with the #2 round tip (in non-contrasting color) about ¼ in. (6 mm) above the third scallop. Then, go back to the beginning of the reverse fourth row and pipe 4 additional scallops with the #2 round tip in a contrasting color. Stage 1 is complete.

STAGE 2

The reverse first and second row is complete.

Move to the reverse third row. Position the #0 round tip in a contrasting color and pipe four scallops directly over the scallops piped with the #2 round tip in a contrasting color. This row is complete.

Move to the reverse fourth row. Position the #0 round tip in a contrasting color and pipe four scallops directly over the scallops piped with the #2 round tip in a contrasting color. This row is complete.

STAGE 3

Reverse first, second, third, and fourth rows are complete.

Directly over the seams above the fourth reverse row, use the #2 round tip to pipe two dots—one under the other. This exercise is complete (see the bottom right of Illustration 4.4).

New Skill: Top Border—Reverse Overpiped Scallops

Quick Prep

4 medium-size paper cones
piping tips: #0, #2, #3, and #5 round tips
6 oz (170 g) Meringue Powder Royal Icing (page 273)

This technique is used primarily in competition.

Fruitcake is the only cake that withstands this upside-down treatment, and that is only if it is covered in marzipan, iced with several coats of Meringue

Powder Royal Icing, and then left to dry for several days—even weeks—to develop an extremely hard surface. (Marzipan is discussed in Lesson 8.)

STAGE 1

Measure the top of the cake into four equal sections. Turn the cake upside down. Place the cake on a tall, narrow, flat surface so you do not injure it. You can use a narrow round or square tall Styrofoam, a stack of 6 inch (51.2 cm) round or square cardboard taped together, or any container that is at 6 inches (15.2 cm) high and a circumference of at least 4 to 6 inches (10.2 to 15.2 cm). (If you are practicing on Styrofoam, the surface doesn't matter.) The first row, in this case, is the bottom row. Thus, the first row is called reverse first row; as for the bottom borders, you work from the bottom of the cake toward the center.

Position the #5 round tip at the bottom left-hand corner of the cake (if right-handed). Raise the tip about ½ in. (1.3 cm) from the bottom of the cake. Apply pressure as you allow the icing to flow from the tip. When you move the tip from one position on the marked cake to the next, gravity will pull the icing down to form a scallop. When you reach the next marked point, drag the tip to the surface. Pipe the next three scallops in the same way. This is the reverse first row.

For the reverse second row, position the #3 round tip about ¼ in. (6 mm) above the reverse first row. Pipe four scallops from the left to the right side of the cake, using the same technique as for the reverse first row.

For the reverse third row, position the # 2 round tip about ¼ in. (6 mm) above the reverse second row and pipe four scallops. Let each reverse row dry for 15 to 20 minutes. Stage 1 is complete (see the top left of Illustration 4.5).

STAGE 2

Return to the reverse first row. Position the #3 round tip directly on top of the border piped with the #5 round tip. Overpipe four scallops.

Return to the reverse second row. Position the #2 round tip directly over the border piped with the #3 round tip. Overpipe four scallops.

Skip the reverse third row, piped with the #2 round tip. Stage 2 is complete (see the third scallop section from the top left of Illustration 4.5). Allow this to dry for 15 to 20 minutes.

Decorator's Hint

It may be advantageous to measure both the top and bottom border and work on them simultaneously. Note that the bottom border is a bit more complicated. It is discussed after this exercise is complete.

Illustration 4.5
Top: the steps for creating reverse overpiped scallops. Bottom: the steps for piping overpiped garlands with ruffles and reverse scallops.

STAGE 3

Using the #0 round tip and a contrasting color, overpipe four scallops on each row, totaling 12 scallops.

Position the #0 round tip about ¼ in. (6 mm) above the reverse third row and pipe a continuous *U* embroidery following the scalloped pattern. Stage 3 is complete, and so is this exercise. Turn the cake right side up to see the results (see the top right of Illustration 4.5).

New Skill: Bottom Border—Overpiped Garland (Crescent) with Ruffles and Reverse Scallops

Quick Prep

5 medium-size paper cones
2 large paper cones
piping tips: #0, 2 #2s, #3, and #5 round tips; #18 star tip; #101 petal-shaped tip
8 oz (228 g) Meringue Powder Royal Icing (page 273)

To prepare, place the round tips in the medium-size paper cones. Place the star tip and the petal-shaped tip in the large cones. Load 1 Tbsp (14 g) icing in the round tips, using a contrasting color in the #0 and one of the #2s. Load 2 oz (57 g) icing in the star tip and the petal-shaped tip.

This bottom border design is divided into two sections—the very bottom and the middle of the cake. First, divide the very bottom into four equal sections. Then, divide the middle of the cake into five sections. The very left and right sections of the cake measurements are half reverse scallops. Then there are three equal reverse scallops between the two half reverse scallops. (See the bottom of illustration 4.5).

STAGE 1

Starting near the bottom of the cake, position the star tip at the left edge of the corner (if right-handed). Remember that garlands are made like zigzags, only tighter and with more pressure. Apply pressure as you drag the tip to the cake's surface in a tight zigzag motion, starting with low pressure and building up to high pressure at the midpoint of the garland. Reverse the procedure by applying heavy pressure and then easing off as you taper the first garland to the next marking. Repeat this for the next three markings for a total of four garlands. Allow this to dry for 15 to 20 minutes. This is the reverse first row (see the bottom left of Illustration 4.5).

Invert the cake, as you did for the top border. Move the #5 round tip up about 1 in. (2.54 cm) from the garlands in the reverse first row. Position the tip at the left-hand side of the cake and pipe a half-reverse scallop—that is, half the distance of a full scallop—starting at the left side of the cake and ending above the center point of the first reverse row. Then pipe three full-reverse scallops and another half-reverse scallop. This is the reverse second row (see the middle row in the center of Illustration 4.5).

Position the #3 round tip about ¼ in. (6 mm) above the reverse second row and pipe a half-reverse scallop followed by three full-reverse scallops. Pipe another half-reverse scallop to complete the row, following the pattern of the reverse second row. This is the reverse third row.

Position the #2 round tip about ¼ in. (6 mm) above the reverse third row.

Pipe a half-reverse scallop, three full-reverse scallops, and another half-reverse scallop to complete the row, following the pattern of the reverse third row. This is the reverse fourth row. Stage 1 is complete. Let dry for 15 to 20 minutes.

STAGE 2

Turn the cake right side up and return to the reverse first row. Position the petal-shaped tip at the left side of the garlands; you are now going to pipe ruffles that align at the middle of the garlands. Apply a controlled burst of pressure as you move in an up-and-down motion, following the shape of the garland. When you reach the seam, ease the pressure and drag the tip to end the seam. Start the next ruffle where the first ruffle ends and continue for the next three garlands (see the ruffle second from the bottom left of Illustration 4.5). Let dry for 15 to 20 minutes.

Invert the cake again and return to the reverse second row. Position the #3 round tip at the reverse second row. Pipe a half-reverse scallop over the reverse scallops piped with the #5 round tip. Pipe three full-reverse scallops, then another half-reverse scallop to complete this row.

Position the #2 round tip at the reverse third row, piped in Stage 1 with the #2 round tip. Overpipe the row by piping a half-reverse scallop, three full-reverse scallops, and another half-reverse scallop (see the middle right section of Illustration 4.5).

Position the #2 round tip with a contrasting color at the reverse fourth row. Pipe a half-reverse scallop, three full-reverse scallops, and another half-reverse scallop to complete this row. Let dry 15 to 20 minutes.

STAGE 3

Turn the cake right-side up and return to the reverse first row. Position the #5 round tip at the top edge of the ruffles that are piped on top of the garlands. Pipe a scallop for each ruffle, allowing the scallops to drape and conform to the shape of the ruffles (see the third scallop section from the bottom right of Illustration 4.5). Let dry for 15 to 20 minutes.

Invert the cake again. Position the #2 round tip in contrasting color at the reverse second row. Pipe a half-reverse scallop, three full-reverse scallops, and another half-reverse scallop to complete this row.

Position the #2 round tip in contrasting color at the reverse third row. Pipe a half-reverse scallop, three full-reverse scallops, and another half-reverse scallop to complete this row. Skip the reverse fourth row. Stage 3 is complete. Let dry 15 to 20 minutes.

STAGE 4

Turn the cake right-side up again and return to the reverse first row. Position the #3 round tip directly over the scallops piped with the #5 round tip. Pipe four scallops to complete this row.

Go back to the first row with the #2 round tip in contrasting color and overpipe a scallop for each row just piped with the #3 round tip. Let dry for 15 to 20 minutes (see the bottom right of Illustration 4.5).

Position the #0 round tip in contrasting color at the reverse first row. Pipe four scallops. This row is complete. Allow this to dry for 15 to 20 minutes.

Invert the cake. At the reverse second, third, and fourth rows, pipe scallops with the #0 round tip in contrasting color. These rows are now complete.

Position the #0 tip ¼ in. (6 mm) above the reverse fourth row. Pipe a *U* embroidery just above each of the reverse scallops to complete this exercise.

Decorator's Hint

Piping is done on the reverse second, third, and fourth rows in Stage 4.

Part II: Advanced Top and Bottom Border Designs

You will need the following equipment and recipes to complete this section:

Meringue Powder Royal Icing (page 273)

small and medium-size paper cones

piping tips: #0, #2, #3 round tips; #18 star tip; #103 petal-shaped tip

gel food colors

rounded toothpicks

small metal bowls

offset metal spatulas

rubber spatulas (brand-new)

rectangular Styrofoams

These top and bottom border designs are not as difficult as those presented in the Part I exercises. Part I was designed to be academic, giving you a thorough grounding in the principles and practices of pressure control and precision piping. While not common, Part I exercises are essential in forming good piping habits and paying strict attention to details.

Part II exercises are those most commonly seen on high-end celebration cakes. Done properly, these designs are showy and beautiful—but often they are not done well at all.

As in Part I, top and bottom borders can be piped simultaneously. Because little overpiping is done is this part, drying time between layers is minimal.

New Skill: Top Border—Reverse Shells with Scalloped Strings

Quick Prep

2 medium-size paper cones
1 large paper cone
piping tips: #0 and #3 round tips; #18 star tip
4 oz (114 g) Meringue Powder Royal Icing (page 273)

To prepare, place the round tips in the medium-size paper cones and the star tip in the large cone. Load 1 Tbsp (14 g) icing in the round tips, using a contrasting color in the #0. Load 2 oz (57 g) icing in the star tip.

Divide the top section of the cake form (or Styrofoam) into five equal parts, using adding machine paper or a ruler. Measure from the left to the right side of the cake and divide the length by five. Mark the five equal sections on your cake dummy with a pencil. Mark the top edge of the cake. Do not mark the bottom, as the bottom borders are not divided into sections. Use a little Meringe Powder Royal Icing to make your Styrofoam stick to a foiled-covered rectangular cake board.

Position the star tip at the inside edge of the top of the cake. Recall the reverse shell exercises from Lesson 1. Pipe reverse shells along the inside edge of the top of the cake.

This step produces the scallops and embroidery on the top side edge. Position the #3 round tip at the marked position near the top edge of the cake. (Remember, this edge is divided into five sections.) Apply a burst of pressure, allowing icing to flow from the tip. Move the tip from the first marked position to the next, allowing gravity to pull the line down into a scalloped shape. When you reach the next marked position, drag the tip to the surface to end the scallop. Pipe scallops for the next four marked positions.

Position the #0 round tip in contrasting color about ¼ in. (6 mm) under the scalloped border piped with the #3 round tip. Drag the tip to the surface as you pipe a continuous *M* embroidery, following the shape of the scalloped border above it. The top border is complete (see the top of Illustration 4.6).

> ### Decorator's Hint
>
> The center point of the scallop should be ½ in. (1.3 cm) from the top edge of the cake.

Illustration 4.6
Top: reverse shells and the steps for piping scalloped strings. Bottom: zigzags with large shells and reverse scallops.

New Skill: Bottom Border—Zigzags with Large Shells and Reverse Scallops

Quick Prep

> 2 medium-size paper cones
> 1 large paper cone
> piping tips: #0 and #2 round tips; #18 star tip
> 4 oz (114 g) Meringue Powder Royal Icing (page 273)

To prepare, place the round tips in the medium-size paper cones with the #2 round tip in a contrasting color. Place the star tip in the large cone. Load 1 Tbsp (14 g) icing in the round tips, using a contrasting color in the #0. Load 2 oz (57 g) icing in the star tip.

Position the star tip near the bottom edge of the cake surface. This is a layered border, like the overpiped borders done in Part I of this lesson, but no drying time is required between the layers. Pipe a zigzag along the bottom of the border.

The next step is to pipe large shells directly on top of the zigzag, using the star tip. The right edge of the shells will come in contact with the cake's surface.

Position the #2 round tip in contrasting color about ¼ in. (6 mm) above the large shells just piped. These are reverse scallops. (Normally, when piping reverse scallops, the cake is turned upside down. Because these are short reverse scallops, however, the tip is dragged to the cake's surface as the scallops are piped. This allows you to achieve the same look, as if the cake were inverted.)

Position the #0 round tip about ¼ in. (6 mm) above the short reverse scallops just piped. Drag the tip as you pipe a continuous *U* embroidery in a straight line. This bottom border is complete (see the bottom right section of Illustration 4.6).

New Skill: Top Border—Large Shells with Overpiped *S* Scrolls

Quick Prep

> 2 medium-size paper cones
> 1 large paper cone
> piping tips: #0 and #2 round tips; #18 star tip
> 4 oz (114 g) Meringue Powder Royal Icing (page 273)

To prepare, place the round tips in the medium-size paper cones and the star tip in the large cone. Load 1 Tbsp (14 g) icing in the round tips, using a contrasting color in the #0. Load 2 oz (57 g) icing in the star tip.

Position the star tip at an angle between 45 and 90 degrees along the inside edge of the top of the cake. If you want to produce a scroll look on the sides of the shell, go closer to 90 degrees. Raise the tip slightly from the surface. Apply a burst of pressure and allow a small amount of icing to protrude from the tip. Move the tip slightly forward and continue with pressure as the head of the shell builds up, then gradually pull the tip toward you and lower it to scratch the surface. Ease off the pressure and stop. Continue with the next large shell until the top border is completed. (See the top of Illustration 4.6.)

The *S* scrolls are piped on the sides of the cake near the top edge. First, measure the cake from left to right. Mark the cake into 1-in. (2.54 cm) segments. Now, go back to the markings and mark ¾ in. (1.9 cm) of each 1-in. (2.54 cm) measurement. This will be the length of each scroll. The remaining ¼-in. (6 mm) sections will be the spaces between each scroll.

Decorator's Hint

Exact measurements here are not of primary importance. What *is* important is the placement of the scroll plus a space between each scroll. Thus, the scrolls could be 1 in. (2.54 cm) long instead of ¾ in. (1.9 cm), and the space between each scroll could be ⅛ in. (3 mm) rather than ¼ in. (6 mm).

Illustration 4.7
Top: large shells with overpiped *S* scrolls.
Bottom: shells with scallops.

Position the #2 round tip at the first marking at a 90-degree angle and slightly above the surface. Squeeze the paper cone and drag the tip to the surface in a clockwise direction, forming a horizontally oriented backward *S*. Continue to drag the tip and complete the shape of the backward *S*. It should be ¾ in. (1.9 cm) long (see the top right of Illustration 4.7). The remaining ¼ in. (6 mm) is the space before the next backward *S*. Move the tip to the next marking and continue piping scrolls until they are all complete. Allow the scrolls to dry for 10 minutes.

Position the #0 round tip with a contrasting color at the first scroll. Carefully overpipe the scrolls to add depth to each. Position the #0 tip between two scrolls with the tip about ¼ in. (6 mm) below them. Pipe a dot, then round off the tip to the right or left (so there is not a peak left on the dot). Pipe a small backward curve to the left and right of the dot to complete this section (see the top right of Illustration 4.7).

New Skill: Bottom Border—Shells with Scallops

Quick Prep

> 2 medium-size paper cones
> 1 large paper cone
> piping tips: #0 and #2 round tips; #18 star tip
> 4 oz (114 g) Meringue Powder Royal Icing (page 273)

To prepare, place the round tips in the medium-size paper cones and the star tip in the large cone. Load 1 Tbsp (14 g) icing in the round tips, using a contrasting color in the #0. Load 2 oz (57 g) icing in the star tip.

Position the star tip at the left-hand corner of the bottom of the cake. Pipe large shells as described in the top border exercise in this lesson and in Lesson 1. Next, position the #2 round tip about ¼ in. (6 mm) above the shells and pipe scallops approximately the length of each shell. Remember, when piping scallops, touch the surface with the tip and apply a controlled burst of pressure. Allow the icing to flow from the tip and move the tip from one point to another. Gravity pulls the icing down into a scalloped shape. Continue until all the scallops are piped. Allow the scallops to dry for 10 minutes.

Position the #0 round tip in contrasting color by the scallops piped with the #2 round tip. Overpipe each scallop to give it depth. Position the #0 round tip ¼ in. (6 mm) above the scallops you just overpiped. Touch the surface and drag the tip against the cake as you pipe a *U* embroidery that conforms to the shape of the scallops below. This border is complete (see the bottom of Illustration 4.7).

New Skill: Top Border—Garlands with Double Strings and Drop Strings

Quick Prep

> 2 medium-size paper cones
> 1 large paper cone
> piping tips: #0 and #2 round tips; #18 star tip
> 4 oz (114 g) Meringue Powder Royal Icing (page 273)

To prepare, place the round tips in the medium-size paper cones and the star tip in the large cone. Load 1 Tbsp (14 g) icing in the round tips, using a contrasting color in the #0. Load 2 oz (57 g) icing in the star tip.

Decorator's Hint

Exact measurements here are not of primary importance. What *is* important is the placement and natural flow of the scallops.

Measure the cake from left to right into five or six equal sections to produce garlands about 2 in. (5 cm) in length. Mark each section with a half-circle shape. Practice five or six half-circles or scallops on another surface, making sure each is connected.

Position the star tip and pastry bag at a 45-degree angle. Position your body at the 9 o'clock position (if right-handed) or the 3 o'clock position (if left-handed). Apply a burst of pressure as you drag the tip to the surface in a tight zigzag motion. Start out with light pressure, increasing as you reach the center of the scallop. Start decreasing the pressure as you move the tip back and forth to the scallop's end. Repeat this technique for the next pattern (see the top left of Illustration 4.8). Continue piping garlands until all the marked sections are piped. Let dry for 15 to 20 minutes.

Position the #0 round tip with contrasting color at a 45-degree angle at the top edge of the first finished garland. Apply pressure to the bag and slowly pull the tip out of the garland. Continue pressure, slowly easing off as you reach the end of the garland. Gravity will pull the string down to form the scallop shape of the garlands. The first set of strings should lie across the center of each garland. Repeat for additional garlands. For a double string line, repeat this procedure, starting with the first garland and allowing the second line to drop below the centered line. Taper the end of the string to the garland (see the top right of Illustration 4.8).

Position the #2 round tip about ¼ in. (6 mm) lower than the first set of garlands with double strings. Pipe scallops from left to right, allowing the string to conform naturally to the shape of the garlands above. Reposition the #0 round tip with contrasting color at the left side of the scallops with the tip about ¼ in. (6 mm) lower than the previous scallops. Pipe scallops under the second row of scallops. The top border is complete.

Illustration 4.8
Top: the steps to pipe garlands with double strings and drop strings. Bottom: a single ruffle bottom border.

New Skill: Bottom Border—Single Ruffles

Quick Prep

1 large paper cone
piping tips: #103 or #104 petal-shaped tip
3 oz (85 g) Meringue Powder Royal Icing (page 273)

To prepare, place the tip in the paper cone and load it with 2 oz (57 g) icing.

This lovely, simple, clean border is from Lesson 1. You can never get enough practice on ruffles.

To start, turn your body slightly to the left (if right-handed) or right (if left-handed). Position the tip flat on your work surface with the narrow end pointing toward you. Angle the tip to 45 degrees. Apply a burst of pressure, allowing some of the icing to protrude. Raise the tip slightly and then drop it down to the surface. Continue this up-and-down motion as you apply pressure. The ruffles should appear uniform and even. Ease the pressure when you reach the end of the edge of the cake. The bottom border is complete (see the bottom of Illustration 4.8).

New Skill: Top Border—Fleur-de-Lis with Overpiping and Drop Strings

Quick Prep

2 medium-size paper cones
1 large paper cone
piping tips: #0 and #2 round tips; #18 star tip
4 oz (114 g) Meringue Powder Royal Icing (page 273)

To prepare, place the round tips in the medium-size paper cones and the star tip in the large cone. Load 1 Tbsp (14 g) icing in the round tips, using a contrasting color in the #0. Load 2 oz (57 g) icing in the star tip.

This elaborate border is the type seen on wedding cakes. Producing it here reviews the fleur-de-lis with drop strings skills taught in Lesson 1. The overpiping adds elegance to this striking technique.

For the fleur-de-lis, measure the top edge of the cake from left to right into six or eight sections. Position the star tip at the top edge of the cake. Raise the tip slightly from the surface and apply a burst of pressure, allowing some of the icing to extend. Move the tip forward slightly. Continue with pressure to build the head of the shell, then gradually pull the tip toward you. Extend the tail of the shell about ¾ in. (1.9 cm), ¼ in. (6 mm) longer than a regular large shell. Ease the pressure as you scratch the surface.

Position the tip at the bottom of the shell. Move it ¼ to ½ in. (6 mm to 1.3 cm) to the left of the shell. Move it upward ¼ to ½ in. (6 mm to 1.3 cm). Then position the tip and pastry bag at an angle between 45 and 90 degrees. Raise the tip slightly from the surface and apply a burst of pressure. Move the tip clockwise. At the 11 o'clock position, apply a burst of pressure and swing the tip around and down to the 6 o'clock position. The tail end of the reverse shell should overlap the centered shell. Stop the pressure and ease away. Move the tip to the right about ¼ to ½ in. (6 mm to 1.3 cm) and then upward ¼ to ½ in. (6 mm to 1.3 cm). Raise the tip slightly from the surface and apply a burst of pressure. Move the tip in counterclockwise. At the 1 o'clock position, apply a burst of pressure and swing the tip around and down to the 6 o'clock position. The tail should overlap the left and centered shell. Stop the pressure and ease away. Proceed to the next markings and pipe the remaining fleurs-de-lis (see the top left of Illustration 4.9). Allow to dry for 15 to 20 minutes.

Position the #2 round tip at the first completed fleur-de-lis. Following its shape, overpipe it beginning in the center of the left reverse shell and spiraling clockwise. Drag the tip to the surface of the reverse shell while overpiping the string. End at the tail end of the centered shell. To do the same in reverse for the right reverse shell, start in its center and spiral counterclockwise. Remember to drag the tip while overpiping the string. Both left and right strings should end side by side at the tail end of the centered shell.

Position the #2 round tip above the cake where the shell extends above its sides, in the center of the centered shell. Touch the surface and raise the tip slightly, allowing the string to conform to the shape of the centered shell. Allow the string to drop to the centered shell (rather than dragging the tip, as you did on the left and right reverse shells) and taper it to the bottom. The center string should be in the middle of the reverse strings (see the top middle of the Illustration 4.9). Repeat the overpiping on the rest of the fleur-de-lis. Allow to dry for 15 to 20 minutes.

Position the #0 round tip with contrasting color directly on top of the fleur-de-lis piped with the #2 round tip. Overpipe the overpiped strings. Allow to dry for 10 minutes.

For drop strings, position the #2 round tip at the tail end of the centered shell of the fleur-de-lis. Touch the surface and pull the tip toward you. Move the tip to the next centered shell. Stop the pressure and taper the icing to the shell. Gravity pulls the strings down and forms beautiful scalloped shapes. Continue with the drop strings and complete the rest of the overpiped fleurs-de-lis. Let dry for 10 minutes.

Go back to the first overpiped fleur-de-lis with drop strings and pipe an additional drop string slightly under the previous one. This is called a double drop-string. The strings should drop about ¼ in. (6 mm) at the center point of the scallop. Be careful when tapering the end of the string over the previous strings. Complete the remaining strings. The top border is complete (see the top right of Illustration 4.9).

Illustration 4.9
Top: the steps for piping fleurs-de-lis with over-piping and drop strings. Bottom: a bottom border of rosettes and drop strings.

New Skill: Bottom Border—Rosettes with Drop Strings

Quick Prep

1 medium-size paper cone
1 large paper cone
piping tips: #0 round tip and #18 star tip
4 oz (114 g) Meringue Powder Royal Icing (page 273)

To prepare, place the round tip in the medium-size paper cone and the star tip in the large cone. Load 1 Tbsp (14 g) icing in a contrasting color in the #0. Load 2 oz (57 g) icing in the star tip.

This is a quick and easy yet effective border. Rosettes are not often used as a bottom border. This technique gives you a new use for them.

Position the star tip at the bottom of the cake to the left (if right-handed) or right (if left-handed). Remember, a right-handed person will be in the 9 o'clock position and the left-handed person at the 3 o'clock position. Because these rosettes are slightly angled to the cake rather than flat on the cake board, position the tip at the crease where the cake ends and the cardboard begins. Raise the tip slightly from the surface. Pipe a tight circle—that is, without any interior space. After one revolution, stop the pressure but continue to move the tip as you ease it away from the rosette. Leave about ¼ in. (6 mm) before starting the next rosette. Continue piping rosettes until you reach the end of the cake (see the bottom of Illustration 4.9). Let dry for 10 minutes.

Position the round tip with contrasting color at the center of the first completed rosette. Touch the surface and apply a controlled amount of pressure. Move the tip to the center of the next rosette, allowing gravity to pull the strings down into a natural scallop shape. Continue piping strings until all the rosettes are connected. This bottom border is complete (see the bottom right of Illustration 4.9).

END-OF-LESSON REVIEW

What is another name for a scallop?

What are the two types of royal icings? What is the difference between them?

What term is used to describe lines of icing that are piped directly on top of one another?

True or False: Royal Icing cannot be colored with food colors.

Why is it recommended that paper cones be used for piping fine and intricate work?

What is the correct procedure for piping a drop string?

What types of colors are used to color Royal Icing?

What is the purpose of using a contrasting color when piping lines of icing on top of one another?

When piping lines of icing on top of one other, should the last line be piped with a round tip or small opening tip? Why?

PERFORMANCE TEST

Select one top and one bottom border from Part I of Lesson 4. Review the procedures in Lesson 4 to complete the following exercise:

Top: Overpiped Scallops and Short Overpiped Scallops

Bottom: Overpiped Garlands (Crescents) with Scallops and Ruffles with Overpiped Scallops

Select one top and one bottom border from Part II of Lesson 4. Review the procedures in Lesson 4 to complete the following exercise.

Top: Reverse Shells with Scalloped Strings and Large Shells with Overpiped S Scrolls

Bottom: Zigzag with Large Shells and Reverse Scallops and Shells with Scallops

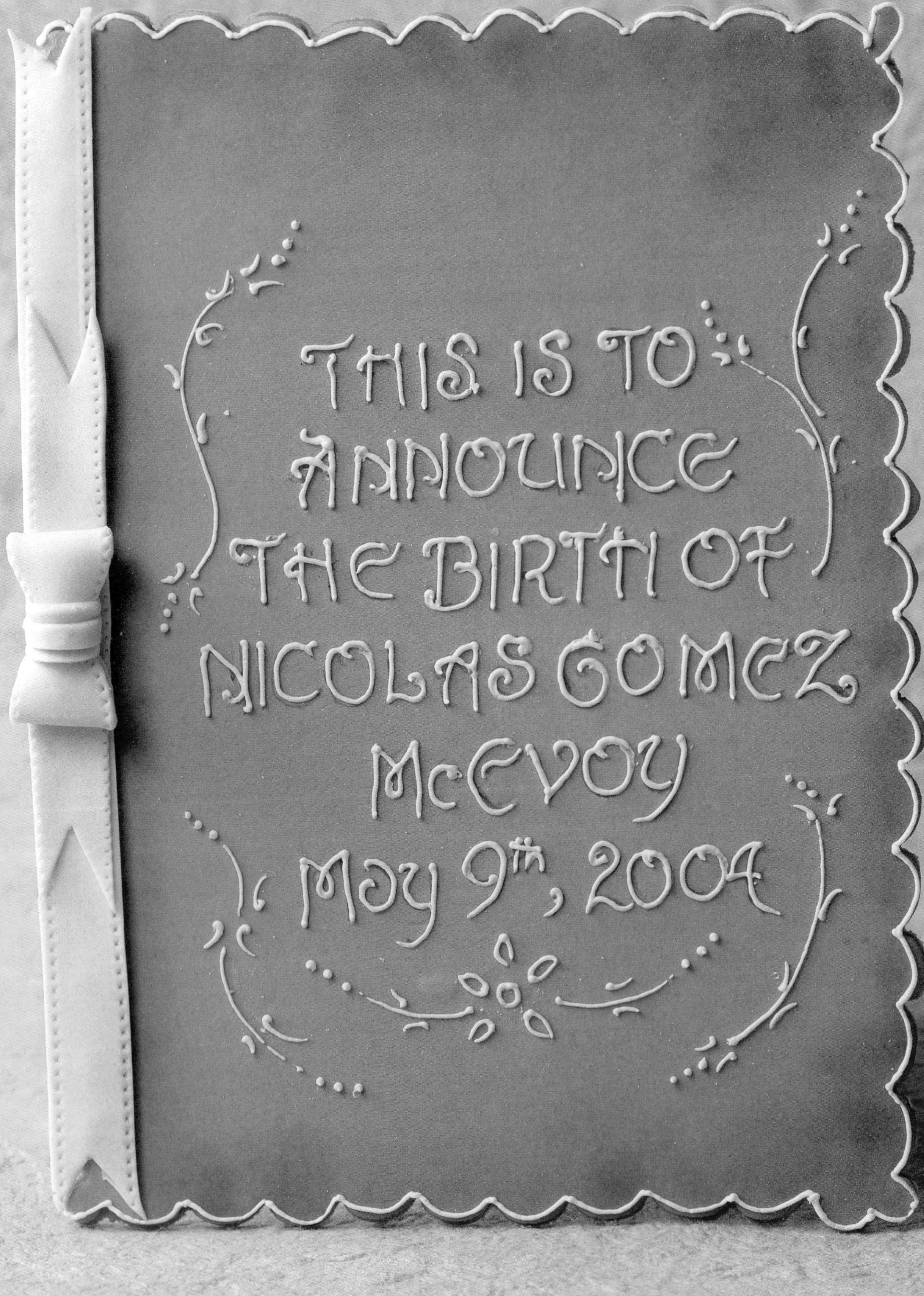
THIS IS TO
ANNOUNCE
THE BIRTH OF
NICOLAS GOMEZ
McEVOY
May 9th, 2004

THE ART OF WRITING

Writing Workshop

You will need the following icings and items to complete this lesson:

Chocolate Glaze for Piping (page 268)

Meringue Powder Royal Icing (page 273)

Flood Icing (page 274)

piping gel

light corn syrup

fresh or pasteurized egg whites

rounded toothpicks

small and medium-size paper cones for tips and paper cones without tips

piping tips: #0, #2, and #3 round tips; #101 petal-shaped tip

gel food colors

small metal bowls

offset metal spatulas

rubber spatulas (brand-new)

cardboard circles and squares

plastic wrap

masking tape

scissors

warming tray

Welcome to Lesson 5 and the art of writing. Writing on cakes is perhaps one of the most difficult tasks to do, especially when out of practice. A beautiful cake can almost be ruined by poor writing skills. A cake should not be sold if the writing is poor and certainly not if the name is misspelled. This chapter reveals my secrets for successful writing on cakes and ways of overcoming writing anxiety.

Constant practice is probably the key to cake writing. The next most important aspect is finding an icing medium that you're comfortable with. Some people find chocolate to be a good writing medium. Others prefer piping gel (a transparent medium available at cake decorating stores and used chiefly for writing on iced cakes in retail/wholesale bakeries), buttercream, or royal icing. To be an accomplished cake writer in any medium, one must develop the skill so it is as natural as writing with a pencil on paper. Working in a bakery, where the demand for cake writing is constant, is the best way to develop speed and confidence. However, you must practice. A style of writing, or transfer techniques, can lead to success.

Alphabet Practice

The alphabet is a great place to start. Choosing an alphabetic design can be as easy as selecting a font from your computer, calligraphy book, or art book. Choose lowercase and uppercase characters in a basic block style with either a fancy script or calligraphic hand. Some find block writing the easiest. Others prefer a cursive or calligraphic style. The best mediums are piping gel, melted chocolate with a little corn oil, or light corn syrup added as a thickening agent, although some people use buttercream or meringue powder royal icing. Of course, the only way to know what works for you is to try several mediums and choose the one with which you are most comfortable and successful.

Knowing how to form letters with a paper cone is different than using a pencil or pen. The key when learning how to write is to trace. The approach is to trace the letters over and over before advancing to freehand work. Develop a fluid style by writing phrases and learning to connect large characters with small characters. Finally, practicing at every opportunity builds confidence.

Writing on an Iced Cake

Writing on an iced cake is the first challenge for the new cake decorator. If the surface is buttercream, it is best to refrigerate the cake before writing. This allows you to make corrections without damaging the icing. If chilling isn't possible, practice on a round cardboard the same size as the cake, marking exactly where to place the lettering. If you plan to add a spray of piped flowers, you may wish to place the writing on the right side of the cake and the piped flowers on the left, or vice versa.

Keep the writing small and uniform so you can fit all the lettering on the cake. As a guideline, use a toothpick to pinprick the letter positions. Also, remember that the entire inscription does not need to be on one line. You can usually write Happy on one line and Birthday on the second, adding a person's name on the third. The personalization of a cake is the most important part to many customers. Never misspell a name or company title on a cake.

Writing on a Sugar Plaque

For a greeting on a cake that is very formal, write on a sugar plaque made from marzipan, rolled fondant, pastillage, or gum paste rather than directly on the cake. This technique, which can be a lifesaver, allows you to correct mistakes by removing the writing with a toothpick or a damp cloth. After the plaque dries, try again. When you have the writing perfected, place the plaque on the cake. If the cake is iced with rolled fondant, stick the plaque on with a dab of icing. If the cake is iced with buttercream, set the plaque directly on the cake. The buttercream will hold the plaque in place. Before service, you can remove the plaque from the cake and give it to the person of honor as a keepsake. (See recipes for the rolled icings for plaques in Lesson 19.)

Remember, if cake writing were easy, everyone would do it. Take pride in your writing and don't be afraid or shy when the opportunity arises.

New Skill: Alphabet Writing Workshop

Quick Prep

4 oz (114 g) Chocolate Icing for Writing (Chocolate Glaze for Piping, page 268)
4 oz (114 g) piping gel
4 oz (114 g) Meringue Powder Royal Icing (page 273)
warming tray for the Chocolate Icing for Writing
alphabet practice sheets: A, B and C

Prepare the practice surface by placing Writing Exercise Pattern A on flat surface (see Writing Exercise Pattern A on page 315). Sheet A is a calligraphy workshop. Turn the alphabetic exercises to the left (if right-handed) or to the right (if left-handed) for a more natural writing position. Tape the corners with masking tape. Place a piece of plastic wrap or parchment paper over the alphabet sheets and tape it down securely. You should be able to see the alphabet practice sheets through the plastic wrap or parchment paper. You could also use wax paper, Plexiglas, Mylar, or any other transparent medium.

Load a paper cone with 1 Tbsp (14 g) Chocolate Icing for Writing. Snip the end of the paper cone with a pair of scissors. If a tiny hole is cut straight across the tip of the tapered cone, the icing flow will be smooth and perfect. Position your body comfortably. Begin with the uppercase characters. Hold the paper cone as if you were holding a pencil. Place your opposite hand on the paper cone too for added control.

Start with the uppercase A. Touch the surface and apply controlled pressure to begin the writing. The tip of the paper cone should be slightly above the surface as you trace the outline of the letter underneath the see-through surface. Trace part of the letter from north to south or vice versa. When ending a curve or stroke, slightly drag the tip of the cone to the surface. Position the tip of the cone at another position on the letter and repeat until the entire letter is completed. Go on to the next letter.

Trace each character one at a time and then go on to the lowercase letters. When you have completed, clean the surface and trace the alphabets all over again (see Illustration 5.1 a-e). If the icing becomes too thick, replace the paper cone with fresh icing.

Practice Writing Exercise Pattern B (Appendix 1, page 316). This is a block-with-flourish-style exercise—that is, block-style writing with attractive curves. Chocolate Icing for Writing is also appropriate for this style. Place the block lettering exercise under plastic wrap or glass as in Exercise A.

Decorator's Hint

Preparing a paper cone for writing without a tip is a little different than making the traditional paper cone form with a triangle. To write without an icing tip, you need a paper cone that is narrower and pointier than the cones prepared for tips. This is fully illustrated in Lesson 1.

Decorator's Hint

Paper cones can be made without cutting the tip end of the paper. Fold the tip inward to complete the cone. You can adjust the tip by gently pulling up or down on the tail to open or close the tip to the desired size. The goal is for the chocolate to flow out of the bag in an even stream without catching and veering to the side, which makes it hard to control.

Squeeze the bag to see how the chocolate icing flows from the bag. If it flows too quickly, allow the icing to set up a little bit more before you begin your practice. Leave the icing in the bag at room temperature and squeeze it periodically to check its consistency.

Decorator's Hint

It does not matter where you start writing. Some people find it easier to start at the top of the letter. I start some alphabet styles from the bottom and others from the top. The angle at which you hold the bag depends on the size of the paper cone and how it is held. If the cone is held like a pencil, then 45 degrees is an appropriate angle. If a larger cone is held like a pastry bag, then the angle should be closer to 90 degrees.

(a)

(b)

(c)

(d)

(e)

Illustration 5.1
Writing letters with a pattern: (a) The tip of the cone is just above the surface; (b, c, d) Drag the tip to the surface to end the line; (e) It's important to practice writing to become proficient and comfortable with the process.

Load a paper cone with 1 Tbsp (14 g) Chocolate Icing for Writing. Snip the very end of the cone with a pair of scissors. Position your body to the practice surface. Begin with the uppercase characters, holding the paper cone as if it were a pencil. Touch your opposite hand to the cone for added control. Squeeze the bag to see how the chocolate icing flows from the bag. If it flows too quickly, allow the icing to set a little bit more before you begin your practice. Leave the icing in the bag at room temperature and squeeze the bag periodically to check its consistency. Begin piping. Remember, drag the tip to the surface to start the letters and raise the bag slightly above the surface to complete them. When ending each character, drag the bag to the surface.

When you finish the uppercase letters, go on to the lowercase characters. When those are completed, look at the piped letters carefully and check to see which of them could have been made better. Clean the surface and repeat the alphabets.

Place Writing Exercise Pattern C (Appendix 1, page 316) under the work surface. For this block-style writing exercise, you have the choice of piping gel or Meringue Powder Royal Icing. Piping gel gives a softer look (like the Chocolate Icing for Writing). Meringue Powder Royal Icing has a firmer and sharper look. For this exercise, pipe half of the uppercase and lowercase letters with piping gel and the other half with Meringue Powder Royal Icing. (Both of these can be colored with paste or gel food colors or left neutral.) Load a paper cone with 2 Tbsp (28 g) piping gel. Load a second cone with 2 Tbsp (28 g) Meringue Powder Royal Icing.

Practice Writing Exercise Pattern C under the same conditions as A and B. Remember to drag the tip of the paper cone to the surface when starting and to lift the cone just above the exercise to complete it. Drag the tip to the surface when ending a stroke or curve.

Note: When practicing extremely large lettering or small continuous borders, such as *e*, *c*, *mm*, and w scrolls, raise the tip of the paper cone filled with chocolate about 1 to 3 in. (2.54 to 7.6 cm) above the surface. Squeeze the bag and allow the icing to fall to the surface. This technique is beautiful and graceful and will help you develop confidence in piping intricate designs.

> *Decorator's Hint*
>
> Try some of the other alphabetic writing patterns in Appendix 1, pages 315–318.

New Skill: Writing Styles and Techniques— Simple Block Lettering

Quick Prep

small, medium, and large paper cones
piping tips: #2 and 3 round tips; #101 petal-shaped tip
12 oz (340 g) Meringue Powder Royal Icing (page 273)

Perhaps the most widely used style in cake writing is simple block lettering. This is an extension of the natural writing hand that pays more attention to each letter. A simple writing hand can be most profitable in a busy bakery. In a supermarket bakery, writing on cakes is an everyday assignment. There is no time to worry if the writing isn't perfect. As long as the name and greetings are spelled correctly, the cake can be sold!

Gourmet supermarkets that include an on-site bakery give more time to cake writing than ordinary chain supermarket bakeries do. These goods are sold at higher prices because more time is spent producing beautiful, delicious cakes.

Pull the templates for Happy Birthday, Bon Voyage, Haute Couture, and With Sympathy (see Appendix 1, pages 319–322). We will practice these block-style writing examples first.

Illustration 5.2
Happy Birthday piped freehand.

Place the Happy Birthday template under a piece of parchment paper, Plexiglas, or Mylar (see Illustration 5.2). Load a #2 round tip with 1 Tbsp (14 g) of royal icing. Practice this simple greeting three times, then practice three times without the template.

The letters of the Bon Voyage message are in an informal, natural block handwriting style. This example is achieved with the #2 round tip and 1 Tbsp (14 g) royal icing. Hold the icing tip just above the template, as in the other exercises. Pipe the greeting three times with the template and then another three times without it (see Illustration 5.3).

For the Haute Couture greeting, soften the consistency of the royal icing with a little water. Softening the royal icing will help give this writing exercise a blocked but more rounded and stylized look. Place 1 Tbsp (14 g) royal icing in a small container with ¼ tsp (1 ml) cold water and stir gently. Load a paper cone with the #3 round tip and the softened royal icing. Position the greeting under parchment or Mylar, as for the previous exercises. Raise the tip slightly above the surface at a 45-degree angle. Pipe the greeting three times with the template and another three times without it.

The With Sympathy greeting is a little more challenging and a lot of fun. Rather than a traditional round tip, use the #101 petal-shaped tip. Place 2 Tbsp (28 g) royal icing in a large paper cone with the #101 petal-shaped tip. Place the greeting under parchment or Mylar to begin the exercise. Remember, when using a petal-shaped tip, position its wide end on the surface when piping.

Position the tip just above the greeting and gradually apply pressure as you form each of the letters. The tip should slightly drag the surface as you form each of the letters. This is called the contact method for writing. Making contact with the surface when you do certain types of calligraphy writing gives a fluid stroke and the ability to make both thin and heavy lines. Some of the characters are formed in two parts, such as the *y* and the *t*. Practice this greeting several times with the template and then practice freehand as well (see Illustration 5.4).

Decorator's Hint

When piping the Haute Couture message, be careful to end each letter by easing off the pressure. The idea is to form a rounded look at the end of each letter.

Illustration 5.3
Freehand writing allows for creativity in forming letters.

Illustration 5.4
Using the #101 petal-shaped tip to write letters adds an extra dimension to any writing activity.

New Skill: Elegant Writings

Quick Prep

small and medium paper cones
piping tips: #0, #2, and #3 round tips
10 oz (283 g) Meringue Powder Royal Icing (page 273)
2 oz (47g) Chocolate Icing for Writing (Chocolate Glaze for
    Piping, page 268)
warming tray for the Chocolate Icing for Writing
4 oz (114 g) piping gel

This set of skills creates beautifully tailored writing. Each exercise has its own rewarding challenges. Pay close attention to detail. Neatness is essential to success with these writing styles. Pull the templates for Wedding Bliss, Glorious Divorce, Season's Greetings, and the stylized Happy Birthday (see Appendix 1, pages 320–322).

For the Wedding Bliss exercise, load 1 Tbsp (14 g) royal icing with the #0 round tip in a small paper cone. Place the exercise under Mylar, plastic wrap, or parchment paper. The keys to this exercise are patience and accuracy. When pip-ing curves and circles, carefully drag the tip just above the surface. When forming down strokes, move the tip in a zigzag motion from top to bottom (rather than side to side, as in Lesson 1). This tech-nique forms small beads on top of the downstroke and adds elegance to the writ-ing. Be sure to use strokes of different weight: lighter strokes for curves and cir-cles and heavier strokes for downstrokes. This is similar to copperplate calligraphy writing.

Repeat this exercise three times with the template and then three times without it (see Illustration 5.5).

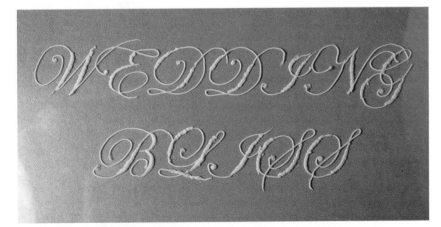

Illustration 5.5
This writing technique involves lighter strokes on the curves and heavier strokes on the downstrokes.

Illustration 5.6
To achieve the best results with Chocolate Icing for Writing, it is important that the icing flows with the right consistency.

Glorious Divorce is made in the same way as piped alphabets. A small amount of corn syrup or corn oil is added to melted chocolate to give it body and allow greater piping control.

Place the exercise under the parchment paper. Load a paper cone with 1 Tbsp (14 g) Chocolate Icing for Writing. Remember, there is no tip in the paper cone when using this icing.

Cut a small hole in the bag and place the tip just above the exercise template. Follow the line of the pattern, lightly dragging the tip at the beginning and end of each letter. Practice Glorious Divorce several times with the template and then several times without it (see Illustration 5.6).

The Season's Greetings and the stylized Happy Birthday are the finale of this lesson. Each greeting requires a technique known as *outline and flooding*. Each letter of the greeting is outlined with Meringue Powder Royal Icing and its interior is filled in with softened Meringue Powder Royal Icing or piping gel. This exercise is done just once because it calls for so much drying time.

First, transfer the greetings to a piece of cardboard, using the transfer technique covered in Lesson 7. Next, color 1 Tbsp (14 g) Meringue Powder Royal Icing with chocolate brown gel food color. Place the colored icing in a paper cone fitted with the #2 round tip. Carefully outline each of the letters in Season's Greetings. Next, load 2 Tbsp (28 g) Meringue Powder Royal Icing in a paper cone with the #3 round tip. Carefully outline each of the letters in Happy Birthday.

Now, divide the 4 oz (114 g) piping gel into 1 oz (28 g) containers. Color the gel with holiday colors (red, yellow, green, etc.). Load each color in a paper cone without a tip. Carefully cut the bags. Place the tip of the paper cone inside the outlined letters. Squeeze some of the gel into the outline. Use a toothpick to spread the piping gel so it fills in the outline. Continue to fill the Season's Greetings outlines with the colored piping gel (see Illustration 5.7). Let dry.

Illustration 5.7
Using piping gels in different colors to fill outlines makes for a festive presentation.

For the Happy Birthday greeting, measure out 6 oz (170 g) Meringue Powder Royal Icing and color with gel food colors. Soften the colored icing by gently stirring in 1 to 2 tsp (3.5 to 7 g) tap water. The icing should become soft and have a flood consistency. Check for the right consistency with the technique in Lesson 7 on Flood Icing techniques. Load a medium or large paper cone with the flood icing and cut a small hole in the cone. Squeeze some of the softened icing into the first letter in the Happy Birthday outline and spread it over the space with a toothpick. Carefully flood each of the remaining letters. Let dry for 2 hours.

Once the greeting is dried, pipe fine cornelli lace over each of the letters. This is achieved by placing 1 Tbsp (14 g) Meringue Powder Royal Icing in a small paper cone with the #0 round tip. Holding the tip at a 45-degree angle, drag it to the surface of each letter, moving in tight and random little curves. Do not allow the lines to intersect. The lace should look like one continuous long, curvy line (see Illustration 5.8). (See Lesson 7 for more information on cornelli lace.)

This lesson is complete. With plenty of practice, you can make cake writing an art.

Illustration 5.8
Additional details can be piped onto outline-filled letters.

END-OF-LESSON REVIEW

1. Why is it important to write well on cakes?

2. How can you achieve good writing skills?

3. What mediums can you use to write on a cake?

4. When learning how to write, why is it important to learn how to trace first?

5. What is the fallen technique?

6. What is the contact or drag technique?

PERFORMANCE TEST

Make a half-recipe of Meringue Powder Royal Icing (page 273) and a half-recipe of Chocolate Icing for Writing (Chocolate Glaze for Piping, page 268).
Pipe the following greetings:

1. All three alphabetic charts (Writing Exercise Patterns A, B, and C)

2. Happy Birthday

3. Bon Voyage

4. Glorious Divorce

5. With Sympathy (requires the #101 petal-shaped tip)

ROYAL ICING PIPED FLOWERS

Blossoms, Violets, Daisies, Pussy Willows, Sweet Peas, Primrose, and Pansies

You will need the following icings and items to complete this lesson:

Meringue Powder Royal Icing (page 273)

rounded toothpicks

12-in. (30 cm) flex or disposable plastic pastry bags

couplers

piping tips: #2 and #3 round tips; #101 or #102 petal-shaped tip

gel food colors

small metal bowls

offset metal spatulas

rubber spatulas (brand-new)

cardboard circles and squares

2 × 2 in. (5 × 5 cm) pieces of parchment paper

#6 or #7 icing nail

#0 sable paintbrush

plastic wrap

masking tape

scissors

small paper cones

Royal icing flowers made from egg whites or meringue powder are a staple in the cake decorating industry. These hard-drying yet edible flowers can be piped weeks in advance and stored in containers with lids or in a small box. The flowers are used to adorn formal cakes, cupcakes, and iced cookies. As a quick fix, they can dress up any cake. Attach them to an iced cake with a dab of royal icing, or place them directly on cupcakes iced in a soft icing. Royal icing flowers can also be petal dusted for contrast.

In the nineteenth century, royal icing was used chiefly to ice rich fruitcakes that were already coated with marzipan or almond paste. Royal icing sealed in the cake's flavor and freshness, so the cake could be made several days or weeks in advance yet taste moist and delicious when cut and served. Cakes covered with this icing were the choice of English royalty and, thus, the entire English community.

Royal icing is used today in the same fashion. Fruitcakes in Great Britain are still iced in marzipan and several coats of royal icing. Cake coverings are covered fully in Lesson 8.

New Skill: Orange, Apple, Cherry, and Peach Blossoms

Quick Prep

6 oz (170 g) Meringue Powder Royal Icing (page 273)
12-in. (30 cm) flex or disposable plastic pastry bags
gel food colors: orange, pink, and peach
2 × 2 in. (5 × 5 cm) pieces of parchment paper
piping tips: #2 round tip; #101 or #102 petal-shaped tip
#6 or #7 icing nail
4 couplers
2 small paper cones
#0 sable paintbrush

Orange, apple, cherry, and peach blossoms are all five-petal blossoms piped in exactly the same way. What makes each different is the color of the icing used. Measure 4 oz (114 g) Meringue Powder Royal Icing and color it a light pink (for cherry blossoms), peach (for peach blossoms), light orange (for orange blossoms), or natural white (for apple blossoms). Also, measure out ½ oz (14 g) icing and color it lemon yellow for use as the flowers' stamens.

Load a pastry bag with a #101 or #102 petal-shaped tip and the colored icing. Have a #6 or #7 icing nail and twelve pieces of parchment paper handy.

Pipe a dot of icing on the icing nail. Put the parchment square on the dot. Hold the pastry bag in your writing hand and the icing nail in the other hand. Position the wide end of the piping tip in the center of the icing nail. Tilt your hands and the piping tip slightly to the right. With steady and even pressure, squeeze the pastry bag and drag the piping tip from the center of the nail, moving up about ½ in. (1.3 cm) and pivoting to the right about ¼ in. (6 mm). Then drag the piping tip back down to the point where you began. Both the starting and ending positions should come to a point. As you squeeze the pastry bag and move the piping tip, slowly rotate the icing nail counterclockwise.

For the next petal, position the piping tip's wide end at the center point, next to the point of the first petal. Start slightly under the first petal. Repeat the procedure you used for the first petal, placing the petal next to the first. Repeat for the third and fourth petals. Overlap the fifth petal with the first, raising the tip slightly when moving back to the center point (see Illustration 6.1).

To finish the flower, load 1 Tbsp (14 g) lemon-yellow icing, softened with a few drops of water to prevent takeoff points, in a paper cone with the #2 round tip. Pipe five dots in the center to complete flowers.

Decorator's Hint

When working with royal icing, it is important not to use a pastry bag that once had buttercream icing in it or a rubber spatula that has touched grease. Any particle of grease will break down the royal icing. Washing icing tips in hot sudsy water will remove all traces of grease, but it is impossible to clean plastic or flex bags well enough for this purpose. Use a brand-new rubber spatula when working with royal icing.

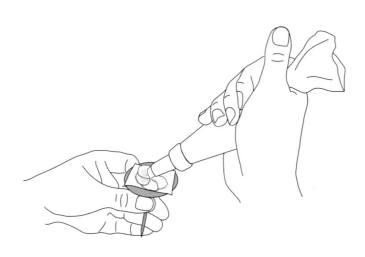

Illustration 6.1
Rotate the icing nail as you pipe the icing and move the tip.

Illustration 6.2
The steps to piping royal icing flowers (from top to bottom): fruit blossom, violet, daisy.

Use this same technique to pipe all of these flowers, whether apple, orange, peach, or cherry blossoms (see the top row of Illustration 6.2).

New Skill: Primrose

Quick Prep

6 oz (170 g) Meringue Powder Royal Icing (page 273)
12-in. (30 cm) flex or disposable plastic pastry bags
gel food colors: lemon yellow and moss green
2 × 2 in. (5 × 5 cm) pieces of parchment paper
piping tips: #2 round tip; 101 or #102 petal-shaped tip
#6 or #7 icing nail
2 small paper cones
#0 sable paintbrush

Primrose five-petal blossoms are bright yellow compared to egg yellow, with green stamens in the center. The petals are shaped like hearts.

Load a pastry bag with 4 oz (114 g) lemon-yellow Meringue Powder Royal Icing. Attach the #101 or #102 petal-shaped tip to the bag. Load a small paper cone with the #2 round tip and ½ oz (14 g) moss-green royal icing softened with a few drops of water to avoid takeoff points. Have an icing nail and small pieces of parchment paper handy.

Pipe a dot of icing on the icing nail. Put a parchment square on the dot. Hold the pastry bag in your writing hand and the icing nail in the other hand. Position the wide end of the piping tip in the center of the icing nail. Tilt your hands and the piping tip slightly to the right. With steady and even pressure, squeeze the pastry bag and drag the piping tip from the center of the nail, mov-

Decorator's Hint

1. The last petal is usually difficult to pipe. You need to be careful when overlapping the fifth petal to the first. If it doesn't come out as neatly as you wish, use a wet paintbrush dipped in water to reshape the piped petals. In a fast-paced environment, you may not have enough time to work to this degree of detail. However, cake designers may make time for this important step when working on expensive cakes.

2. An easier way to pipe these blossoms is to draw the five-petal flower on a piece of parchment paper. This is your template. Tape the drawing on the icing nail with scotch tape and tape securely. Then, place an additional piece of parchment over the template—secured with dots of icing. You should be able to see the template through the parchment paper. Pipe the five-petal flower and carefully remove the flower and parchment without disturbing the template.

ing up about ½ in. (1.3 cm) and pivoting slightly to the right about ⅛ in. (3 mm). Drag the tip down slightly and up again to form the heart shape. Then drag the piping tip back down to the center point where you began. Both the starting and ending positions should come to a point. As you squeeze the pastry bag and move the piping tip, slowly rotate the icing nail counterclockwise.

For the next petal, position the piping tip's wide end at the center point, next to the point of the first petal. Start slightly under ther first petal. Repeat the procedure you used for the first petal, placing the petal next to the first. Repeat for the third and fourth petals. Overlap the fifth petal with the first, raising the tip slightly when moving back to the center point.

To finish the flower, pipe several dots of moss-green icing in the center with the #2 round piping tip. Remember to use a damp paintbrush to help ease the petals into shape (see Illustration 6.3).

Illustration 6.3
The steps (clockwise from top right) for piping a primrose.

New Skill: Violets

Quick Prep

6 oz (170 g) Meringue Powder Royal Icing (page 273)
12-in. (30 cm) flex or disposable plastic pastry bags
gel food colors: lemon yellow and violet
2 × 2 in. (5 × 5 cm) pieces of parchment paper
piping tips: #2 round tip; #101 or #102 petal-shaped tip
#6 or #7 icing nail
2 small paper cones
#0 sable paintbrush

Vibrant violets, another five-petal blossom, are unlike the primroses in that not all the petals are the same size. The first two petals are the same size, but the last three are larger. The flower is completed with two yellow stamens pointing toward the two smaller petals.

Load a pastry bag with 4 oz (114 g) Meringue Powder Royal Icing in a deep violet. Attach the #101 or #102 petal-shaped tip to the bag. Load a small paper cone with the #2 round tip and ½ oz (14 g) lemon-yellow royal icing. Have an icing nail and small pieces of parchment paper handy.

Pipe a dot of icing on the icing nail. Put a parchment square on the dot. Hold the pastry bag in your writing hand and the icing nail in the other hand. Position the wide end of the piping tip in the center of the icing nail. Tilt your hands and the piping tip slightly to the right. With steady and even pressure, squeeze the pastry bag and drag the piping tip from the center of the nail, moving up about ½ in. (1.3 cm) and pivoting to the right about ¼ in. (6 mm). Drag the piping tip back down to the center point where you began. Both the starting and ending positions should come to a point. As you squeeze the pastry bag and move the piping tip, slowly rotate the icing nail counterclockwise.

To pipe the second petal, position the piping tip's wide end at the center point, right next to the point of the first petal. Repeat the procedure you used for the first petal. Skip a space on the icing nail by rotating the icing nail one blank space. (Right-handed users turn the nail counterclockwise; left-handed users turn it clockwise.) The third, fourth, and fifth petals are slightly separate from the first two as well as a little larger. Starting at the flower's center with the tip's wide end down, squeeze the pastry bag and move the tip upward about ¾ in. (1.9 cm) and over about ¼ in. (6 mm) and then drag the tip back to the flower's center, coming to a point. Repeat this for the fourth and fifth petals. Remember to ease up a little when bringing the fifth petal to the flower's center.

To finish the flower, pipe two points with yellow royal icing and the #2 metal round piping tip, starting at the center of the flower and dragging the points over the two smaller petals (see row 2 of Illustration 6.2).

New Skill: Pansies

Quick Prep

> 10 oz (283 g) Meringue Powder Royal Icing (page 273)
> 2 12-in. (30 cm) flex or disposable plastic pastry bags
> gel food colors: lemon yellow, violet, burgundy, brown, lavender, and pink
> 2 × 2 in. (5 × 5 cm) pieces of parchment paper
> piping tips: #2 round tip; #101 or #102 petal-shaped tips
> #6 or #7 icing nail
> 2 small paper cones
> #0 sable paintbrush

Pansies are striking and come in a variety of shades. Some are multicolored and some are a single color. On this five-petal flower, the fifth petal is the largest. Pansies have a violet painting in the center of the flower and a round circle piped with the #2 round tip and lemon-yellow royal icing.

Load two pastry bags with 4 oz (114 g) each Meringue Powder Royal Icing in two of the color choices given in the quick prep. Attach the #101 or #102 petal-shaped tip to each bag. Load a small paper cone with ½ oz (14 g) lemon-yellow royal icing and the #2 round tip. Have an icing nail and small pieces of parchment paper handy.

Pipe a dot of icing on the icing nail. Put a parchment square on the dot. Hold the pastry bag in your writing hand and the icing nail in the other hand. Position the wide end of the piping tip in the center of the icing nail. Tilt your hands and the piping tip slightly to the right. With steady and even pressure, squeeze the pastry bag and drag the piping tip from the center of the nail, moving up about ½ in. (1.3 cm) and pivoting to the right about ¼ in. (6 mm). Drag the piping tip back down to the center point where you began. Both the starting and ending positions should come to a point. As you squeeze the pastry bag and move the piping tip, slowly rotate the icing nail counterclockwise (or, if left-handed, clockwise).

To pipe the second petal, position the wide end of the piping tip at the center point, right next to the first petal's point. Repeat the procedure you used for the first petal. For the third petal, position the tip at the flower's center point. Rotate the tip slightly to the left and turn the icing nail slightly clockwise. This will allow you to make the third petal larger. The third and fourth petals overlap the first two petals and are slightly larger and lower in position than the first two. With heavy pressure, squeeze and move the bag and tip back and forth as you turn the nail counterclockwise. As the third petal overlaps the first, drag the tip back to the center point.

For the fourth petal, apply heavy pressure as you squeeze and move the pastry bag and piping tip back and forth and turn the icing nail counterclockwise.

Decorator's Hint

As an alternative to two pastry bags, place two colored royal icings in one pastry bag, one color in the left side and the other in the right. Squeeze the bag until both colors merge.

Decorator's Hint

Try piping the first two and the fifth pansy petals in one color and the third and fourth in a different one.

Illustration 6.4
The steps (from left to right) for piping a pansy.

As the fourth petal overlaps the second, extend the petal slightly so the fourth petal is larger; then drag the tip back to the center point.

The fifth petal is the largest and is piped opposite the first four. Position the piping tip at the end of the fourth petal. With heavy pressure, squeeze the pastry bag and rotate the piping tip back and forth. Turn the nail as you rotate the tip, easing off the pressure as you pull the nail toward the flower's center. This petal is slightly ruffled.

When the flower is dry, dip a small sable paintbrush in water and then in violet food color. Paint tiny lines in the center of the flower over the third and fourth petals. Then paint tiny lines over the fifth petal. Pipe a tiny circle with the #2 round tip and yellow royal icing in the center of the flower (see Illustration 6.4).

New Skill: Sweet peas

Quick Prep

6 oz (170g) Meringue Powder Royal Icing (page 273)
12-in. (30 cm) flex or disposable pastry bags
gel food colors: moss green, lavender, pink, and lemon yellow
2 × 2 in. (5 × 5 cm) pieces of parchment paper
piping tips: #2 round tip; #101 or #102 petal-shaped tip
#6 or #7 icing nail
2 small paper cones
#0 sable paintbrush

Sweet peas have a wide petal, like pansies, and two smaller petals in front of the larger petal. These flowers can be subtle or brightly colored. They are often seen in pink, yellow, and lavender, and they can be two-toned as well. They are finished with a sepal and calyx, similar to the rosebud and half-rose in Lesson 2.

Load a pastry bag with 4 oz (114 g) Meringue Powder Royal Icing in one of the colors on the quick prep list. Attach the #101 or #102 petal-shape tip to the bag. Load a small paper cone with ½ oz (14 g) moss-green royal icing and the #2 round tip. Have an icing nail and small pieces of parchment paper handy.

Pipe a dot of icing on the icing nail. Put a parchment square on the dot. Hold the pastry bag in your writing hand and the icing nail in the other hand. Position the wide end of the piping tip in the center of the icing nail. Squeeze the pastry bag and turn the nail counterclockwise to form a large back petal. Position the piping tip back at the flower's center. Pipe two smaller petals in front of the back petal, using the same technique as for the apple, cherry, peach, and orange blossoms. For the sepal and calyx, position the #2 round tip with moss-green icing at the left side of the flower. Pipe a small upward curve and end at the center. Do the same on the reverse side. Start at the bottom; squeeze the paper cone and pull in an upward curve. Stop the pressure and pull the tip toward you, leaving the center sepal suspended. For the calyx, position the tip at the bottom of the flower. Finish the flower by applying heavy pressure and then easing off as you pull a small tail (see Illustration 6.5).

Illustration 6.5
The steps (clockwise from left) for piping a sweet pea.

New Skill: Daisies

Quick Prep

6 oz (170g) Meringue Powder Royal Icing (page 273)
12-in. (30 cm) flex or disposable plastic pastry bags
gel food colors: lemon yellow
2 × 2 in. (5 × 5 cm) pieces of parchment paper
piping tips: #2 and #4 round tips; #101 or #102 petal-shaped tip
#6 or #7 icing nail
2 small paper cones
#0 sable paintbrush

Daisies are twelve-petal flowers with yellow centers. The petals are often white but can be made in shades of yellow. The flowers can be finished with small dots of yellow icing piped in the center with the #2 round tip or one large dot piped in the center with the #4 round tip.

Load a pastry bag with 4 oz (114 g) Meringue Powder Royal Icing. The icing can be naturally white—that is, you don't have to add food coloring. Attach either the #101 or #102 petal-shaped tip to the bag. Load a small paper cone with ½ oz (14 g) lemon-yellow royal icing and either the #2 or #4 round tip. Have an icing nail and small pieces of parchment paper handy.

Pipe a dot of icing on the icing nail. Put a parchment square on the dot. Hold the pastry bag in your writing hand and the icing nail in the other hand. This time you want the small end of the piping tip at the center of the nail. Move the tip out about ½ in. (1.3 cm) at the 12 o'clock position. With steady and even pressure, squeeze the pastry bag, holding the piping tip at a 45-degree angle. Raise the tip barely off the icing nail and pull the icing toward you at the 6 o'clock position. Drag the tip to the center of the nail as you ease off the pressure. Turn the nail counterclockwise ¹⁄₁₂ the distance around the circle.

Repeat the procedure to pipe 11 more petals. When piping the last petal, ease the end gently to the flower's center. When the flower is dry, finish it with dots of yellow icing piped with the #2 round tip or one large dot piped with the #4 round tip (see the third row from the top in Illustration 6.2 and see Illustration 6.6).

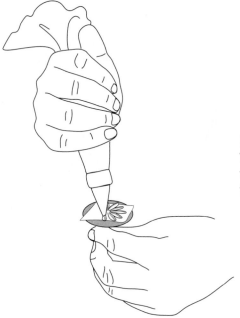

Illustration 6.6
To pipe a daisy, position the metal tip ½ in. (1.3 cm) out from the center of the icing nail and then squeeze the pastry bag—pulling the tip and icing to the center of the icing nail.

New Skill: Pussy Willow

Quick Prep

6 oz (170g) Meringue Powder Royal Icing (page 273)
2 small paper cones
gel food color: chocolate brown
piping tips: #2 and #3 round tips
parchment paper or Mylar
plastic wrap (optional)

Decorator's Hint

The other flowers in this lesson were piped on parchment paper and can be removed from the paper upon drying. Pussy willows, while simple to pipe, are fragile and will break if moved. Should you wish the flower to dry and be removable, line your work surface with a piece of plastic wrap.

Decorator's Hint

Softening the royal icing for the pussy willow buds avoids leaving a takeoff point when exiting. To slightly soften royal icing, add ½ tsp (3.5 g) water to 1 Tbsp (14 g) Meringue Powder Royal Icing and mix gently.

Pussy willows are small brown branches with white bulbs at the ends. They are simple to pipe and do not require an icing nail. This exercise can be piped on parchment paper or Mylar.

Load a small paper cone with the #3 round tip and 1 oz (28 g) chocolate-brown royal icing. Load a small paper cone with the #2 round tip and 1 oz (28 g) white royal icing slightly softened with drops of water.

Place the pattern of the pussy willow under your work surface, or quickly trace the flower from the book and place the sketch under your work surface to use as a guide. First pipe the branches with the tip slightly above the surface of the plastic wrap. Drag the tip lightly to the surface when attaching smaller branches to the main branch. Let dry for a few minutes. Position the #2 round tip with the softened white icing at a 45-degree angle just above a branch. Apply a small burst of pressure. Keep the tip steady as you form a small ball. Stop the pressure and slightly drag the tip down. Do this to each branch tip. Allow to dry for a few minutes.

To finish the pussy willow, pipe a small curve around each of the bulbs with the #3 round tip and chocolate-brown icing (see Illustration 6.7).

Illustration 6.7
Pussy willow (from left): the branches and bulbs of the pussy willow and the completed pussy willow with piped curves to hold the bulbs.

END-OF-LESSON REVIEW

1. Why are royal icing flowers useful?

2. Can these flowers be made up ahead of time?

3. Can royal icing be colored with food colors?

4. How are flowers stored once they are piped and dried?

5. How are royal icing flowers attached to an iced cake?

PERFORMANCE TEST

Pipe each of the following flowers three times:

peach blossom   violet   primrose   daisy   pansy

ROYAL ICING DESIGN SKILLS

Embroidery Piping in Royal Icing

You will need the following icings and items to complete this lesson:

Meringue Powder Royal Icing (page 273)

Flood Icing (page 274)

Buttercream Icing for Flooding (page 267)

egg whites

rounded toothpicks

piping tips: #0, #1, #2, #3, #4, and #5 round tips; #79, # 80, or #84 lily-of-the-valley tip

gel food colors

small metal bowls

offset metal spatulas

rubber spatulas (brand-new)

#0, #1, and #3 sable paintbrushes

8-in. (20.3 cm) square Plexiglas

8-in. round or rectangular cardboards

parchment paper

plastic wrap

masking tape

scissors

commercial rolled fondant

small nonstick rolling pin

4-in. (10.2 cm) round, scalloped, oval, or square-metal cookie cutter

small 4- and 5-petal cutters

stickpin or hatpin

#2 graphite pencil

small and medium paper cones

Embroidery piping in royal icing or any other icing medium is one of the highest forms of the decorating art. It requires expert control; a creative eye; and a fluid, artistic hand. All three skills must work uniformly to create a dazzling display of piping artistry.

Many forms of fine piping are done in royal icing, and most have an embroidered look. Brush embroidery, freehand embroidery, satin stitching, eyelet embroidery, Swiss dots, cornelli lace, and sotas are typical royal icing embroidery styles. Some embroidery piping is accompanied by small clusters of plunger flowers.

Embroidery can be either simple or intricate in design and detail. It can lay flat or rise beautifully. Embroidery can also be used in conjunction with outlining and flooding. Stitched lines added to a large flooded monogram can be breathtaking!

Before practicing embroidery skills, it is important to know how to transfer embroidery designs.

Design Transfers

Design transfer is the technique used to transfer a design onto a cake. Many approaches are used in the cake decorating industry. The three discussed below are the most popular.

Pinprick Method

This method is used to transfer a design to a rolled iced cake. A pattern is traced onto see-through paper that is then carefully attached to the cake with stickpins or masking tape. The entire pattern is then carefully gone over with a pin, puncturing both the paper and the rolled icing. Once the pattern is pinpricked, the paper is removed. The design is ready for the appropriate embroidery technique.

Carbon Copy Method

This is another method of transferring a pattern to a rolled iced cake or gumpaste or marzipan plaque. (See recipes for Gumpaste and Marzipan in Lesson 19.) A pattern is traced onto see-through paper. The paper is then turned over and the pattern is traced in reverse onto a piece of parchment paper. The parchment is then reversed to the right side and placed over a sugar plaque or a rolled-iced cake with a firm cake base. The pattern is carefully taped in place with masking tape. Then the pattern is retraced and removed. A copy of the pattern is revealed on the cake or sugar plaque.

Buttercream/Gel Transfer Method

This is a delicious method of transferring a design onto a buttercream-iced cake. It can be done in piping gel (generally used for writing on cake) or buttercream (which is softer).

A pattern is traced and then placed on a piece of Plexiglas. Plastic wrap is taped over the pattern, which is then outlined with icing. The outline is then filled in with a softer icing. The iced Plexiglas is placed in the freezer until the icing is firm. Then the iced design is carefully removed from the Plexiglas and transferred to an iced cake.

Embroidery Techniques

Brush Embroidery

Brush embroidery resembles the fine embroidery seen on table linen and napkins. Just as the raised and flat stitching gives lushness to linens, brush embroidery piping adds elegance and style to any cake with a rolled-iced surface. With practice, brush embroidery is much easier to do than it looks. A floral design is transferred directly to the cake's surface with a stickpin or to a rolled-iced plaque or plain cardboard. In the case of a plaque or cardboard, the design can be transferred using the tracing method. (See Design Transfer at the end of this lesson.)

Each petal of the transferred floral design is outlined and the outline is then brushed with a paintbrush dipped in pasteurized egg whites. A thin film of the icing is brushed to the root of the flower, leaving a thin outline edge. A thin transparent coating of the icing is brushed on the petals, leaving a clear view of the surface beneath. The contrast of light and dark surfaces is important here. If the icing is white, then the surface should be dark.

Each petal and leaf is brushed separately. Once the leaves and petals are brushed, tiny lines are piped onto the leaves to resemble leaf veins. Dots of icing are placed in the center of the flowers to resemble stamens. Once dried, the entire surface of the brushed work can be dusted with Super Pearl (a pearl luster powder that gives sheen to the design).

Freehand Embroidery

Nothing completes a cake like fine pipework. All beautiful cakes have a simple yet clean and elegant design. Truly breathtaking cakes are made with the addition of fine detailed piping. Freehand embroidery is a good example. It is amazing enough that this is achievable with a metal tip and icing, but it seems absolutely impossible to do it freehand. And yet, with practice, you can learn this skill.

Freehand embroidery consists of dots, circles, curves, ovals, quotation marks, commas, and so on. All or some of these marks are organized into a pattern that forms beautiful embroidery that is the hallmark of Australian cake piping. Only in Australia are dots, curves, circles, and so forth organized into dazzling displays of piping artistry. This type of piping art is part of this country's heritage, along with bridge and extension work, which will be discussed in Lesson 11.

First, mark the cake into sections that reflect a pattern you selected from a book. Note the center point of the design. The pattern will be mirrored on each side of the center point—that is, whatever you pipe on the left side of the center point you will also pipe on the right. If you are uncomfortable piping freehand onto a finished cake, trace the pattern on see-through paper. Place the pattern on the cake and pinprick the design onto it. Then remove the pattern and pipe over the pinpricked pattern. This is an acceptable technique that allows you to execute accurate designs until you master freehand piping.

Cornelli Lace and Sotas

Cornelli lace is one of the easiest forms of embroidery piping. It is not organized like freehand embroidery or brush embroidery. In essence, a #0 round tip is dragged to the surface of the cake at a 45-degree angle and moved in one continuous loose curve. If the cake is iced in buttercream, the tip is held just slightly above the cake's surface and the same technique applied. The finished design looks like one continuous line in tiny small curves that do not intersect.

Sotas are similar to cornelli lace in that the curves are random. The difference is that the tip is held at a 90-degree angle and raised slightly above the surface of the cake so the icing falls in random curves. Unlike the cornelli, these curves can intersect. The curves are also much wider and looser. Typically, a #1 or #2 round tip is used with a slightly softened icing.

Swiss Dots

This is perhaps the easiest of all of embroidery piping styles. Dots are piped all over the cake, either randomly or in an organized pattern. The key to Swiss dots is to soften the royal icing with a little water or pasteurized egg whites to the consistency of yogurt. No tip is used; instead, a tiny hole is snipped at the end of a small paper cone. When a dot is piped on the cake and the cone is pulled away, the tip of the dot rolls back to a round ball, leaving no head.

Satin Stitch

Raised monogrammed stitching on beautiful linen is the envy of all, and satin stitching resembles the finest in exquisite linen embroidery. Satin stitch is a combination of tube embroidery and monograms. Tube embroidery consists of lines piped with a fine tip to fill in a pattern, like flowers and foliage. Different colors can be used in the pattern for a festive look. Piping these lines on a raised monogram is the classic use for satin stitching.

The smallest round tips are used to complete this embroidery. Satin stitch is most dramatic when piped over a raised surface, like an outline and flooded monogram.

Eyelet Embroidery

This is the only embroidery that doesn't require piping, although adding piping to eyelet embroidery is the difference between nice and wow! What's needed here is rolled icing and several small floral cutters. The icing is rolled thin, as for a plaque, and small floral cutters are carefully pushed into the icing while it's still soft, then released. The imprint is carefully removed, leaving the negative of the cutter. (The center can also be left in for a different look.) This, combined with piping, adds a lot of dimension to an embroidered design.

Now that you have an understanding of these techniques, it is time to put them into practice.

New Skill: Design Transfer Techniques

Quick Prep

8 oz (228 g) commercial rolled fondant
2 8-in. (20.3 cm) round or square cardboards
small pieces of parchment or see-through paper
stickpin
#2 graphite pencil
8-in. (20.3 cm) square Plexiglas
plastic wrap
4 oz (114 g) Decorator's Buttercream Icing (page 260)
12 oz (340 g) Buttercream Icing for Flooding (page 267)
6 medium-size parchment cones
piping tips: #2, #3, #4, and #5 round tips
4-in. (10.2 cm) round, scalloped, oval, or
　　square-metal cookie cutter
gel food colors

PINPRICK TECHNIQUE

Roll out 2 oz (57 g) commercial rolled fondant on a little cornstarch. Cut out a plaque with the 4-in. (10.2 cm) metal cookie cutter. Select a pattern from Appendix 1. Trace the pattern on a piece of see-through paper.

Place the traced pattern on the plaque and secure the ends with masking tape. Transfer the pattern to the plaque by outlining it with a stickpin. Be sure the pinpricks are close together to reveal a good likeness of the pattern.

Remove the pattern from the plaque. You now have a duplicate of the pattern (see the top left of Illustration 7.1).

Cut out two more plaques and select another pattern transfer design.

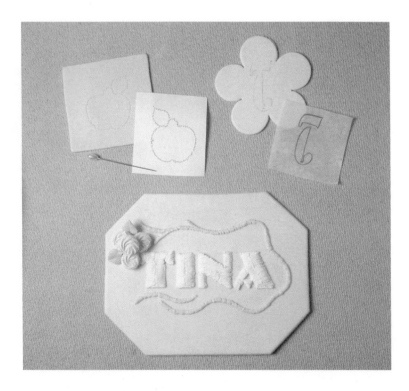

Illustration 7.1
Top left: pinprick method transfer technique.
Top right: carbon copy transfer technique.
Bottom: satin stitching.

CARBON COPY TECHNIQUE

Select a pattern from Appendix 1. Trace the pattern on a piece of see-through paper. Reverse the pattern and trace the opposite side of the pattern.

Place the traced pattern right side up on an 8-in. (20.3 cm) round or square cardboard or a small plaque made of rolled fondant or gumpaste. Tape the pattern securely with masking tape. Carefully trace the pattern once more with a #2 graphite pencil. Press firmly, as you make a carbon copy of the reverse side of the pattern. Once the pattern is retraced, carefully remove the masking tape (see the top right of Illustration 7.1).

Select another transfer pattern design and use the carbon copy technique to transfer the pattern.

BUTTERCREAM DESIGN TRANSFER TECHNIQUE

Select a pattern from Appendix 1. Carefully trace the pattern on a piece of see-through paper.

Trim the pattern to fit on an 8-in. (20.3 cm) Plexiglas. Place the pattern on the Plexiglas and tape it securely with masking tape so that the pattern is right side up on the Plexiglas. Turn the Plexiglas over and place a piece of plastic wrap directly over it. Tape the corners securely with masking tape. You are now looking at the pattern backward (see the top left of Illustration 7.2). In fact, the entire transfer technique is backward, but it will be reversed once frozen and removed from the Plexiglas.

Carefully outline the pattern in a dark-colored icing with the #2 round tip and 1 oz (28 g) Decorator's Buttercream Icing in a piping consistency. Start with the most difficult area and then move on to the less difficult parts. If you make a mistake, use a toothpick to remove the error and a damp paintbrush to clean up the area. Dry with a dry brush and continue outlining the pattern.

Decorator's Hint

Commercial rolled fondant can also be used for the carbon copy method of pattern transfer. To do this, roll out the paste on a little cornstarch and cut out a plaque with a cookie cutter. Allow the plaque to dry for 2 to 4 hours on one side, then turn it over and allow it to dry for another 2 to 4 hours. For best results, let it dry overnight. The dried plaque can be used to transfer a design with the carbon copy method.

Decorator's Hint

Use a dark-colored pencil to trace the pattern. The pattern can cover the entire surface of the cake or be restricted to a small picture or monogram.

Illustration 7.2
The buttercream transfer technique (clockwise from top left): the backward pattern, the partially filled outlined pattern, and the completed buttercream pattern.

Fill in the outline with Buttercream Icing for Flooding (see the top right of Illustration 7.2). Be creative and color your softened buttercream with gel colors. Fill the parchment cones with different colors. Cut a small hole in each cone to release the icing. Squeeze the icing within the outline. Use a toothpick to move the softened buttercream to the outline (see Illustration 7.2). Work carefully and quickly. Once the entire pattern is flooded, place the Plexiglas outline in the freezer for 20 minutes. When the icing is firm, give depth to the pattern by carefully outlining the outside edge with the #4 or #5 round tip and then carefully spreading a thin layer of buttercream icing, preferably white, within the outline.

Place the Plexiglas buttercream design in the freezer for about 1 hour. Freeze very large patterns for several hours. Working quickly, carefully remove the masking tape securing the plastic wrap to the Plexiglas. Turn the buttercream design onto your hands or place on a piece of cardboard. Peel back the plastic wrap and carefully place the buttercream plaque on the iced cake. The transfer is complete.

New Skill: Brush Embroidery Techniques

Quick Prep

4 oz (114 g) Meringue Powder Royal Icing (page 273)
piping tips: #0, #2, and #3 round tips
2 8-in. (20.3 cm) round or rectangular cardboards
#1 and #3 sable paintbrushes
medium-size paper cones
1 oz (28 g) egg whites

Select a floral design pattern with several of the same flowers and leaves in the pattern section of the book (see Brush Embroidery Floral Patterns on page 298 in Appendix 1). Using the carbon copy design transfer method, carefully trace the pattern with a #2 graphite pencil. Use the dark side of the cardboard to transfer the pattern, as uncolored Meringue Powder Royal Icing will be used. The light icing against the dark background will give the best results.

Once the design is transferred, load a medium-size paper cone with the #2 or #3 round tip and 2 Tbsp (28 g) uncolored Meringue Powder Royal Icing. Start from the outside of the pattern and work your way toward the center of the pattern.

Outline a leaf by slightly dragging the tip to the surface. Before the outline dries, dip the #1 or #3 sable paintbrush in a little egg white and carefully brush some of the outline icing toward the base of the leaf. Use long strokes to lightly brush a thin layer of icing over the entire leaf pattern. The background should be visible through the layer. Continue to dip the brush in egg white and brush the outline icing, leaving the bulk of the outline icing intact (see the first two steps in Illustration 7.3). Continue with the rest of the leaves, brushing one leaf at a time (see step 3 of Illustration 7.3). Let the leaves dry before beginning the petals.

Outline one petal to start. Before the outline icing dries, dip the #1 or #3 sable paintbrush in the egg white and lightly brush the outline icing toward the center of the flower. Use long strokes to lightly brush a thin layer of icing over the entire petal. Remember, the background should be visible through the icing. Brush the remaining petals, one at a time, until all the petals are done. Remember to maintain the integrity of each petal—that is, its outline.

When the petals are dry, begin the leaves. Load 1 Tbsp (7 g) Meringue Powder Royal Icing with the #0 round tip. Drag the tip slightly from the base of a leaf toward its point in a slight curve. Go back to the slightly curved line and pull out little veins by inserting the tip and applying a slightly burst of pressure.

Illustration 7.3
Brush embroidery (from left to right): outline of a leaf, some of the outline lightly brushed toward the base of the leaf, several brushed leaves, and the completed brushed pattern.

Decorator's Hint

Remember to pipe one leaf at a time and one petal at a time. Otherwise, the petals and leaves will dry before being brushed with egg whites.

Illustration 7.4
An example of brush embroidery.

Drag the tip about ¼ in. (6 mm) and ease off the pressure. Do this to the left and right sides of the curved line.

Repeat this process for all the leaves. For the center of the flower, position the #0 tip at the center and pipe dots of icing in a rounded cluster (see step 4 of Illustration 7.3). When the pattern is dry, petal dust the entire design with a little super pearl for a luxurious look. Illustration 7.4 is another example of brush embroidery.

New Skill: Freehand Embroidery Techniques

Quick Prep

> 4 oz (114 g) Meringue Powder Royal Icing (page 273)
> piping tips: #0 round tip; #79, # 80, or #84 lily-of-the-valley tip
> medium-size paper cones
> 2 8-in. (20.3 cm) round or rectangular cardboards

Select a freehand embroidery pattern from Appendix 1, one that is not too intricate. Trace the pattern onto see-through paper. Tracing the pattern will give you a sense of the placement of the organized dots, circles, curves, and commas.

Place 1 Tbsp (14 g) Meringue Powder Royal in a medium-size paper cone with the #0 round tip. Transfer the pattern from the see-through paper onto a cardboard using the carbon copy design transfer method (page 94). Transferring the pattern in this exercise will give you good control and a sense of immediate gratification.

Piping begins at the center of the pattern and moves from left to right. Pipe directly over the transfer so you know exactly where to place the circles, ovals, dots, and curves. Slightly drag the tip to the cardboard surface when piping the embroidery. Remember to apply light pressure with the #0 tip when piping freehand embroidery.

Once the pattern is complete, repeat the exercise freehand, without transferring the pattern to the cardboard. Look at the traced pattern and copy the pattern by sight onto a new piece of cardboard. Remember, start at the center of the pattern and carefully work from left to right. Continue to practice freehand to become more comfortable with the technique.

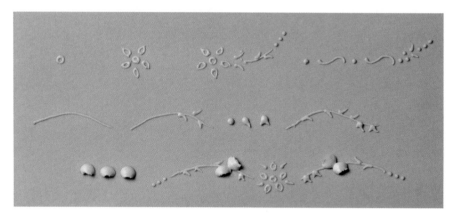

Illustration 7.5
Examples of freehand embroidery.

LILY-OF-THE-VALLEY

When piping lilies-of-the-valley, load a medium-size paper cone with the #79, #80, or #84 tip and 2 oz (28 g) Meringue Powder Royal Icing. Note that these tips have rounded curves with one end slightly larger than the other. Position the tip at a 45-degree angle with the wide end of the tip tilted slightly to the left. With steady and even pressure, squeeze the bag and rotate the tip from the left to the right. Stop the pressure and gently ease away by dragging the tip to the 5 o'clock position. Repeat this several times.

For the lily-of-the-valley buds, position the #0 tip at a 45-degree angle at the end of a freehand embroidered curve. Keeping it steady, slightly squeeze the tip and make a large dot. While the tip is still in the icing, drag the tip down and slightly to the left. Reposition the tip in the large dot and drag it down with a slight curve to the right. Do this a few more times to practice. See Illustration 7.5 for additional examples of freehand embroidery.

New Skill: Cornelli Lace and Sotas Techniques

Quick Prep

    4 oz (114 g) Meringue Powder Royal Icing (page 273)
    piping tips: #0 and #2 round tips
    medium-size paper cones
    2 8-in. (20.3 cm) round or rectangular cardboards

To begin the cornelli lace technique, load a medium-size paper cone with 1 Tbsp (14 g) Meringue Powder Royal Icing and the #0 round tip. Place a cardboard on the work surface and tape down the corners with masking tape so it won't move during the exercise.

Divide the cardboard into four sections. Position the tip at a 45-degree angle to one of the sections. With steady pressure, squeeze the bag and move the tip

Decorator's Hint

When piping cornelli lace out of melted chocolate, the technique is slightly different in that no piping tip is used. The tip of the bag is held at a 90-degree angle and about 1 in. (2.54 cm) from the cake's surface. The chocolate is allowed to fall to the surface as the bag is moved in small curves. To end, the bag is slowly lowered until the tip touches the cake's surface.

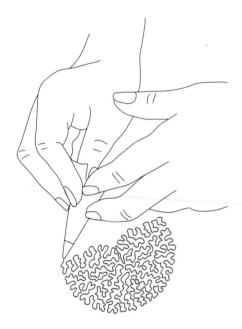

Illustration 7.6
In cornelli lace, the curves are randomly piped but never cross one another.

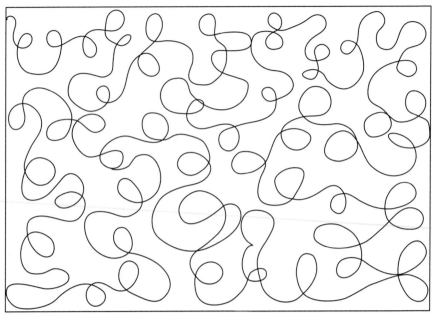

Illustration 7.7
An example of sotas technique.

in small curves, slightly scratching the surface of the cardboard. The curves should be random and never cross each other (see Illustration 7.6). When you finish one section, do another. Continue until all four sections are completed (see bottom right of Illustration 7.8).

To begin the sotas technique, load a medium-size paper cone with 2 tbsp (28 g) Meringue Powder Royal Icing and a #2 round tip. Place cardboard on the work surface and tape down the corners with masking tape so it won't move during the exercise. Divide the cardboard into 4 sections.

Raise the tip about 1 in. (2.54 cm) from the cardboard. With the tip at a 90-degree angle, apply a controlled burst of pressure and allow the icing to flow from the tip. Move the tip in a random pattern, allowing the icing to fall to the surface. The curves should be larger than those of cornelli lace, and they are allowed to cross (see Illustration 7.7).

Continue with each section of the cardboard until all four sections are completed.

New Skill: Swiss Dot Technique

Quick Prep

2 oz (57 g) Meringue Powder Flood Icing (page 273)
2 small paper cones
8-in. (20.3 cm) round or square cardboard

Load a small paper cone with 1 Tbsp (14 g) Meringue Powder Flood Icing, which is Meringue Powder Royal Icing softened with water or egg whites to the consistency of sour cream. Divide the cardboard surface into four sections.

No tip is used in the paper cone. Snip the paper cone with a pair of scissors and hold the tip at a 45-degree angle to the cardboard's surface. Apply light pressure and allow a small ball of icing to flow from the tip of the paper cone. Keep the tip stationary as you build up the ball of icing. Stop the pressure and remove

Illustration 7.8
Clockwise (from top left): a shape is removed from the paste to begin an eyelet embroidery design, a completed eyelet embroidery design, cornelli lace, sotas, and Swiss dots.

the tip of the cone from the ball of icing. The icing will drop back and settle to make the surface of the ball completely smooth.

Randomly pipe balls of icing to form Swiss dots. Once you complete one section of the cardboard, pipe Swiss dots on the other three sections. As part of the practice, make balls of different sizes in each section (see the bottom left of Illustration 7.8).

New Skill: Satin-Stitch Technique

Quick Prep

    4 oz (114 g) Meringue Powder Royal Icing (page 273)
    4 oz (114 g) Flood Icing (page 274)
    2 small and 2 medium-size paper cones
    piping tips: #0 and #3 round tips
    2 8-in. (20.3 cm) round or square cardboards
    plastic wrap
    masking tape
    toothpicks

Decorator's Hint

Cover the tip of the paper cone with plastic wrap or a damp towel to prevent the icing from clogging it.

Select a pattern from Appendix 1 on Satin Stitch. Use the carbon copy design transfer method to trace the pattern.

Place 1 Tbsp (14 g) Meringue Powder Royal Icing and the #3 round tip in a small paper cone. Carefully outline the monogram. When outlining long lines of a pattern, remember to lift the tip and let the icing drop to the surface. Keep the tip to the surface when outlining curves and short lines.

Next, place 1 Tbsp (14 g) Meringue Powder Royal Icing and the #0 round tip in a small paper cone. Carefully pipe over the embroidery around the monogram, remembering to keep the tip close to the cardboard surface (see step 1 of Illustration 7.9).

Next, place 2 oz (57 g) Meringue Powder Flood Icing in a medium-size paper cone without a tip. Cut the tip of the paper cone so the flood icing begins to flow from the cone. Position the tip of the cone inside of the monogram and begin to carefully squeeze the bag. Allow some of the icing to build up inside the monogram. Using a toothpick, move the softened icing so it fills the monogram within the outline. Continue flooding until the monogram is complete. Let dry for 2 hours or until the flooded monogram is dry to the touch.

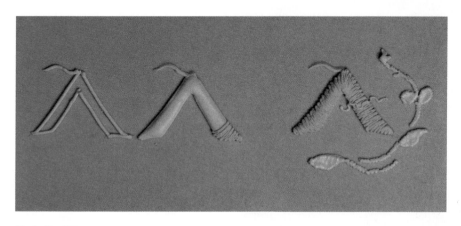

Illustration 7.9
Satin stitching (from left to right): the outline of a pattern, the flooded patter with the beginning of the stitching, and a completed satin stitching design.

When the monogram is dry, the satin stitching can begin. Position the #0 tip with the Meringue Powder Royal Icing at the upper left-hand corner of the monogram. Squeeze the bag as you drag the tip from left to right over the surface of the monogram. The lines should be extremely tight, with no spaces between them (see step 2 of Illustration 7.9).

For an extremely wide monogram, drag the tip from the left of the monogram to the center and then back to the left. Go back and forth, ending at the center. When you have filled in the left side of the monogram, move the tip to the upper right-hand corner. This time, drag the tip from the right edge left to the center and then back to the right side. Continue the pattern until the right side of the monogram is stitched.

To stitch the embroidery around the monogram, position the #0 tip at one end of the embroidery and then move the tip in back and forth, covering the embroidery in satin stitch (see step 3 of Illustration 7.9 and the bottom of Illustration 7.1).

New Skill: Eyelet Embroidery Designs

Quick Prep

4 oz (114 g) commercial rolled fondant
cornstarch
small nonstick rolling pin
small metal or plastic blossom cutters (4- or 5-petal cutters)
4-in. (10.2 cm) round, scalloped, oval, or
    square-metal cookie cutter
half-size piece of parchment paper
masking tape

Tape the corners of the parchment paper to your work surface. Knead 4 oz (114g) commercial rolled fondant until pliable. If the fondant is sticky, sprinkle a little cornstarch on the paste and knead it in.

Sprinkle a little cornstarch on your work surface. Roll out the rolled fondant to about ⅛ inch (3 mm) thick. Cut out two or three shapes for plaques with the 4-in. (10.2 cm) cookie cutter. Remove the excess fondant and wrap in plastic wrap.

Press a small metal or plastic blossom cutter carefully but firmly into one of the plaques. Carefully remove the cutter, revealing an imprint in the fondant (see the top left of Illustration 7.8). Carefully remove the shaped fondant from the blossom cutter. Shape the cutout with a dogbone or ball tool (see Lesson 14 on Gumpaste Flowers). This blossom shape, along with some royal icing piping, can be added to the plaque for a more attractive piece. Use other cutters to make more eyelet impressions in the plaque (see the top right of Illustration 7.8).

Continue to practice eyelet impressions with additional plaques and blossom cutters.

END-OF-LESSON REVIEW

1. Which transfer design technique would be used to transfer a large monogram onto a rolled iced plaque that has been air-dried? Why?

2. When piping Swiss dots on an iced cake, why should Meringue Powder Royal Icing be softened with water or egg whites?

3. When piping cornelli lace, why is it important to raise the tip of the paper cone from the surface and allow the melted chocolate to form small curves?

4. What technique is similar to cornelli lace?

5. What medium can be used for a buttercream transfer besides Buttercream Icing for Flooding?

6. Which transfer technique should be used to transfer the face of a clown onto an iced cake in which both the cake and the transfer are to be eaten?

7. Could a plaque with a transfer design be placed onto a buttercream iced cake?

8. What country is most noted for piping freehand embroidery?

PERFORMANCE TEST

Select two of the following exercises:

1. Select a pattern from Appendix 1. Using the buttercream transfer technique, transfer the design onto an 8-in. (20.3 cm) square cardboard.

2. Select a monogrammed pattern from Appendix 1 and satin stitch it.

3. Select a pattern from Appendix 1 and practice freehand embroidery on a small plaque made from commercial rolled fondant.

Lesson

8

THE ART OF ICING A CAKE

Buttercream, Marzipan, Rolled Fondant, Royal Icing, and Ganache

You will need the following icings and items to complete this lesson:

3 8 × 3 in. (20.3 × 7.6 cm) round cakes

2 or 3 10 × 3 in. (25.4 × 7.6 cm) round cakes

2 10-in. (25.4 cm) cakes

2 6-in. (15.2 cm) cakes

9-in. (22.9 cm) spiked pillars

Swiss Meringue Buttercream Icing (page 262)

Meringue Powder Royal Icing (page 273)

Marzipan (page 270)

Spackle Paste (page 285)

commercial rolled fondant

melted chocolate

heavy cream

rounded toothpicks

piping tips: #18,# 20, or #22 star tips

12-in. (30 cm) flex pastry bag

gel food colors

corn syrup

cornstarch

quart-size plastic containers (heat resistant)

confectioner's sugar

small and medium size metal bowls

offset and straight metal spatulas

serrated knife (bread knife)

bench or side scraper

long metal smoother

adding machine paper or strips of parchment paper

pastry brushes (wet and dry)

turntable (great, but not essential)

rubber spatulas

plastic wrap

masking tape

Xacto knife

scissors

6 to 8 in. (15.2 to 20.3 cm) decorative cake foil

8 × 3 in. (20.3 × 7.6 cm) round Styrofoam

large rolling pin

pair of plastic smoothers

#2 graphite pencil

fine sandpaper

cardboard circles: 6 in. (15.2 cm), 8 in. (20.3 cm), and 10 in. (25.4 cm)

damp sponge and side towels

couplers

cooling rack

12-in. (30 cm) round corkboard or English board

The actual icing of a cake is the most important task of the cake decorator or pastry chef—as essential as knowing how to make up the icings. A cake that is iced cleanly in buttercream, ganache, rolled fondant, marzipan, or royal icing shows pride and professionalism, and it helps elevate this skill to an art form. A cake that is smoothly iced needs no further decoration to be complete and saleable, although skillful decorating can significantly add to its value.

The key to successful cake icing is making sure the cake is level and free of crumbs before putting the icing on it. If the cake is split into several layers, each layer should be as even as possible. Additionally, the cake must be properly structured (or crumb-coated), especially if the layers are filled with jam, preserves, citrus curd, or buttercream.

Choosing the right icing for each cake is also important. This is often the responsibility of the decorator. The choices are constrained by time and environment—by time, if the cake is to be out for several hours before service, and by heat and humidity.

Practice each technique for cake smoothing until you can perform it effortlessly. Without constant practice, it is easy to lose the touch. This is not a skill to neglect.

New Skills: Leveling, Splitting, Assembling, Damming, and Filling a Cake

Quick Prep

several 8-in. (20.3) round cardboards
8 × 3 in. (20.3 × 7.6 cm) round yellow cake
serrated knife (bread knife)
offset metal or flat spatula
2 10-in. (25.4 cm) round cardboards
decorative cake foil
metal bowls
rubber spatulas
12 oz (340 g) cake filling of choice
8 oz (228 g) Swiss or Italian Meringue Buttercream Icing
    (pages 262 and 265)
damp sponge and side towels
piping tip: #18 star tip
12-in. (30 cm) flex pastry bag
couplers
turntable (if available)

LEVELING

Place an 8-in. (20.3) cake on your work surface. A turntable is helpful but not essential. If one is available, place the cake on it.

Carefully level the cake. If right-handed, place your left hand on the cake and hold the serrated knife in your right hand. Position the knife at the 3 o'clock position at the right edge of the cake. Move the cake counterclockwise as you lightly saw slivers of the cake (see Illustration 8.1a). Place the cake slivers in an empty bowl (see Illustration 8.1b). Continue until the cake is level (see Illustrations 8.1c and 8.1d). If you are left-handed, reverse hands and direction.

Illustration 8.1
Leveling a cake.

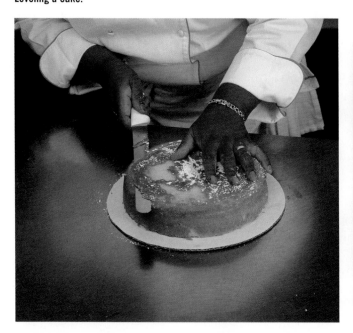

(a) With one hand on the cake, lightly saw the knife back and forth.

(b) Remove cake slivers as they are separated from the cake.

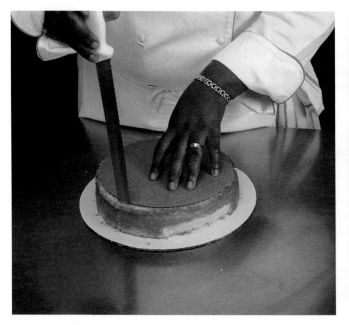

(c) Even the sides by placing a round cardboard on top of the cake and passing the knife around the edge in an up-and-down motion.

(d) Remove these slivers from the side of the cake for a completely leveled cake.

Illustration 8.2
After scoring the cake, move the knife back and forth to sever the layer.

SPLITTING

For this exercise, you will split the cake into three layers. Measure the height of the cake and place toothpicks at the split points. If you are right-handed, place your left hand on the cake and hold the serrated knife at the 3 o'clock position. Move the knife back and forth lightly as you turn the cake counterclockwise, scoring a line in the cake. Continue to score the cake until one circle is completed. Now, move the knife back and forth with more force to begin severing the first layer (see Illustration 8.2).

After sawing completely around the cake, slide an 8-in. (20.3 cm) cardboard under the severed layer. This prevents the layer from breaking. Carefully remove the layer and set it aside. Continue with the next layer and place it on another 8-in. (20.3 cm) cardboard. Slip a third cardboard under the last layer. You now have three cake layers.

Place the layers side by side and compare their height. Carefully cut slivers off the taller layers until all the layers are even.

ASSEMBLING THE CAKE LAYERS

Tape two 10-in. (25.4 cm) cardboard rounds together. Place masking tape at the 12 o'clock, 3 o'clock, 6 o'clock, and 9 o'clock positions. Cover both cardboards in decorative foil (see Lesson 17 for Covering a Foiled Board).

Place the foil-covered board on a turntable or work surface. Place a dab of buttercream in the center of the board and spread it to cover a circle 7 in. (17.8 cm) in diameter—that is, 1 in. (2.54 cm) smaller than the diameter of the cake layers. Pick up one of the cake layers on its cardboard round. Hold the cake with the cardboard support in your right hand and use your left hand to turn the cake clockwise. This releases the cake from the cardboard support. Angle the cake and cardboard at 45 degrees. Stick your right thumb under the cake and bend back the cardboard. Carefully slide the cake off the cardboard and onto the iced board. Adjust the cake to make sure it is in the center of the board, then press the support cake board (the one just used to transfer the cake) firmly on top of the cake layer. This ensures that the cake sticks to the iced board.

Illustration 8.3
A cake is dammed by piping a ring of icing just inside the top of the layer.

DAMMING THE CAKE

This technique allows a soft filling to remain stable between the cake layers without oozing out the sides. Load the pastry bag with 8 oz (228 g) buttercream icing and the #18 star tip. Starting at the 9 o'clock position (right-handers) or the 3 o'clock position (left-handers), pipe a circular border just inside the cake layer, about ¼ inch (6 mm) from the outside edge. Hold the bag at a 45-degree angle and raise the tip slightly off the surface. Allow the icing to drop as you move the pastry bag counterclockwise. Lower the bag and ease off the pressure when the cake is completely encircled (see Illustration 8.3).

Although the filling adds both moisture and flavor to the cake, adding another moisture source is a common practice for extending its shelf life. Simple syrup is often applied, especially to genoise cake layers. Some bakeries use plain water to moisten cake layers. Determining how much liquid is needed depends on the type of cake. Simple syrup is made by heating equal parts water and granulated sugar until the granules dissolve. Dip a pastry brush into the cooled syrup and brush liberally on dry cakes or lightly on moist cakes.

Illustration 8.4
Use an offset metal spatula to smooth the filling inside the icing dam.

FILLING THE CAKE

Choosing the right filling is important, especially if the icing and smoothing task requires rolled icing. If the cake is going to be eaten within a few days, then a curd made of lemon, lime, pineapple, or passion fruit can be delicious. However, if the cake must last a week or two, a jam or preserve is best, as rolled icing cakes are generally not refrigerated.

To fill a cake, place about 4 oz (114 g) cake filling inside the bottom cake layer. With a small offset metal spatula, spread it evenly out to the dam (see Illustration 8.4).

Place the second cake layer onto the bottom layer and repeat the procedure for assembling, damming, and filling. Finally, place the third layer on the cake. Do not dam this layer or place filling on top (see Illustration 8.5).

Illustration 8.5
Place the top cake layer onto the dammed and filled bottom layer by gently sliding it off the support cardboard.

New Skills: Crumb-Coating, Piping the Icing, and Smoothing the Icing

Quick Prep

3-layered cake
2 lbs (908 g) buttercream icing of choice
offset metal or straight metal spatula
metal bowls
piping tip: #18 star tip
12-in. (30 cm) flex pastry bag
quart-size plastic containers (heat resistant)

CRUMB-COATING THE CAKE

This technique stabilizes the loose crumbs on the cake. Spread a little buttercream on the top and sides of the cake and, if time permits, refrigerate the cake for 1 hour to allow the buttercream to set. Often in the industry time does not permit.

Some decorators don't crumb-coat their cakes. They simply dump a lot of buttercream icing on top of the cake and carefully move the buttercream to the sides with a long offset metal spatula. Then they work back and forth from the top of the cake to the sides to smooth the icing. While this technique requires more skill, in time it can be easily accomplished.

Begin by measuring 6 oz (170 g) buttercream icing into a metal bowl. Beat the icing lightly if it has been sitting for more than 1 hour. Dip a metal spatula into the buttercream and load it with icing.

Place the spatula with icing at the 9 o'clock position (for right-handers) or the 3 o'clock position (for left-handers). Using the inside of the spatula, begin by spreading the icing back and forth, keeping the spatula at a 45-degree angle to the cake. Spread the icing from the top of the cake to the foiled cardboard. Reload the spatula and continue to spread the icing as you move the spatula counterclockwise (for right-handers) and the cake clockwise. (see Illustration 8.6).

Once you have gone around the cake, spread a thin layer of icing on the top of the cake. Use a paddle-type motion as you spread the icing on the top, then smooth the icing by positioning the spatula at the 6 o'clock position. Hold the spatula at a 45-degree angle. The spatula should be at the very edge of the cake. Carefully move the spatula across the cake in a light motion. Once you pass the center of the cake, carefully ease off the pressure and lift up the spatula before you reach the opposite end of the cake. Turn the cake clockwise as you continue to smooth the icing across the cake. Each time, you should start at the edge of the cake and move the spatula across the cake in a light motion.

Piping the Icing on the Cake—Load the pastry bag with buttercream icing and the #18 star tip. This is one of the easiest ways to ice a cake. By piping the icing onto the cake, all the icing needed to successfully and smoothly ice a cake is there. Now only the excess needs to be carefully removed.

First, position the tip and pastry bag at a 90-degree angle and at the 6 o'clock position. The tip should be at the top edge of the cake. Apply a burst of

Illustration 8.6
When crumb-coating a cake, move the spatula counterclockwise to spread the icing.

Decorator's Hint

In the photo, the author is using a straight spatula instead of an offset metal spatula. The height of the cake dictates which type to use. If the cake is 3 in. (7.6 cm) tall or higher, then a small off-set metal may not be adequate. Once the filling, crumb-coating, and icing is applied to the cake, the cake might be almost 4 inches (10.2 cm) tall.

Illustration 8.7
Piping icing on a cake.

(a) Move the icing tip up and down the side of the cake while applying steady pressure to the pastry bag.

(b) To pipe icing on the top of the cake, hold the tip at a 45-degree angle and move it left and right until the entire cake is piped.

pressure and lightly drag the tip to the cake from the top edge of the cake to the bottom of the cake board. Then apply steady pressure as you drag the tip back up to the top of the cake. Continue piping the icing, moving the tip up and down the cake until the entire cake has been circled (see Illustration 8.7a).

Next, position the tip on top of the cake at the upper left-hand corner of the cake. The pastry bag and tip should be at a 45-degree angle. Apply a burst of pressure as you lightly drag the tip from the left side of the cake to the right side of the cake. Then drag the tip from the right side of the cake back to the left side. Continue with this back and forth technique (like a long zigzag) until the entire top of the cake is covered (see Illustration 8.7b).

The cake now has all the icing it needs on the cake. The next step is to smooth the cake.

Smoothing the Icing on the Cake—This is a technique and skill that requires plenty of practice. The more cakes you ice and smooth the better you will become. To begin, heat some water and place it in a large heat-roof plastic container. You will use the hot water later to heat the spatula (see Illustration 8.8a).

Position the cake on a turntable, if available. Position an offset or straight spatula at a 45-degree angle to the cake at the 9 o'clock position (for right-handers) or the 3 o'clock position (for left-handers). Apply light pressure as you move the spatula counterclockwise. Remove the excess icing from the spatula and continue smoothing the cake. Remember that the spatula should be at a 45-degree angle toward the cake. If the angle is too sharp, you will remove too much icing. Continue to smooth until you have gone completely around the cake. This is the pre-smoothing stage (see Illustration 8.8b).

Now, position the spatula at the 6 o'clock position and at a 45-degree angle at the very edge of the cake. Use the same technique as for crumb-coating—that is, carefully move the spatula across the cake in a light motion, easing off the pressure once you pass the center of the cake. Lift the spatula before you reach the opposite side. Turn the cake clockwise as you continue to smooth the icing.

Decorator's Hint

You should still be able to see the cake after the cake has been crumb-coated. You are only applying a thin layer of icing to seal in the crumbs.

Decorator's Hint

If no turntable is available, place a round cardboard circle under the cake board. This circle should be 1 or 2 in. (2.54 to 6.4 cm) smaller than the cake board. The circle will act as a turntable.

Illustration 8.8
Smoothing the cake.

(a) Dipping the spatula in hot water helps smooth the cake.

(b) Pre-smooth the icing by holding the spatula at a 45-degree angle while moving it around the side of the cake. Remove any excess icing from the spatula.

(c) To pre-smooth the top, start at the edge and move the spatula at a 45-degree angle toward the center in a light motion.

(d) A smoothed cake.

Start each pass at the edge of the cake and move the spatula across it in a light motion. The cake is now pre-smoothed.

For a final smoothing, dip the spatula in the hot water and dry it off with a side towel. Position the heated spatula flat against the cake at a 90-degree angle and at the 9 o'clock position (for right-handers) or the 3 o'clock position (for left-handers). Move the spatula counterclockwise and the cake clockwise. Again dip the spatula in hot water and dry it off. Pick up where you left off by placing the spatula flat against the cake. Continue to move the spatula clockwise until the icing is completely smooth around the cake.

For smoothing the top of the cake, dip the spatula into the hot water and dry it off with a side towel. Hold the heated spatula at a 45-degree angle and at the 6 o'clock position. Using the same technique as crumb-coating the top of the cake, move the spatula in a light motion toward the opposite end of the cake. You want to push the edge of icing that built up from smoothing the sides of the cake (see illustration 8.8c). When you reach the center of the cake, slightly ease off the pressure and lift the spatula from the cake. Turn the cake clockwise and pick up where you left off.

Continue smoothing until you have gone completely around the cake. You may need to go around the sides and then the top edge again (see Illustration 8.8d). Never let the spatula touch the cake—it should touch the icing only—thus eliminating picking up crumbs.

New Skill: Spackling a Cake

Quick Prep

3-layer cake (already filled)
16 oz (454 g) buttercream icing of choice (Swiss, Italian, Decorator's)
16 oz (454 g) Spackle Paste (page 285)
offset or straight spatula
8-in. (20.3 cm) cardboard circle or square

I developed the spackling technique because I saw a need to present high-end cakes like those produced in British and Australian sugarcraft. In the United Kingdom and Australia, fruitcake is used as a base. The fruitcake is covered with a layer of marzipan and then with several coatings of royal icing or a layer of rolled fondant. When the cake is cut, the icing is ½ in. (1.3 cm) thick.

Cakes like these would not be popular in the United States, as fruitcakes, marzipan, and rolled icings are not considered everyday foods. However, Europeans and many people from the Caribbean who live in the United States would love to eat such a cake. Spackling involves icing a layered cake (of any kind) with a mixture of cake crumbs, cake fillings, and buttercream. The cake is then refrigerated until firm, given a light coating of buttercream icing, and finally covered with a layer of rolled fondant.

With this procedure, the icing is ¼ in. (6 mm) thick. The delicious paste improves the taste of the rolled fondant, and the cake exhibits the perfect smoothness seen in British and Australian sugarcraft.

To begin, lightly beat the spackle paste with a rubber spatula or wooden spoon. Place 8 oz (228 g) of the spackle paste on a small round or square cardboard along with 4 to 6 oz (114 to 170 g) of buttercream icing. This gives you latitude when spreading the paste, as it is quite thick.

Begin by loading some of the paste on a metal spatula. Start at a 45-degree angle at the 9 o'clock position (for right-handers) or the 3 o'clock position (for left-handers).

Decorator's Hint

If you are using an offset metal spatula, turn it toward the inside and apply it flat against the cake. This way, it raises the edge of the icing to slightly higher than the top of the cake. This is exactly what you want when you are ready for the final smoothing.

Decorator's Hint

Water can be used with the spackle paste instead of buttercream to make spreading the paste easier. Buttercream, of course, adds more delicious flavor to the already flavorful spackle paste.

Spread the spackle paste on the cake as if you were crumb-coating it. Spread the paste from the top edge of the cake to the foiled-covered cake board. Put a little buttercream on the spatula to help spread the spackle paste. When the cake is completely spackled, apply an additional thin layer of spackle paste to the top of the cake using the same technique (see Illustration 8.9).

Illustration 8.9
Spackling a cake.

(a) Spackle the side of the cake first.

(b) Spackle the top by starting at the edge and moving the spatula toward the center of the cake.

(c) A spackled cake.

Loosely cover the spackled cake with plastic wrap and refrigerate until firm. You can leave the cake in the refrigerator overnight or up to one week.

When ready to ice in rolled fondant, spread a thin layer of buttercream icing over the spackled cake to act as glue for the rolled icing. The cake is now ready to be covered with rolled fondant.

New Skill: Icing a Cake with Rolled Fondant

Quick Prep

2 lbs (908 g or 0.91 kg) commercial rolled fondant
pair of white plastic smoothers
metal spatula
cornstarch
confectioner's sugar
gel food colors
rounded toothpicks
large rolling pin

Nothing looks more exquisite than a cake properly covered in rolled fondant. The cake can be finished with a spray of royal icing flowers, gumpaste flowers, or a spray of hand-shaped chocolate roses. A simple greeting or just an individual's name can also complement the cake. A string of bead piping at the bottom of the cake and a simple thin ribbon tied around it with a tiny ribbon bow says wow! The cake is complete, and the look is perfect.

The one drawback to rolled fondant is its taste. It is a sugary-sweet icing that tastes like doughy marshmallows. Also, fondant, especially commercial brands, sometimes has a slight aftertaste, although you can flavor it with extracts or candy oils. You can also mix in marzipan or white modeling chocolate for a more palatable taste. The ratios are 2 parts rolled fondant to 1 part white chocolate plastic, or 2 parts rolled fondant to 1 part marzipan.

The reason rolled fondant is so popular is its gorgeous, classy look. High-end wedding cakes and special celebration cakes are often adorned with this icing.

Begin by kneading the rolled fondant thoroughly. Color it with gel colors, if desired. Kneading the fondant warms it so it can be readily rolled out. If the rolled icing is sticky, sprinkle a little confectioner's sugar or cornstarch on the work surface. Shape the rolled icing into disk 5 or 6 in. (12.7 or 15.2 cm) in diameter.

Sprinkle the work surface with cornstarch or confectioner's sugar, or a combination of both. You can reduce the amount of sugar or cornstarch by rolling the fondant on a Roul'Pat or Silpat (silicone) surface. Place the disk of rolled fondant in the center. Beginning at the 6 o'clock position, roll out the fondant, starting with light to medium pressure. Roll the rolling pin to the 12 o'clock position. Rotate the fondant disk in small increments. Continue rolling out the paste and rotating the disk so it does not stick to the work surface.

For an 8 × 3 in. (20.3 × 7.6 cm) cake, roll the fondant disk to about ¼ in. (6 mm) thick and about 16 in. (40.6 cm) across. (See the Decorator's Hint on calculating rolled fondant size on p. 117.)

Use a plastic smoother to smooth over the paste. This also stretches the paste more and it swashes any air bubbles that may arise when rolling out the fondant. Next, position the rolling pin at either the 12 o'clock or 6 o'clock position. Roll the fondant onto the rolling pin, brushing aside any residue of cornstarch or confectioner's sugar with a pastry brush (see Illustration 8.10).

Place the spackled cake in front of you. If it just came out of the refrigerator, lightly coat the cake with a little buttercream icing. If the cake is just out of the

Decorator's Hint
Knead in ½ tsp (1g) of solid vegetable shortening into the rolled icing before covering a cake with it. This reduces cracks on the shoulder of the cake.

Decorator's Hint
Try sprinkling the work surface with confectioner's sugar or cornstarch. Unlike cornstarch, confectioner's sugar adds sweetness to the fondant. On the other hand, cornstarch can dry out the fondant, which confectioner's sugar does not. I prefer cornstarch or, as a compromise, a combination of equal parts cornstarch and confectioner's sugar.

Illustration 8.10
In preparation for transferring rolled fondant to the cake, roll it onto a rolling pin

refrigerator but already coated with a thin layer of buttercream, use a pastry brush to brush it with water or a little brandy, liqueur, or rum.

Position the rolled fondant to the cake at the 6 o'clock position. The rolled fondant should start at the edge of the foiled-covered board; otherwise, it will be too short on one side. Transfer the rolled fondant to the cake by unrolling it from the rolling pin and allowing it to drape over the cake. The fondant should be transferred in one quick movement (see Illustration 8.11).

Once the rolled fondant is positioned on the cake, place the rolling pin on top of the cake at the 6 o'clock position and about 1 in. (2.54 cm) inside the cake's edge. Apply light pressure as you roll the pin toward the 12 o'clock position. Stop the rolling pin when you are about 1 in. (2.54 cm) from the cake's farther edge.

Illustration 8.11
Transferring the fondant to the cake.

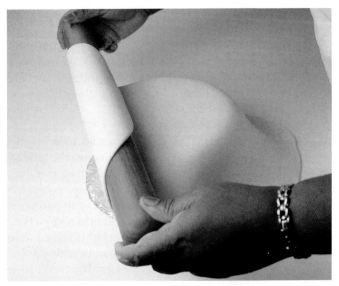

(a) Position the fondant between you and the cake.

(b) Roll the fondant from the rolling pin onto the cake in one quick motion.

Immediately focus on the folds on the cake. Lift up a fold with one hand to relax it, and use the other hand to smooth the fondant to the cake. Go on to the next fold and repeat the procedure (see Illustration 8.12).

With an offset metal spatula, pizza wheel, or Xacto knife, cut away excess fondant at about ½ in. (6 mm) from the edge of the cake. To do this, place the spatula at the 6 o'clock position just inside the edge of the fondant on the board. Angle the spatula to 45 degrees. Push the spatula and the fondant toward the edge of the cake and gently press down to cut away the excess fondant. Turn the cake clockwise and continue until the entire cake is done (see Illustration 8.13a).

To complete the edge and seal the fondant to the cake, position the spatula at a 45-degree angle and the 6 o'clock position at the very edge of the cake. Press the spatula firmly while turning the cake clockwise. This removes excess fondant and seals the fondant to the cake's edge (see Illustration 8.13b).

For a perfect finish, go over the sides and top of the cake with plastic smoothers to eliminate cracks and wrinkles. Position the plastic smoothers at the 6 o'clock and 9 o'clock positions. Apply medium to firm pressure as you move the smoothers back and forth (see Illustration 8.14).

To soften dryness on the cake's shoulders, apply a little solid vegetable shortening. Rub the shortening into the fondant and then use the center of your writing hand to smooth it. Smooth the shoulders back and forth with your hands until the dryness disappears.

Illustration 8.12
Smooth the fondant to the cake by lifting the folds with one hand to relax them and smoothing the fondant to the cake with the other hand.

Decorator's Hint

Press hard enough to ensure that the fondant adheres to the cake. Otherwise, air pockets will develop. To remove an air pocket, puncture it with a hatpin or stickpin held at a 45-degree angle, then gently smooth the fondant with plastic smoothers.

Illustration 8.13
Removing excess fondant.

(a) Remove excess fondant about ½ in. (6 mm) from the bottom edge of the cake.

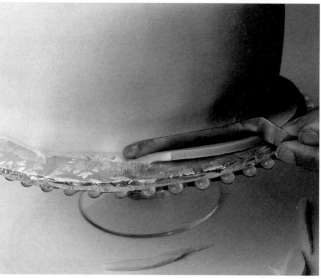

(b) With the spatula at a 45-degree angle, press firmly to remove excess fondant while sealing the fondant to the cake.

Decorator's Hint

Dryness on the shoulders of an iced cake is usually the result of using too much cornstarch or confectioner's sugar when rolling out the fondant, or taking too much time to roll it out. Generally, spend no longer than 3 to 5 minutes to roll out fondant, and then apply it immediately to the crumb-coated or spackle-iced cake. To minimize the drying on the cake's shoulder, rub a little solid vegetable shortening into the cracks.

Illustration 8.14
Move plastic smoothers back and forth along the side and top of the cake to iron out any wrinkles or cracks.

New Skill: Covering a Square Cake with Rolled Fondant

Quick Prep

8 × 3 in. (20.3 × 7.6 cm) Styrofoam square
10-in. (25.4 cm) foil-covered cardboard square
4 oz (114 g) Meringue Powder Royal Icing or
    Buttercream Icing (page 273)
2 lbs (908 g) commercial rolled fondant
cornstarch or confectioner's sugar
2 oz (57 g) corn syrup
pastry brush
2 plastic smoothers
rolling pin
fine sandpaper

Covering a square cake with fondant is trickier than covering a round cake. In fact, covering any odd-shaped cake is tricky. The key is to roll out the fondant a little larger than for a round cake. This gives you more latitude when lifting up the folds and smoothing the fondant.

For this skill, use a square Styrofoam to practice. Prepare the Styrofoam by softening the shoulder's edge with a piece of fine sandpaper. This technique is called *beveling*. Without beveling, the fondant will tear at the shoulder's edge. On a real cake, the edge of a square cake is not nearly as sharp and does not pose the same problem.

Fold the fine sandpaper into quarters and apply light pressure around the edge of the cake. If you sand the cake form too hard, it will tear the edge. Once you have gone completely around the cake, glue the cake form to a finished board with a little royal or buttercream icing. Using a pastry brush, brush the entire Styrofoam with a little corn syrup. The corn syrup will help the fondant adhere to the cake.

Shape the fondant to a 5-in. (12.7 cm) square. Sprinkle the work surface with a little cornstarch or confectioner's sugar, or a combination of both. Place the rolled icing at the center of the work surface. To roll out the fondant, place the rolling pin at the 6 o'clock position, apply light to medium pressure, and roll the pin

Decorator's Hint

You can brush Styrofoam with water instead of corn syrup to help the rolled fondant adhere.

toward the 12 o'clock position. Turn the rolled fondant a quarter-turn and continue rolling out until the fondant is ¼ in. (6 mm) thick and 17 to 18 in. (42.7 to 45.7 cm) across.

Once the fondant is rolled out, use the plastic smoothers to prevent air bubbles, even the surface, and stretch the fondant.

Position the rolling pin at the 12 o'clock position and roll the fondant onto the rolling pin. Place the practice Styrofoam in front of you and unroll the fondant onto it (see Illustration 8.15a). Roll the top of the fondant with a rolling pin to secure it to the cake (see Illustration 8.15b). Lift the folds with one hand and use the other hand to secure the fondant to the cake.

For the cake corners, lift the fondant with one hand. Cup your writing hand and use its shape to gently ease the fondant to the cake (see Illustration 8.15c). Use gentle pressure when shaping the fondant to the corners; otherwise, you will leave folds.

Illustration 8.15
Covering a square cake with fondant.

(a) Unroll the rolled fondant from the rolling pin onto the square cake.

(b) Lightly roll the rolling pin along the top of the fondant to secure it to the cake.

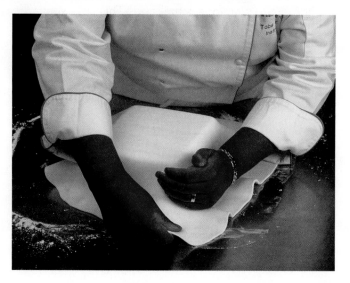

(c) Cup your hand to gently ease the fondant to the corners of the cake.

Continue smoothing the fondant to the cake, carefully cupping your hand when securing the fondant to the corners.

Once the cake is covered with rolled fondant, cut away the excess fondant and secure the edge to the cake (as you did for the round cake). Smooth the fondant with plastic smoothers.

New Skill: How to Ganache a Cake

Quick Prep

6 × 3 in. (15.2 × 7.6 cm) crumb-coated layer cake on an
    iced support board
1 recipe Ganache Icing (page 264)
cooling rack
medium-size metal bowl
1 small metal offset spatula
1 very large offset metal spatula

Decorator's Hint

An alternative technique is to lift the cake and rotate and tilt it to remove excess ganache from the top. This must be done quickly to prevent drips from forming on the sides of the cake.

Position a cooling rack on top of a large metal bowl. This is used to catch the ganache icing as it drips off the cake. Place the crumb-coated or spackled cake on a cardboard round of the same diameter. This is to prevent damage when lifting the cake. Slide a large metal offset spatula under the cardboard. Carefully lift the cardboard with the cake onto the cooling rack.

Check the ganache to see if it is sufficiently cool and thick enough to be poured onto the cake. Continue to cool the ganache until it reaches spreading consistency. Position the bowl of cooled ganache with both hands. Beginning over the center of the cake, start pouring the ganache in a circular motion (see

Illustration 8.16
Icing a cake with ganache.

(a) Pour the ganache in the center of a cake in a circular motion.

(b) The ganache will begin to drape over the sides of the cake. Continue until the entire cake is covered.

Illustration 8.16a). Widen the circle and continue to pour as the ganache begins to drape over the sides of the cake. Continue pouring until the entire cake is coated with ganache (see Illustration 8.16b).

Place the bowl next to the work surface and quickly use a metal spatula to spread the ganache (see Illustration 8.16c). Let the iced cake sit until the ganache stops dripping into the bowl. Carefully transfer the iced cake from the cooling rack to the work surface with a large offset metal spatula. Let the cake cool completely, or place it in the refrigerator to firm the ganache.

New Skill: Royal Icing a Marzipan Cake

Quick Prep

8 × 3 in. (20.3 × 7.6 cm) Styrofoam or
   8 × 3 in. (20.3 × 7.6 cm) fruitcake or pound cake
3 lbs (1,362 g or 1.36 kg) Marzipan (page 270)
1 lb (454 g) Meringue Powder Royal Icing (page 273)
6 oz (170 g) sieved apricot jam
12-in. (30 cm) round corkboard or English board
   (these boards are ½-in. [1.3 cm] thick)
6-in. (15.2 cm) and 8-in. (20.3 cm) round cardboards
bench or side scraper
adding machine paper or strips of parchment paper
   12 to 14 in. (30 to 35.6 cm) long
metal smoother or long straight metal spatula
small and large offset metal spatulas
wide offset metal spatula
pastry brush

(c) Use a spatula to spread and smooth the ganache.

Icing cakes in royal icing is not customary in the United States. Decorators who have lived in the United Kingdom, the Caribbean, or former British colonies commonly use royal icing and marzipan.

The royal icing and marzipan technique is typically applied to fruitcake, although any type of cake can be used. The cake is first covered with a layer of marzipan and then with several coats of royal icing. This approach contrasts with that of covering a cake in rolled icing and then decorating it with royal icing.

To begin this skill, fill any holes in the fruitcake with small pieces of marzipan. Use a metal spatula to smooth the marzipan over the holes. If using a pound cake or another firm cake, this step should not be necessary.

When the cake is ready to be iced, roll out 1 lb (454 g) marzipan on a surface lightly dusted with confectioner's sugar. Roll the paste to ¼ in. (3 mm) thick and a diameter greater than that of the cake. This will allow the entire cake surface to be covered and the excess to be trimmed. Place a cardboard circle that is the same size as the cake in the center of the rolled marzipan. Score around the cardboard with a quilting wheel or toothpick. Remove the cardboard circle and brush sieved apricot jam inside the scored circle.

Carefully lift the cake onto the marzipan circle, directly on top of the sieved jam. Lightly press down on the cake with cardboard to secure the cake to the marzipan. Cut around the circumference of the cake with an offset spatula (see Illustration 8.17). Remove the excess marzipan and wrap it in plastic wrap to be used another time. Set the cake aside.

To ice the other side of the cake, weigh out another 1 lb (454 g) marzipan. You can include the excess from the first pound. Sprinkle confectioner's sugar on the surface and roll out the marzipan to ¼ in. (6 mm) thick. Using the cardboard circle, score the marzipan to the exact size of the cake and brush the circle with sieved apricot jam. Carefully lift the cake with a very large offset spatula. Place a plain cardboard round on top of the cake and flip the cake onto the cardboard, revealing the marzipan underneath. Place the cake on the second marzipan circle, pressing lightly to seal the cake to the marzipan. Cut away the excess with an offset spatula and wrap the excess in plastic wrap. You have just encased the top and bottom of the cake in marzipan.

To ice the sides of the cake in marzipan, measure the height and the circumference of the cake. Make a pattern by taping together strips of parchment paper with masking tape or adding machine paper. Roll out another 1 lb (454 g) marzipan in a strip ¼ inch (3 mm) thick that is longer and wider than the pattern.

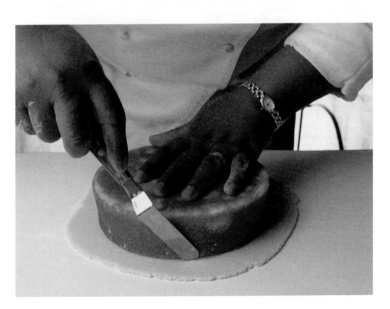

Illustration 8.17
After placing the cake on the rolled-out marzipan, remove excess marzipan by cutting around the cake with a spatula.

Illustration 8.18
Carefully unroll the strip of marzipan around the side of the cake.
The ends should just come together.

Place the pattern on the marzipan and cut with a pizza wheel, Xacto knife, or metal spatula. Remove the excess and wrap in plastic wrap.

Carefully roll up the marzipan like a jellyroll. Brush the sides of the cake with sieved apricot jam and unroll the marzipan around the cake. If the marzipan stretches while unrolling, cut off the excess with an Xacto knife. The ends of the marzipan strip should just meet. Use a smoother to press the marzipan into place and help it adhere to the cake (see Illustration 8.18).

Spread a little royal icing in the center of a finished board and carefully lift the encased marzipan cake onto it. Press the cake lightly with a cardboard round to secure it to the board. The cake is now ready to be iced with royal icing.

Decorator's Hint
Seal the seam by spreading a little royal icing on it with a metal spatula.

ICING THE SIDES IN ROYAL ICING

Royal icing softens when it sits for any length of time. If the icing is too soft, re-beat it with a paddle attachment until the consistency has a medium to stiff peak. Be sure to keep it covered with plastic wrap.

Place the marzipan cake on a turntable. Put some royal icing on an offset metal spatula, hold it at the 9 o'clock position and a 45-degree angle, and paddle the icing onto the cake in a back-and-forth motion. Continue until you have gone completely around the cake (See Illustration 8.19).

When ready to smooth the icing, place a round cardboard, 1 to 2 in. (2.54 cm to 5.1 cm) smaller than the diameter of the cake, on top. If right-handed, place your left hand on the cake and vice versa. Turn the cake clockwise as far as you can without moving your hands. Position a side scraper or bench scraper at a 45-degree angle, as close to the 12 o'clock position as possible. In one continuous movement, turn the cake counterclockwise and drag the scraper to the cake clockwise (see Illustration 8.20). Continue until you have completely encircled the cake. Stop turning the cake and gently ease off the pressure on the scraper.

This completes the first coat of icing. To remove the excess from the top edge, hold a metal spatula flat against the top edge of the cake and gently take off the edge of icing as

Illustration 8.19
Paddle the royal icing back and forth around the sides of the cake.

Illustration 8.20
Drag the scraper around the side of the cake to smooth the royal icing while your other hand turns the cake from the top.

you turn the turntable. This first coat must dry for at least 1 hour or until the sides of the cake are dry.

ICING THE TOP OF THE CAKE

Touch the sides of the cake to confirm that the first layer of icing is dry. Load the metal spatula with royal icing and begin spreading the icing on top of the cake. Paddle the icing on the cake in a back-and-forth motion, as you did on the sides. Reload the spatula and continue to paddle the icing onto the cake.

To smooth the icing on top, place a long smoother or a long metal spatula at the 12 o'clock position and a 45-degree angle. Place your hands close together on the smoother and apply even and firm pressure as you pull it toward you (see Illustration 8.21). When you reach the end of the cake at the 6 o'clock position,

Illustration 8.21
Pull the smoother toward you while applying even pressure.

gently pull the smoother toward you to exit the cake. Use a small metal spatula to scrap the excess icing on the top edge of the cake. Allow the cake to dry for at least 1 hour.

Before adding another layer of royal icing to the sides of the cake, use a piece of very fine sandpaper to lightly sand any take off lines or icing build-ups. Using the same technique as before, ice the sides of the cake with royal icing again and smooth it with a side or bench scraper. Remove the excess from the top edge of the cake and let dry at least 1 hour. Repeat the procedure for the top of the cake and let dry for 1 hour or overnight.

Add a third side and top layer of royal icing to the cake. Carefully use fine sandpaper between the layers to ensure the smoothest look. After three layers, check if the marzipan is still visible through the icing. If it is, add another layer of royal icing, or perhaps even two.

ICING THE CAKE BOARD

Icing a finished board in royal icing extends the size of the cake and adds to its dimension. This technique is not necessary, but the tradition is entrenched.

Paddle the icing on the board with a metal spatula. Avoid building up icing at the bottom edge of the cake. When the cake board is iced all around, place a cardboard round on top of the cake to protect it. Place your writing hand on the cake and turn the cake clockwise as far as you can without moving your hands. This is the same technique as for icing the sides of the cake. Position the side or bench scraper close to the 12 o'clock position and at a 45-degree angle. In a single movement, turn the cake counterclockwise as you drag the side scraper on the cake board (see Illustration 8.22). Once around the cake, carefully lift the side scraper, avoiding take-off lines. Use a metal spatula to scrap any icing build-ups on the edge of the cake board. Let dry for 1 to 2 hours. Lightly sand the cake board with very fine sandpaper before adding the next layer. Repeat the procedures above.

Check whether the board is visible through the icing. If it is, then add another coat of icing.

Illustration 8.22
To smooth the icing on the cake board, drag the scraper around the board while rotating the cake from the top.

New Skill: Stacking Cake Tiers

Quick Prep

10-in. (25.4 cm) cake iced in commercial rolled fondant and
   placed on a finished board
6-in. (15.2 cm) cake iced in commercial rolled fondant and
   place on an iced support board
5 oz (140 g) buttercream or Meringue Powder Royal Icing
   (page 273)
6-in. (15.2 cm) cardboard circle
toothpicks
small and large offset metal spatulas
6 to 8 in. (15.2 to 20.3 cm) lollipop or cookie sticks
Xacto knife
#2 graphite pencil

Most people marvel when they see a beautifully decorated cake, gorgeously iced
and featuring fine pipework and perhaps a spray of piped or hand-shaped flowers. A tiered cake, even a plain one, has a beauty all its own. How *can* the top cake
not crush the bottom one? Even cake tiers separated by plastic pillars can be
stunning, especially when the space is filled with a beautiful floral arrangement.

Here you will practice constructing a two-tier cake. The bottom tier is a 10-in.
(25.4 cm) cake on a finished board and the top tier a 6-in. (15.2 cm) cake. Both
cake tiers are finished in commercial rolled fondant.

DOWELING THE CAKE

The first step is to anchor the bottom tier. For many years, this was achieved
with wooden dowels, which are still used in many countries. Today, however,
many decorators use drinking straws. I myself like using lollipop or cookie
sticks. These are made from tightly wrapped paper and are food approved. They
are extremely strong but can be easily cut.

Place a cardboard round, the same size as the top tier, on the bottom tier in
the spot you plan to set the layer. If you want to center the top tier, place the
cardboard in the center of
the bottom tier, and if you
want the top tier off-center,
place the cardboard where
you wish the tier to be placed.

Use a toothpick to mark
holes around the cardboard.
You will use these pinpricks
as a guide when placing the
top tier on the bottom tier
(see Illustration 8.23). Remove the cardboard to reveal
the pinpricked pattern.

> ## Decorator's Hint
>
> For an off-center top tier, a good spot is
> 1½ to 2 in. (3.8 to 5 cm) inside the edge
> of the bottom tier.

Illustration 8.23
The pinpricks placed around a cardboard the same size as
the next tier will guide its placement.

For a 10-in. (25.4 cm) cake, you will need six dowels to support the top tier. (See the guide for doweling at the end of this lesson.) Place the first dowel in the center of the pinpricked pattern. The dowel should go all the way down to the finished board. Place the five remaining dowels around the centered dowel, about 1 in. (2.54 cm) in from the pattern and one-fifth the distance around the centered dowel.

Use a #2 graphite pencil to mark the point on each dowel where it meets the rolled fondant (see Illustration 8.24a). Remove the dowels one at a time and score each with an Xacto knife at a point slightly lower than the pencil marking, approximately ¹⁄₁₆ to ⅛ in. (1.5 to 3 mm). Break each dowel at the scored line (see Illustration 8.24b). Replace the dowels inside the cake, making sure

Illustration 8.24
Doweling the cake.

(a) Mark the point on the dowel where the dowel and rolled fondant meet.

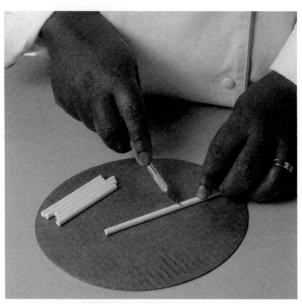

(b) Cut the dowels so they are slightly lower than the rolled icing.

(c) Return the dowels inside the cake, making sure they reach the cake board.

each reaches the finished board (see Illustration 8.24c). The dowels should now be slightly below the level of the rolled icing.

Place a little buttercream or royal icing where the top tier is to be set, inside the pinpricked pattern. Slide a large offset metal spatula under the top tier. Using your hands to help support it, carefully place the cake on the bottom tier, using the pattern as a guide. Carefully remove the spatula from beneath the top tier (see Illustration 8.25a). Adjust the tier with your hands. Place a cardboard on the top tier and press lightly to help it adhere to the bottom tier. The tiered cake is complete (see Illustration 8.25b).

Illustration 8.25
Placing the top tier on the bottom tier.

(a) Using the pinpricked pattern as a guide, carefully place the top tier on the bottom tier. The spatula and your hand under the bottom of the top tier will help support the cake.

(b) The completed tiered cake.

New Skill: Tiers with Columns or Pillars

Quick Prep

> 10-in. (25.4 cm) cake iced in commercial rolled fondant and
>   placed on a finished board
> 6-in. (15.2 cm) cake iced in commercial rolled fondant and
>   placed on a finished board
> 6-in. (15.2 cm) cardboard circles
> toothpicks
> pack of 9-in. (22.9 cm) spiked pillars (4 or 5 pillars)

Tiers separated by pillars and columns are no longer in fashion, although they are still requested by clients looking for grand effects: staircases, fountains, plastic ushers, bridesmaids, and brides and grooms. Pillared and columned cakes were made popular in the United States in the 1950's to 1980's. They are still used, but not as often as cakes stacked on top of each other.

These splashy cakes use plastic separator plates with pins and columns to create a majestic look. This look can be downsized and simulated with a lot less plastic.

Determine the distance wanted between the top and bottom tier. This will dictate the size of the pillars. Spiked pillars are the best choice because the cake can be doweled and still have pillar space between the tiers. With spiked pillars, the procedure is quick and easy. These pillars, narrow at the bottom and square at the top, are available in lengths of 9 to 12 in. (22.9 to 30 cm) or more. The height of both cake tiers also dictates the size of the pillars. Thus, if the bottom tier is 4 in. (10.2 cm) high and the pillars are 9 in. (22.9 cm) high, that leaves a 5-in. (12.7 cm) space between tiers. That may or may not be enough room in which to arrange a floral spray or fountain. If the plan is for something very simple in between the tiers, then the 9-in. (22.9 cm) pillars might be just right.

Place cardboard on the bottom tier that is the same size as the top tier and score the bottom tier, just as you did to stack tiers. This is a guide for placing the spiked pillars. It is best to use five spiked pillars to dowel the bottom tier; however, you can get away with four if necessary.

Place the spiked pillars about ½ in. (1.3 cm) inside the scored pattern, or one-quarter of the distance if using four spiked pillars, or one-fifth of the distance if

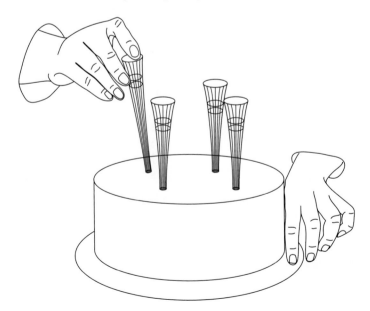

Illustration 8.26
Push the pillars into the cake until they reach the cake board.

Illustration 8.27
Carefully place the top cake tier on its own cake board directly onto the pillars.

using five spiked pillars. Push the pillars into the bottom tier until they reach the finished board. The pillars stay inside the cake. Insert all the pillars (see Illustration 8.26).

Place the top tier and its finished board directly on top of the pillars (see Illustration 8.27). Remember, the pillars are flat on top. Center the cake on the pillars. Your pillared tiered cake is complete. You can place a small- to medium-size floral spray between the tiers, arranging them to hide the pinpricked pattern. This can also be done by adding piped or hand-shaped leaves.

Guide for Doweling a Cake

CAKE DIAMETER	DOWELS NEEDED
4 in. (10.2 cm)	3 to 4
6 in. (15.2 cm)	5 to 6
8 in. (20.3 cm)	7
9 in. (22.9 cm)	8
10 in. (25.4 cm)	9
12 in. (30 cm)	11
14 in. (35.6 cm)	13
16 in. (40.6 cm)	15
18 in. (45 cm)	17
20 in. (50.8 cm)	19

How many dowels are needed to dowel a cake with a 16-in. (40.6 cm) layer, a 12-in. (30 cm) layer, and a 6-in. (15.2 cm) layer? Because the 12-in. (30 cm) layer is sitting on the 16-in. (40.6 cm) layer, it needs support dowels. Because the 6-in. (15.2 cm) layer is sitting on the 12-in. (30 cm) layer, it also needs support dowels. Thus, 11 dowels are needed for the 12-in. (30 cm) layer and 5 to 6 dowels for the 6-in. (15.2 cm) layer.

END-OF-LESSON REVIEW

1. Why would a cake be dammed?

2. Why would a cake be crumb-coated?

3. Is it important to level a cake before splitting, filling, and icing? Why?

4. What is the importance of spackle paste?

5. Why is it important to use cardboard circles or squares to transfer cakes for assembly?

6. What are the advantages of covering a cake in rolled fondant?

7. Can rolled fondant be colored?

8. Why should dowels be placed in the bottom tier of a cake before adding the top tier?

9. Why is it important to pinprick a pattern on the bottom tier before adding the top tier?

10. What is the purpose of using spiked pillars when elevating a cake's top tier from the bottom tier?

PERFORMANCE TEST

Select and execute two of the following projects:

1. Split, fill, crumb-coat, and ice a cake in buttercream icing.

2. Cover a cake or Styrofoam in rolled fondant.

3. Cover a Styrofoam in marzipan and then ice it with three coats of Meringue Powder Royal Icing (page 273).

4. Stack-tier or column-tier a two-tier cake.

HAND MODELING SKILLS

Marzipan Fruits and Vegetables

You will need the following items to complete this lesson:

Marzipan (page 270)	quick glaze
gel food colors	clove slivers
petal dust colors	cheese grater
#0, #1, #3, and #5 sable paintbrushes	Xacto knife
ball tool or dogbone tool	nonstick rolling pin
cone and serrated marzipan tools	rounded toothpicks
28-gauge florist wires	florist tape
confectioner's glaze	small rose calyx cutter

Marzipan modeling is a skill and an art. In Germany, Switzerland, France, Italy, and many other countries, marzipan art is at its zenith. Fruits and vegetables sculpted in marzipan are both beautiful and decoratively useful. Picture a sculpted pomegranate, full size, opened, with its seeds spilling over a gorgeously iced cake. That *wow!* is what food art is meant to accomplish.

The chief ingredient of marzipan is almond paste. Almonds are roasted or blanched, skinned, and then pulverized or ground to a powder. The paste is made by adding almond oil, essence, bitter essence, sugar, and vanilla in varying proportions. Some almond paste, particularly that of Sicily, is very bitter because nothing is added to the ground almonds but bitter essence. Almond paste in the United States is sweeter and usually contains sugar, oil, essence, and vanilla.

To make marzipan, almond paste is combined with confectioner's sugar, corn syrup, vanilla, and/or light rum to heighten the flavor and make the paste more pliable. (Almond paste on its own has no elasticity.) Converting the dark beige almond paste to marzipan also lightens the color, which makes it easier to add food colors.

Marzipan Color Chart

Lemon-yellow marzipan (lemon-yellow color only)

Sunset-orange marzipan (sunset-orange color only)

Granny Smith green marzipan (lemon yellow + leaf green + chocolate brown)

Deep-red marzipan (egg yellow + violet + holiday red + super red)

To complete this lesson, you will need 8 oz (228 g) marzipan in each of these colors. Measure the marzipan and use gel food colors to color the paste. (Be sure to wear latex gloves when coloring.) The best way to color marzipan is to stick a toothpick into the food color and wipe it directly onto the paste. It's important to add the colors in the order in which they appear in the color chart. You can make adjustments as the colors emerge in the marzipan, but remember that colors, once added, cannot be removed.

Knead the paste with a little confectioner's sugar until the desired color is achieved. Wrap the colored marzipan in plastic wrap until ready to use. The color chart in Lesson 17 has additional tips on coloring.

This lesson develops hand-eye coordination, which is essential to making gumpaste flowers (Lesson 14).

New Skill: Oranges and Lemons

Quick Prep

1 oz (28 g) yellow marzipan

1 oz (28 g) orange marzipan

¼ oz (7 g) Granny Smith green marzipan

2 clove slivers

dogbone tool

Xacto knife

cheese grater

orange, lemon yellow, and moss-green petal dust colors

#3 or #5 sable paintbrush

Illustration 9.1
The left side of the image shows the steps to creating a marzipan orange. A pea-sized ball of apple-green marzipan is kneaded into the orange marzipan and then formed into a round ball; the bottom left is the completed orange. The right side of the image shows the steps to creating a marzipan lemon. This time a pea-sized ball of apple green is added to yellow marzipan and then formed into a ball; the bottom right is the completed lemon. Both fruits are rolled on a cheese grater for texture.

ORANGE

Add a pea-sized amount of Granny Smith green paste to 1 oz (28 g) orange marzipan. Knead the green paste into the orange paste, but don't let it disappear entirely—that is, leave some shadows of green throughout the orange. Place the paste in your nonwriting hand and put your writing hand directly on top. Rotate your hands in opposite directions until the paste forms a round ball (see Illustration 9.1).

Roll the ball of paste over a cheese grater to give it an orange-like texture. Do not apply too much pressure, as you want to maintain the ball shape. Next, to soften the texture, lightly rotate the ball between your hands.

Place the paste on the work surface. With the small end of the dogbone tool, press lightly on the top of the ball to form a slight indentation. Place a small clove in the center of the indentation and push it until it is flush with the orange. This is the stem of the orange.

The orange is complete. However, you can add depth to its appearance by dusting the orange lightly with a sable paintbrush dipped in orange petal dust, which is nontoxic chalk with cornstarch added. For even more depth, blend a little moss-green petal dust near the stem of the orange into the orange petal dust (see the bottom left of Illustration 9.1).

LEMON

Add a pea-sized amount of Granny Smith green paste to 1 oz (28 g) lemon-yellow paste. As for the orange, knead in the green paste, but leave shadows of green throughout the yellow. Place the paste in your nonwriting hand and your writing hand directly on top. Rotate your hands in opposite directions until a ball forms (see Illustration 9.1).

Roll the ball of paste over a cheese grater for a textured surface. Use your fingers to hold the textured ball in your nonwriting hand. With your thumb and index fingers of your writing hand, pinch the top of the ball to a dull point and rotate the ball back and forth. Reverse the paste so the dull point is on the bottom. Pinch the paste again to form another dull point. The lemon is starting to take shape.

Hold the lemon at one end and score the other end with an Xacto knife, pressing the knife into the middle of the dull point, turning the paste one-quarter turn, and pressing the knife again, forming a cross. Press a tiny clove sliver in the center of the cross for the lemon's stem.

Hold the lemon at each end and gently push the paste toward the center. The lemon is complete (see the bottom right of Illustration 9.1).

For greater depth, lightly dust the lemon with lemon-yellow petal dust and a little moss-green petal dust near the stem. For a shiny look, brush the lemon with a little Confectioner's Glaze (page 269) or a quick glaze made with equal parts corn syrup and water that is heated until the corn syrup melts and then cools. This glaze can be brushed over fresh fruit or marzipan fruit or anywhere a shine is needed.

New Skill: Granny Smith Apple, Red Delicious Apple, and Bosc Pear

Quick Prep

> 1 oz (28 g) red marzipan
> 1 oz (28 g) yellow marzipan
> 2 oz (57 g) green marzipan
> ½ oz (14 g) orange marzipan
> clove slivers
> nonstick rolling pin
> Xacto knife
> petal dust: moss green, lemon yellow, orange,
>   and cosmos (pinkish)
> #3 or #5 sable paintbrush

GRANNY SMITH APPLE

Partially knead together 2 parts Granny Smith green marzipan (approximately ⅝ oz [18 g]) and 1 part lemon-yellow marzipan (approximately ⅜ oz [9 g]). Roll the paste into a ball. Place the ball on the work surface. Place the middle finger of each hand at the 9 o'clock and 3 o'clock positions on the paste at the bottom of the ball. Apply pressure as you rotate the paste clockwise or counterclockwise to make the bottom of the paste smaller or narrower—about the size of a nickel. Alternatively, pick up the paste with your nonwriting hand and pinch one end as you rotate the ball left and right. Next, turn the paste over so the round part is on top. The apple shape is developing but needs refinement.

Place the cone side of the cone and serrated tool directly in the center of the apple. Push the tool ¼ to ½ in. (6 to 1.3 cm) into the apple. This expands the center of the apple and condenses the overall shape of the ball. Next, soften the shoulder of the apple with a dogbone tool. To do this, position the tool inside the cavity of the apple and rotate the tool, starting with the smallest ball. When you reach the top of the apple, switch to the larger ball and continue to rotate until the shoulder of the apple is smooth. Place a long curved clove sliver in the center of the apple.

To create a small leaf, roll out a small piece of the Granny Smith green marzipan on a little cornstarch. Always use a nonstick rolling pin to roll out marzipan. The paste should be as thin as possible. Rub a little vegetable shortening on the work surface. Place the thin marzipan paste on the shortening. Roll over the paste with the rolling pin to secure the paste to the shortening. Place an Xacto knife at a 45-degree angle to the paste. Drag the tip through the paste, cutting a small oval shape. Carefully pick up the oval cutout with the Xacto

Illustration 9.2
From left to right: the steps to create a
marzipan Granny Smith apple, Bosc pear,
and a Red Delicious apple.

knife. Attach the leaf by brushing one side of the inside of the apple shape with
a little water and setting the leaf on it.

For a more dramatic look, brush a little pinkish petal dust on each cheek of
the apple (see the left side of Illustration 9.2).

RED DELICIOUS APPLE

Form 1 oz (28g) red marzipan paste into a ball. Form the apple's shape using the
same technique as for the marzipan Granny Smith apple. However, when pinching one of the ends to make the bottom of the apple, make it as small as a dime
rather than a nickel. In addition, shape the bottom of the apple to a square. Press
the cone side of the cone and serrated tool into the rounded part of the paste.
Soften the shoulders of the apple with a ball or dogbone tool. Insert a clove sliver
in the center of the apple and attach a small marzipan leaf to one side of the
clove.

You can leave the apple as is or brush it with a little quick glaze or confectioner's glaze (see the right side of Illustration 9.2).

BOSC PEAR

Pears come in most colors: red, yellow, green, brown, and many variations of
these. In this exercise, you will make a marzipan Golden Delicious pear in a Bosc
shape.

Measure 3 parts yellow to 1 part orange marzipan, or ¾ oz (21 g) yellow
paste and ¼ oz (7 g) orange paste. You can also add a pea-sized amount of
Granny Smith green, or use moss-green petal dust to add shadow and depth to
the pear. Knead the paste until the colors are almost completely combined.

Roll the paste into a ball and hold it in your nonwriting hand. Place your
index and middle fingers on the ball near the cheek of your hands—that is, the
9 o'clock position, if you are right-handed. Rotate the paste back and forth,
forming the ball into a cone shape. Place the cone on the work surface. Place
your index fingers at each side of the paste, about one-third the distance from
the top of the cone. Rotate the index fingers back and forth, forming a high waist.

Next, pick up the pear shape in your nonwriting hand. Place a rounded
toothpick about ¼ in. (6 mm) from the bottom of the paste and press it into the

Decorator's Hint

Stick a rounded toothpick into leaf-green
gel food color and mark little dots over
the pear.

paste, forming a ridge. Extend the ridge from the bottom edge of the pear underneath it to the opposite side and up about ¼ in. (6 mm) high. Place a curved clove sliver off-center at the top of the pear (see the middle portion of Illustration 9.2).

Dust the cheeks of the pear with pinkish petal dust and blend it a bit for a more natural look.

New Skill: Peach and Apricot

Quick Prep

2 oz (57 g) yellow marzipan
½ oz (14 g) orange marzipan
¼ oz (7 g) green marzipan
cone and serrated tools
clove slivers
ball or dogbone tool
petal dust: peach, mango, cosmos, and apricot
#3 or #5 sable paintbrush
rounded toothpicks

PEACH

Form 1 oz (28 g) lemon-yellow marzipan paste into a round ball. This paste does not need to be blended with other colors because the combination of peach and mango petal dusts are added once the peach is sculpted. This combination will give the desired shade.

Form a cavity inside the paste by pressing in the cone tool ¼- to ½-in. (6 mm to 1.3 cm) deep. Soften the shoulders with the ball tool. Insert a rounded toothpick at the edge of the cavity. Press down on the toothpick, leaving an indentation. Continue to push against the toothpick until the indentation is extended at the bottom of the peach and slightly underneath. Add a small leaf and a clove sliver.

Mix a tiny portion of peach and mango petal dust. (Peach petal dust alone tends to be very light in color, and it needs a little help from the mango.) You can add a tiny pinch of orange and pink or cosmos petal dusts for an even deeper peach color. Petal dust the entire peach with the petal dust combination. Blush the cheeks of the peach with cosmos petal dust for a beautiful finish (see the left side of Illustration 9.3).

Illustration 9.3
Left: unformed marzipan ball to a completed peach. Right: unformed balls of yellow and orange marzipan to a completed apricot.

APRICOT

Blend together 2 parts lemon-yellow marzipan (or ⅝ oz [18 g]) and 1 part orange marzipan (or ⅜ oz [9 g]). Roll the paste into a ball and form a cavity ¼- to ½-in. (6 mm to 1.3 cm) deep. Press the bottom of the paste to slightly elongate the ball. This is the shape of an apricot. Score an indentation from the cavity's edge, extending it slightly under the apricot.

Soften the cavity on top with a ball or dogbone tool. Add a leaf and a clove sliver in the cavity's center. Petal dust the apricot with apricot or mango petal dust. Blush the cheeks of the apricot with cosmos petal dust (see the right side of Illustration 9.3).

New Skill: Strawberry and Raspberries

Quick Prep

2 oz (57 g) red marzipan
¼ oz (7 g) green marzipan
cone and serrated tools
#1 sable paintbrush
cheese grater
nonstick rolling pin
clove slivers
small rose calyx cutter

STRAWBERRY

Form 1 oz (28 g) red marzipan into a ball. Shape the ball into a cone shape as for the Bosc pear.

Score small indentations on the strawberry-shaped marzipan with the serrated tool. Paint dots inside the indentations with the #1 sable paintbrush dipped in lemon-yellow gel color mixed with a little liquid whitener.

Roll out the ¼ oz (6 mm) Granny Smith green paste on a little cornstarch as thin as possible. Cut two calyxes with the rose calyx cutter. Brush the back of the strawberry with a little water. Attach one calyx to the moistened spot, then moisten the center of the calyx and attach the other calyx directly on top, placing the sepals (or petals) between the empty spaces of the bottom calyx. The calyx now looks like a sunflower. Pull the edges back for a more dramatic look. Add a small clove in the center of the calyx and the strawberry is complete (see the left side of Illustration 9.4).

Decorator's Hint

Add liquid whitener to any gel or paste food color to achieve a pastel color or make the color opaque. Otherwise, the gel color is transparent and streaks when applied to marzipan.

Illustration 9.4
Left: a strawberry is created from a piece of red marzipan. Right: Small pieces of red marzipan made into raspberries.

RASPBERRIES

Divide ½ oz (14 g) red marzipan into three equal parts. Roll into three balls, using your fingers rather than your palms because the balls are so small.

Roll the balls on the cheese grater to create texture. Press the serrated tool ¼-in. (6 mm) deep into each of the red balls to form texture. Brush the raspberries with the quick glaze or confectioner's glaze for a shiny look. The raspberries are now complete (see Illustration 9.4).

New Skill: Pumpkin and Grapes

Quick Prep

1½ oz (42 g) uncolored marzipan
1 oz (28 g) orange marzipan
1 oz (28 g) green marzipan
16 28-gauge florist wires, 4 to 6 in. (10.2 to 15.2 cm)
long cone and serrated tools
cloves
chocolate-brown gel food color
#3 or #5 sable paintbrush
petal dusts: brown, orange, moss green, and super pearl
rounded toothpicks
florist tape

PUMPKIN

Take a pea-sized amount of uncolored marzipan, about ⅛ oz (3.5 g), add a little chocolate-brown food color and knead until the paste is brown. Add the brown paste to 1 oz (28 g) orange marzipan and knead until the paste is pumpkin orange.

Roll the paste into a ball. Create a deep cavity by inserting the serrated tool ½ in. (1.3 cm) inside the paste. Carefully remove the tool. Pick up the marzipan shape and indent lines into it with a toothpick following the ridge markings from the serrated tool. Extend the markings under the paste. Place a large clove in the center of the pumpkin.

Petal dust the pumpkin with a mixture of brown and orange petal dust. Add moss-green petal dust near the stem of the pumpkin for depth (see the left side of Illustration 9.5).

Illustration 9.5
Left: A little bit of brown marzipan is added to orange for a pumpkin color. Right: Super-pearl petal dust gives luster to marzipan grapes.

GRAPES

Mix 1 oz (28 g)) uncolored marzipan with 1 oz (28 g) Granny Smith green marzipan. Knead until the paste is thoroughly combined. Divide this into small pieces, about ⅛ oz (3.5 g). Roll the pieces into small balls. You should have about 16 balls. Let dry for 15 minutes.

Dip the tip of the wires in a little water or pasteurized egg white and insert into the marzipan balls. Let dry for 1 hour. Petal dust the grape balls with super-pearl petal dust. Carefully gather the balls by the wires. Adjust the grapes so no one grape is on the same plane. Twist the wires together or wrap a 1-in. (2.54 cm) piece of florist tape around the wires (see the right side of Illustration 9.5).

New Skill: Carrot and Banana

Quick Prep

> 1 oz (28 g) orange marzipan
> 1 oz (28 g) yellow marzipan
> ½ oz (14 g) green marzipan
> Xacto knife
> leaf-green and chocolate-brown gel food colors
> #1 sable paintbrush
> cone and serrated tools
> nonstick rolling pin
> small rose calyx cutter

CARROT

Knead 1 oz (28 g) orange marzipan and shape it into a ball. Place the ball on the work surface and place the fingers of your writing hand on it. Rotate the paste back and forth, applying pressure at the left side of the ball. Continue to rotate the marzipan until the left side comes to a point. Alternatively, pick up the marzipan in your writing hand and use the fingers of your other hand to rotate the tip of the paste into a point.

Score shallow, short lines around the carrot with an Xacto knife, just scratching the surface with random short strokes. Score a three-quarter view; there is no need to score the paste underneath. Insert the cone side of the cone and serrated tools at the large end of the carrot. Make a cavity ½-in. (⅓ cm) deep. Brush a little water inside the cavity.

Illustration 9.6
Left: Short lines scored around the body of the carrot give it texture. Right: Green and brown gel colors are added to the yellow banana marzipan for a natural look.

Roll out ½ oz (14 g) green marzipan on a little cornstarch, making it petal thin. Cut two calyxes with the calyx cutter. Place a dab of water in the center of one of the calyxes. Place the second calyx on top of the first, positioned so the sepals (petals) are between the empty spaces of the bottom calyxes. The finished calyx should look like a sunflower. Using an Xacto knife, fold the calyxes in half and then in quarters. Pick up the calyxes with the knife and carefully push the folded sides into the carrot's cavity, leaving the sepals outside (see the left side of Illustration 9.6).

BANANA

Knead 1 oz (28 g) yellow marzipan into a ball. Place the ball on the work surface and the fingers of your writing hand on the paste. Rotate the paste back and forth, applying heavier pressure at the left side of the ball. Continue to rotate the paste until the larger side of the paste is twice the size of the smaller side.

Carefully pick up the marzipan, holding it in the center with your fingers. Pinch the top of the smaller side with your thumb and index finger, shaping it into a square. Pinch the larger end of the banana, rotating it back and forth until a dull point forms.

Beginning at the smaller, square end, score lines in the banana with an Xacto knife. Start at the square's edge and drag the knife to the dull point on the top of the banana. Turn the banana one-quarter and score a second and third line. There is no need to score four lines, as the banana will lie on the fourth side. Place both thumbs and index fingers on either side of the banana at the center point. Gently curve the banana from the center to form a natural shape.

Place a dab each of leaf-green and chocolate-brown gel food color on a plastic tray. Paint both the top and bottom surface of the banana with chocolate-brown food color. Clean the brush with a little water and paint a line of leaf-green around the bottom of the brown. Clean the brush again. Then brush water with a little green color up the banana and through its seam. Do the same on the opposite end of the banana. Drag a little of the brown food color through the green for a more natural look (see the right side of Illustration 9.6).

END-OF-LESSON REVIEW

1. What are the components of marzipan?

2. Why not use almond paste instead of marzipan for making fruits and vegetables?

3. What are cloves used for in marzipan modeling?

4. Name some of the tools used in modeling marzipan.

5. What is petal dust used for?

PERFORMANCE TEST

Make eight of the following fruits and vegetables from marzipan:

Granny Smith apple	Orange	Banana	Grapes
Bosc pear	Pumpkin	Strawberry	Lemon
Peach	Carrot	Raspberry (make three)	Apricot

MARZIPAN AND CHOCOLATE MODELING

Marzipan Characters and Chocolate Display

You will need the following items to complete this lesson:

Marzipan Modeling Paste (page 270)

modeling chocolate

commercial rolled fondant

gel food colors

petal dust colors

pasteurized egg whites

#0, #1, #3, and #5 sable paintbrushes

#5 round metal tip

ball tool or dogbone marzipan tool

rounded toothpicks

liquid whitener

cone and serrated marzipan tools

quilting wheel

silicone leaf press

cell pad

nonstick rolling pin

white vegetable shortening

1½ to 2 in. (3.8 to 5.1 cm) square cookie cutter or square pattern

large rose petal cutter or pattern shape

This lesson explores the use of marzipan to make three-dimensional animals. Each creature is exquisitely dressed and can stand on its own as a display on top of a small cake or plaque. It also covers the use of modeling chocolate—a mixture of chocolate and corn syrup—to make a three-dimensional handmade rose with leaves and a bow.

The lesson further addresses changing the consistency of marzipan by adding commercial rolled fondant and tylose. The commercial rolled fondant makes the marzipan whiter and, thus, better able to take gel food colors. Tylose, predominantly used in gumpaste formulas, is used to give the marzipan elasticity and strength.

New Skill: Party Girl Mouse

Quick Prep

2 oz (57 g) Marzipan Modeling Paste (page 270)
1 oz (28 g) commercial rolled fondant
ball tool or dogbone tool
rounded toothpicks
gel food colors
1 oz (28 g) pasteurized egg whites
#1 sable paintbrush
cell pad

Place either chocolate-brown or nut-brown gel food color on a toothpick and add it to the 2 oz (57 g) Marzipan Modeling Paste. Knead well until the color is uniform. (Alternatively, color the paste with warm black or a little super black.) This is the base color for the mouse.

BODY

Place 1 oz (28 g) colored paste in your nonwriting hand. Place your writing hand on top and begin to rotate your hands, forming a rounded ball. Shape the ball into a cone by placing your index and middle fingers on one side of the ball. Rotate back and forth until the cone begins to take shape. Be sure to make a dull cone rather than a pointed one. The height of the body should not exceed 1½ in. (3.8 cm) (see Illustration 10.1).

Place the cone on the work surface with the wide end down. Press the cone to the surface to flatten the bottom.

HEAD

Shape a large pea-size piece of colored paste, about ⅛ oz (3.5 g) into a rounded ball and then a cone. Lay the cone on its side and gently press the small end of the dogbone tool against each side of the rounded part to make small indentations. These are the ear sockets (see Illustration 10.1).

EARS

Roll two tiny pieces of the colored paste, about 1/16 oz (1.8 g) each, into balls. Place both balls on a cell pad. Place the small end of the dogbone tool at the center of one ball. Press carefully to make an indentation, then gently pull the ball tool down and drag the ball to the cell pad surface. Repeat to make the other ear (see the middle right of Illustration 10.1). To attach the ears to the head, use a paintbrush to dab a little water in the ear sockets. Set the thinner edge of the ears in the sockets.

Illustration 10.1
Party Girl Mouse (counter clockwise from top left): The body is formed to a cone shape about 1½ in. (3.8 cm) in height, the smaller cone shape is the head of the mouse, the dogbone tool creates a hollow forming the ears, the dress, the pinafore, and the completed Party Girl Mouse.

ARMS

Shape ¼ oz (7 g) colored paste into a round ball. Place the ball onto the work surface and roll it into a cylinder about 1½ to 2 in. (3.8 to 5.1 cm) long. Shape both ends with the small side of the dogbone tool on a cell pad to form the hands, using the same technique used to form the ears. Use an Xacto knife to cut little lines in the shaped hands for fingers (see Illustration 10.1).

PARTY DRESS AND PINAFORE

Color 1 oz (28 g) commercial rolled fondant with a pastel color to form the dress. Color ¼ oz (7 g) commercial rolled fondant a different color, perhaps a little darker than the dress.

Roll out the paste for the dress on a little cornstarch to about ⅛ in. (3 mm) thick. Divide the darker paste into 4 equal parts. Place the colored balls on the rolled-out paste. Roll the paste with a nonstick rolling pin to combine the darker color into the lighter color.

From an area where the paste is the base color, cut out the pinafore with a small rounded scalloped cutter. Next, from the area where the colors are combined, cut out the dress with a scalloped cutter three times the size of the pinafore.

For additional depth, ruffle both the pinafore and the dress with a rounded toothpick. To do this, place a little cornstarch on the work surface and place the paste on the cornstarch. Place ½ in. (1.3 cm) of the toothpick on the paste. Rotate the toothpick with either your index or middle finger, applying medium to heavy pressure. The more pressure you apply, the more the paste will begin to ruffle. Rotate the paste and continue to ruffle. Place the paste under a piece of plastic wrap until you are ready to assemble the entire piece (see Illustration 10.1).

ASSEMBLY

Place the body on the work surface. Brush a little pasteurized egg white or water on the top of the body and place the ruffled dress on top. Fluff the dress with a dry paintbrush. Next, brush a little liquid on the top center of the body, place the arm piece on top, and fold them toward the center. Brush a little liquid on the center of the arm piece. Place the pinafore over the arms so that it hangs down in the front and back of the dress. Brush a little liquid on the pinafore's top center. Carefully place the head on the pinafore.

Paint two small ovals for eyes and add and a dot of warm black gel color inside each for the pupils. Paint a little dot for the nose and a small curve of red food color under it for the mouth (see the top right of Illustration 10.1).

New Skill: Baby Mouse

Quick Prep

½ oz (14 g) Marzipan Modeling Paste (page 270)
½ oz (14 g) commercial rolled fondant
quilting wheel
ball or dogbone tool
pasteurized egg whites
1½ to 2 in. (3.8 to 5.1 cm) square cookie cutter or
    square pattern

Color ½ oz (14 g) Marzipan Modeling Paste a warm brown with a touch of soft pink food color. This brown color should be softer and lighter than the color of the adult mouse.

HEAD AND EARS

Shape ⅛ oz (3.5 g) colored paste into a round ball and then into a cone, as you did for the Party Girl Mouse. With the small end of a dogbone tool, press ear sockets into the larger end of the cone.

Form tiny balls from two tiny pieces, less than 1/16 oz (1.7 g) each, of brown-colored paste. Shape the balls into ears with the dogbone tool, on a cell pad as you did for the Party Girl Mouse. Moisten the ear sockets with water or pasteurized egg white and insert the ears (see the top middle of Illustration 10.2).

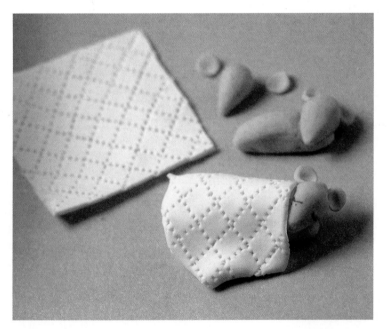

BODY

Roll the balance of the colored paste, about ¼ oz (7 g), into a ball, then shape the ball into a small cylinder about 1½ in. (3.8 cm) long. Slightly press one end of the cylinder with the small end of the dogbone tool. Brush the indentation with a little egg white and set the head in it at an angle. Paint two small curves for the eyes with warm black food color and paint tiny eyelashes on the curves (see the completed Baby Mouse in Illustration 10.2).

Illustration 10.2
Baby Mouse. Left: the blanket. Top row: the head and ears of the mouse. Middle row (left to right): the body and head of the mouse. Bottom row: the completed Baby Mouse.

BLANKET

Color ½ oz (14 g) commercial rolled fondant with a soft pink, lemon yellow, or sky blue. Roll out the paste on a little cornstarch to about ⅛ in. (3 mm) thick. Cut out the blanket with a small square cookie cutter approximately 1½ to 2 in. (3.8 to 5.1 cm) across.

Turn the paste so the opposite corners face each other. Place a ruler at the center point where the angles align. Score a serrated line with the quilting tool from the top to the end. This is the center line. Move the ruler to the left about ½ in. (1.3 cm) and score another line. Continue to score lines until there is no more space on the paste. Next, move the ruler to the opposite side of the centered line and score lines ½ in. (1.3 cm) apart.

Turn the paste one-quarter turn. Score a line down the center and repeat at ½-in. (1.3 cm) intervals. These lines intersect with the previous lines to form a quilting pattern (see the blanket in Illustration 10.2).

ASSEMBLY

Lightly brush egg whites over the mouse's body. Carefully place the blanket over the mouse and tuck in the ends. Do not cover the head of the Baby Mouse (see the bottom of Illustration 10.2).

New Skill: Father Penguin

Quick Prep

> 1 oz (28 g) commercial rolled fondant
> 1 oz (28 g) Marzipan Modeling Paste (page 270), colored black
> large rose petal cutter or pattern shape
> rounded toothpicks
> sunset-orange gel color
> daffodil-yellow petal dust
> #3 or #5 sable paintbrush
> super black gel color
> liquid whitener

BODY

Measure out 1 oz (28 g) commercial rolled fondant and knead it well. If it gets sticky, incorporate ¼ tsp (1.3 ml) white vegetable shortening. Roll the fondant into a ball, then shape the ball into a cone with a dull point.

Indent the bottom of the cone by placing a toothpick about ¼ in. (6 mm) from the bottom. Press the toothpick into the paste and extend the indentation under the cone and around to the opposite side. This is the same technique used in making the pear in Lesson 9.

HEAD

Measure out ⅛ to ¼ oz (3.5 to 7g) black modeling paste. Rotate the paste into a round ball and then shape the ball into a cone. Slightly bend the tip of the head, forming a curve underneath. Set the head aside.

TUXEDO/FINS

Roll out ¼ oz (7g) black modeling paste on a surface that is sprinkled with cornstarch or lightly oiled with white vegetable shortening. (These measures will help you roll the paste very thin and stabilize it for cutting.) Roll the paste to about ⅛ in. (3 mm) thick and cut it with a large rose petal cutter.

Place the cutout pattern on the paste; it will stick. Carefully cut around the pattern with an Xacto knife. Set the tuxedo aside. From the bottom point of the tuxedo, move to the left about ½ in. (1.3 cm) from the center and cut about 1 in. (2.54 cm) high with an Xacto knife. Do the same on the opposite side of the tuxedo. These cuts should resemble the fins of the penguin (see the bottom left of Illustration 10.3).

FEET/SHOES

Divide ⅛ oz (3.5 g) black modeling paste into two balls. Slightly elongate each ball into a small cylinder, about ¼ in. (6 mm) long. Place the small end of a dog-bone tool near one end of a cylinder and apply light pressure as you pull the dogbone tool toward you. Gently ease the pressure to complete the foot (see the bottom left of Illustration 10.3). Repeat for the other foot.

ASSEMBLY

Petal dust the left and right sides of the penguin's body with daffodil-yellow petal dust (see Illustration 10.3). Place a dot of moisture on the top of the penguin's body and set the tuxedo on it. The tuxedo should appear in the back of the penguin with the rounded part slightly over the penguin's body. Gently pull the fins forward, raising the shoulders of the tuxedo. This gives the impression that the penguin is scratching its back or that its fins are behind its back.

Place a dot of moisture on the top of the tuxedo and gently attach the head. Place a dot of sunset-orange food color on a color tray, add a dot of liquid whitener, and mix. The whitener will bring out the pastel tone of the orange food color. Paint two oval shapes on opposite sides of the penguin's head, toward the back. Mix a dot of lemon-yellow gel color with a dot of liquid whitener. Paint a line on each side of the mouth extending to the cheeks.

Place a little moisture at one end of each foot. Stick the feet under the body (see the completed Father Penguin in Illustration 10.3).

Illustration 10.3
Father Penguin (counterclockwise from bottom left): The tuxedo and fins of the penguin, the penguin's feet, the penguin's head, and the completed Father Penguin.

Decorator's Hint

Remember to place the cylinder on a cell pad before shaping the feet with the dog-bone tool.

New Skill: Bear Chef

Quick Prep

3 oz (85 g) Marzipan Modeling Paste (page 270)
1 oz (28 g) commercial rolled fondant
cone and serrated tools
quilting tool
#5 round metal tip
rounded toothpicks
gel food colors: chocolate brown, holiday red or tulip red
pasteurized egg whites
#1 sable paintbrush

BODY

Color 3 oz (85 g) Marzipan Modeling Paste with chocolate-brown food color. Measure out 1 oz (28 g) colored paste and shape it into a round ball and then a cone shape with a dull point.

Indent the bottom of the paste by placing a toothpick about ¼ in. (6 mm) from the bottom of the paste. Press the toothpick into the paste and extend the indentation under the ball and around to the opposite side. This is the same technique used in making the Father Penguin (see page 147) and the pear (see page 135). Insert a rounded toothpick from the dull point on top to the bottom of the paste. This will support the head of the bear chef (see Illustration 10.4).

CAVITY FOR BEAR'S PAW

With the cone tool, make a cavity in the body at the 9 o'clock and 3 o'clock positions. Push the tool in about ½-in. (1.3 cm) deep and rotate it slightly to widen the cavity. Remove the cone tool (see Illustration 10.4).

FEET

The bear's feet are made by positioning the #5 round tip at the bottom of the bear's body. Using the center seam of the bear's body as a guide, move the tip from the center to the left about ½ in. (1.3 cm). Press the tip into the body, making a rounded indentation. Make three more for a total of four. These should be right next to each other. Do the same to the right of the bear's center point. These indentations are for the bear's feet (see Illustration 10.4).

HEAD, NOSE, FACE, AND EAR SOCKETS

Shape ¼ to ½ oz (7 to 24 g) brown-colored paste into a round ball. Place it on your work surface. Make a cavity with the small end of the dogbone tool at the 11 o'clock and 1 o'clock positions on the bear's head. These are the ear sockets. Take a tiny piece of paste—less than 1/16 oz (1.7 g) of the colored paste—and shape it into a tiny ball. Place a dot of egg white on the center of the head and stick the tiny ball of paste there. This is the foundation for the nose.

For the face, roll out a small piece of commercial rolled fondant—about ¼ oz (7 g)—on a little cornstarch. Cut out a circle about ¼ to ½ in. (6 mm to 1.3 cm) in diameter. This can be done freehand, or you can use a very small rounded cookie cutter or the back of the #5 round tip. Brush the fondant circle with a little egg white and center it over the nose of the bear chef. Secure the paste to the head of the bear (see Illustration 10.4).

Decorator's Hint

The cone tool is used because more pressure is needed for the deeper cavity. You could also use the larger end of the dogbone tool here.

Decorator's Hint

The rounded end of a metal tip might be a bit too big for the head and face of the bear chef. Enlarging the head another ⅛ in. to ¼ in. (3 mm to 6 mm) might be perfect.

Illustration 10.4
Bear Chef (counterclockwise from top middle):
The body of the bear with cavities for its paws
and a toothpick to support the head, the bear's
paws, the bear's head with the foundation for
the nose, the bear's ears, the apron with pocket,
the hat cap, the hat band, and the completed
Bear Chef.

PAWS AND EARS

To create the paws, shape ¼ oz (7 g) brown-colored paste into two round balls. Place the balls on the work surface and lightly rotate your middle finger over them to shape them into small logs, each about ¼ in. (6 mm) long. These are the bear's paws. Mark the nails by pressing in the #5 round tip, just as you did for the feet of the bear chef. The nails should be close together and have the same number of nails as the bear's feet.

For the ears, divide about ⅛ oz (3.5 g) colored paste into two small balls. Shape these into ears with the dogbone tool, exactly the same as for the Party Girl Mouse.

APRON, HAT, AND POCKET

Roll out ½ oz (14 g) commercial rolled fondant on a little white vegetable shortening. Trace the bear's apron, hat, and pocket using the patterns in Appendix 1. Cut out the patterns with an Xacto knife and place them over the fondant. Cover the cut-outs with plastic wrap to prevent drying.

For the bear's hat, brush a little egg white at one end of the band. Join the band together. Let the joined band dry for 10 minutes. Brush a little egg white on the perimeter of the band. Attach the cap to the band.

For the apron, stitch the perimeter of the apron with the quilting tool. Apply light pressure as you push the wheel at a 45-degree angle to the edge of the garment.

Stitch the pocket on the apron with the quilting tool. Brush a little egg white on the back of the pocket and attach it to the center of the apron (see Illustration 10.4).

ASSEMBLY

Brush a little egg white around the perimeter of the toothpick supporting the bear's body. Push the head on top of the toothpick to secure it. Place the paws in the cavities. Add more egg white, if necessary, or widen the cavities with the cone tool to make sure the paws fit snugly. Brush the ear sockets and insert the ears. Turn the apron over and brush the back with egg white. Attach the apron to the bear's body and extend the ties around the neck. Carefully raise the hat, brush a little egg white on the bottom, and attach it to the head. Paint two lazy eyes at the 10 o'clock and 2 o'clock positions on the bear's face, just above the white fondant (see the pattern for face painting in Appendix 1). Finally, paint a curve with red gel food color for the mouth and a half-circle just below the center of the mouth to complete the lip (see Illustration 10.4).

New Skill: Kiddy Bear

Quick Prep

> 3 oz (85 g) Marzipan Modeling Paste (page 270)
> ¼ oz (7 g) commercial rolled fondant
> rounded toothpicks
> pasteurized egg whites
> #1 sable paintbrush
> gel food colors: warm brown, nut brown, moss green, lemon
>   yellow, holiday or tulip red, egg yellow

BODY

Color 2 oz (57 g) Marzipan Modeling Paste with nut-brown or warm brown gel food colors. Shape ½ oz (14 g) colored paste into a round ball and then a cone. Make an indentation down the bottom of the body with a rounded toothpick, as you did for the bear chef and the penguin. For the hands-in-the-pocket effect, indent the left and right sides of the body with a rounded toothpick. Place a toothpick at the 4 o'clock position and slightly press the toothpick to the body. Repeat at the 8 o'clock position. The indentations on the sides of the body should be slanted—that is, wide at the bottom and narrow toward the top (see Illustration 10.5).

HEAD AND EARS

Measure out ½ oz (14 g) brown-colored paste for the head, nose, and ears. Roll half of this into a ball. This is the bear's head. Take a tiny piece of paste from the balance, roll it into a tiny ball for the nose, and attach it to the bear's face. Make cavities for the bear's ears with the small end of the dogbone tool and brush both cavities with a little egg white. Roll two tiny balls from the remaining brown paste for the ears. Shape the ears with the small end of the dogbone tool and attach them inside the ear sockets. Retain the balance of the brown paste for buttons.

FACE

Roll out ¼ oz (7 g) commercial rolled fondant and cut a small circle for the bear's face. Attach the circle directly over the bear's nose with a little egg white.

CLOTHES

For the shirt and suspenders, measure out the remaining 1 oz (28 g) Marzipan Modeling Paste and split it into two equal parts. Color one part moss green for the shirt. Color the other part lemon yellow or egg yellow for the suspenders. Roll out both pieces on a little white vegetable shortening. Trace the patterns from Appendix 1 (see page 305) and cut it out. Place the patterns on the green and yellow paste. Carefully cut out the patterns. Place pattern pieces under plastic wrap to prevent drying.

ASSEMBLY

Brush the back of the shirt with a little egg white and attach it around the front of the body. The shirt should go all the way up to the neck and wrap around the back. Trim excess paste from the back of the body. Next, lightly brush egg white on the suspenders and place them over the bear's shoulders. The suspenders should end where the shirt ends. Roll out two tiny balls of brown paste and attach one at the end of each suspender for the buttons. Make two more balls for the buttons on the back.

Brush a little egg white on the top of the bear's body and attach the head. Paint a small curve under the bear's nose with warm brown food color and a little dot of red color under the center of the curve for the lip (see Illustration 10.5).

Decorator's Hint

The suspenders and the shirt can be stitched with the quilting wheel for a nice effect.

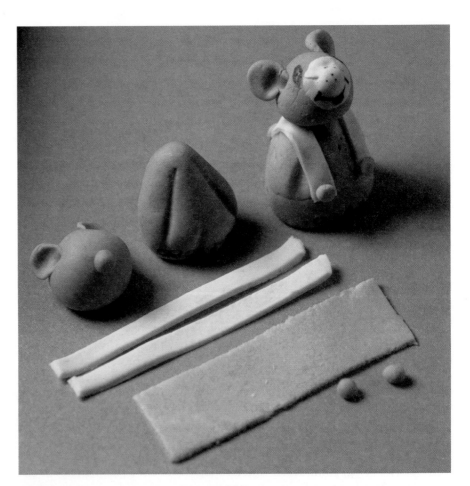

Illustration 10.5
Kiddy Bear (counterclockwise from top middle): The body of the bear, the head of the bear with the ears and nose attached, the suspenders, the shirt, the suspender buttons, and the completed Kiddy Bear.

New Skill: Modeling Chocolate Rose

Quick Prep

½ recipe Modeling Chocolate (page 271)
quilting wheel
ball or dogbone tool
cell pad
silicone leaf press
nonstick rolling pin
#1 or 3 sable paint brush

Modeling chocolate is a term for chocolate that has elasticity. It can be shaped, molded, and rolled thin with a rolling pin or a pasta machine, and it can be used to drape the sides of a cake as a rolled icing.

Its most common name is *chocolate plastic* or *plastique*. It is also known as *chocolate clay*, *candy clay*, and *chocolate leather*. The chocolate is carefully melted over a double boiler or bain-marie. After the chocolate is slightly cooked and all the pieces are melted, light corn syrup is poured in and stirred vigorously until the chocolate starts to thicken and looks like thick fudge. The chocolate is then poured onto a piece of plastic wrap, spread out, covered with additional plastic wrap, and refrigerated overnight. The next day, the chocolate is broken into pieces and kneaded or pounded well with a rolling pin to soften.

In this exercise, you will create a stunning rose with leaves and a bow using modeling chocolate.

BASE

Shape 1 oz (28 g) Modeling Chocolate into a round ball and then a cone shape with a sharp point (see Illustration 10.6). Place the cone inside the pattern marked Rose Base. The cone should fit firmly inside the pattern. If the cone is too large, pare some chocolate away and reshape the cone. Measure again. Place the cone on the work surface.

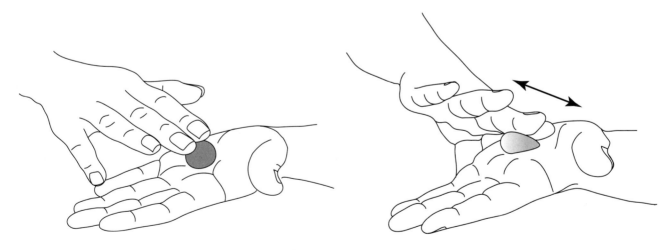

Illustration 10.6
To create the rosebud base, shape the chocolate modeling paste into a cone with a sharp point on one end.

ROSEBUD

Divide ½ oz (14 g) Modeling Chocolate into three parts and shape each into a round ball. Place the balls inside the pattern marked Balls for Rose Petals (see Appendix 1). The balls should fit firmly inside the pattern.

Place one ball on a piece of parchment paper with the corners taped with masking tape. Place a piece of heavy plastic (Mylar, or half a plastic sandwich bag) on top of the ball. Place your thumb on the plastic wrap at 9 o'clock (for right-handers) or 3 o'clock (for left-handers). Drag the thumb with light to medium-heavy pressure across the ball to the opposite position. The petal should have gradual thickness—that is, the left side of the petal should be thick and the right side thin. Continue to flatten the petal into a rounded shape. Remember to use long strokes with your thumb. The petal should be wide enough to fit into the Rose Petal Size pattern. The inside circle is for the first eight petals. The outside circle is for the last seven petals. Put this petal aside.

Make two more petals the same way. Once these petals are flattened, pick up one of them in your writing hand. Hold it at the thick end between your thumb and index finger. Place your other thumb and index finger in back of the petal with your thumb at 9 o'clock and your index finger at 3 o'clock. Holding the petal firmly with your right hand, pull the edge of the petals back to slightly curve their edges. Move your thumb and index finger toward the 12 o'clock position as you continue to curl back the edges of the petal. Pinch the top of the petal to finish it. Place the shaped petal on your work surface. Shape another petal. You now have one unshaped petal and two shaped petals (see Illustration 10.7).

ASSEMBLY

Hold the base in your writing hand. In your other hand, hold the unshaped petal by the thick part. Place the base in front of the petal at the center point. Pull the base down about one-third the length of the petal, about ¼ to ½ in. (6 mm to 1.3 cm) down. Press the base of the petal to the cone's base. Lap the left side of the petal over the base. Next, lap the right side of the petal over the left petal, leaving a tiny opening at the top. With your thumb, lightly roll the right petal back slightly. This gives the illusion that the bud is starting to open. The base is now a bud.

Hold the bud in your nonwriting hand and one of the shaped petals in your writing hand. Place the center of the shaped petal at the seam of the bud. The height of the petal should be the same as or slightly greater than that of the bud. Press the petal to the cone until it sticks. Pull down on the heavy part of the petal so it takes the shape of the cone. Next, place the second shaped petal to the opposite side of the seam. The petal should be the same height as the opposite petal.

Place the bud on the work surface. Turn one of the seams toward you. Tuck your thumb in back of the shaped petal. Push your thumb forward as you push the petal over the seam. Now, place your other thumb behind the second shaped petal and overlap this petal over the previous one. When overlapping petals, be careful not to change the shape of the shaped petal. Turn the bud to the opposite side and do the same thing.

Hold the rosebud between your thumb and index finger of both hands. Lightly squeeze the bottom to slightly open the rosebud. Reshape the petals, if necessary. The rosebud is complete (see Illustration 10.8).

Illustration 10.7
An unshaped petal

Illustration 10.8
Top row: the steps for creating a modeling chocolate rose. Bottom row: the bow and streamers cut from the pattern and the finished chocolate bow.

MEDIUM-SIZE ROSE

Divide 1½ oz (42 g) Modeling Chocolate into five pieces and shape each into a round ball. Place the balls on the pattern to make sure each fits inside. Flatten and shape each ball into a rose petal.

Pick up the rosebud in your nonwriting hand and one of the shaped petals in your writing hand. Place the petal slightly to the left or right of one of the rosebud seams. The new shaped petals should be the same height as the previous petals or slightly higher. Attach the petals in a counterclockwise direction (for right-handers) or clockwise direction (for left-handers).

Push the petal to the rosebud and pull down on the heavy part to shape it to the bud. Do not seal the seams of the petals when they are attached. Pick up the second shaped petal and attach it mirrorwise to the previous petal. Move the petal counterclockwise to the right of the previous petal, then move it back about one-third the distance of the attached petal. Attach the second petal to the first petal. Pull down on the heavy part of the petal to shape it to the rosebud. Do not seal in the seams.

Continue with the next two shaped petals in the same fashion. When attaching the fifth and final petal, lap the petal over the fourth attached petal. Lift up the first petal and tuck the fifth petal inside it. Lap the first petal over the fifth. Go back and look over each petal. To reshape, use your index finger to push the center point of each petal forward and then pinch the petal with your thumb and index finger. The medium-size rose is complete.

FULL-BLOWN ROSE

Divide 2.5 oz (71 g) Modeling Chocolate into seven pieces and shape them into round balls. Place each ball inside the pattern to make sure they are the correct size. If they are too large, shave off some of the paste and reroll them into round balls. Shape each ball into a rose petal shape. These last seven petals can be shaped a little larger than the first eight petals.

Decorator's Hint

A cell pad is similar to a computer's mouse pad. It gives support and give to a petal when you are shaping it with a ball or dogbone tool.

Decorator's Hint

Place another thin strip of chocolate paste over the center strip for a more tailored look. Emboss the edge of the bow pattern and streamers with the quilting wheel for a more realistic look.

To assemble, pick up the medium-size rose in your nonwriting hand and the first petal in your writing hand. Attach the petal to the left or right of any seam. The petal should be the same height as the previous petals, or slightly higher. Assembe each petal as you did for the medium-size rose. Remember, the seventh and final petal goes inside the first, and the first petal overlaps the seventh. Reshape each petal, if necessary. The full-blown rose is complete.

CHOCOLATE LEAVES

Roll out 3 oz (85 g) Modeling Chocolate on the work surface with a nonstick rolling pin. Turn the paste over and roll it until the paste is petal thin.

Position an Xacto knife at a 45-degree angle. Drag the knife through the paste, making an overshaped cut. Cut several oval shapes for leaves. Remove the cut leaves and place each leaf into a silicone leaf press. The press will give texture to both sides of the leaf at the same time. Emboss each leaf.

To soften the edges of the leaves, place them on a cell pad. Position the small end, or neck, of the dogbone tool over the edge of a leaf. Apply light pressure as you move the neck of the tool back and forth to soften the edge of the leaf. Turn the leaf to the opposite side and soften the other edge. Be careful when using the dogbone tool to soften the chocolate leaves. Don't use the ball end of the tool because it will tear or distort the chocolate leaves. Repeat this process for all the leaves.

CHOCOLATE BOW AND STREAMERS

Gather the balance of the Modeling Chocolate for this lesson and reknead the paste until pliable. With a nonstick rolling pin, roll out the paste until it is petal thin

Trace the bow pattern from Appendix 1. Cut out the pattern and place it over the paste. Cut out the chocolate and put it aside. From the remaining rolled-out chocolate paste, cut out a small strip, about 1½ by ¼ in. (3.8 cm by 6 mm), and set it aside. Then cut two strips of chocolate about 4 by ½ in. (10.2 by 1.3 cm) long. Cut the end of the strips on the bias, or cut a *V*-shape at the bottom of each strip. These are the streamers.

To assemble, brush a little water or pasteurized egg white in the center of the bow pattern. Raise one end and attach it to the center of the bow strip. Attach the second end to the center of the bow strip. The bow is taking shape. Now, brush the small strip of chocolate with a little water or egg white and place the center of the bow over the strip. Lap the ends over the center of the bow. Turn the bow over and tuck the center in with your thumb and middle finger. This helps shape and complete the bow (see the bottom row of Illustration 10.8).

END-OF-LESSON REVIEW

1. What is added to Marzipan Modeling Paste to give it strength and elasticity?

2. What tool is used to ruffle the dress and pinafore of the Party Girl Mouse?

3. Why is commercial rolled fondant used to make the Father Penguin's body?

4. How is a cell pad used to soften the edges of chocolate leaves?

5. Give three additional names for *chocolate plastique*.

PERFORMANCE TEST

Make a medium or full-blown chocolate rose plus three of the following six projects:

Party Girl Mouse   Father Penguin   Kiddy Bear   8 chocolate leaves, bows, and streamers

Baby Mouse   Bear Chef

ADVANCED ROYAL ICING PIPING AND DESIGN SKILLS

Runouts, Extension Work, Filigree, Lace, Trellis, and Lattice

You will need the following items to complete this lesson:

Meringue Powder Royal Icing (page 273)

Egg White Royal Icing (page 273)

Flood Icing (page 274)

#2, #3, #4, #5, #6, and #7 round metal tips; # 18 star tips

paper cones

cardboard circles or squares

masking tape

rounded toothpicks

8-in. (20.3 cm) round styrofoam covered with rolled fondant

10-in. (25.4 cm) foil-covered round cardboard

PME 0 stainless-steel tip

adding machine paper or strips of parchment paper

ruler

stickpins

lace pattern design

metal spatulas

metal bowls

scissors or paring knife

coupler

12-in. (30 cm) flex or disposable pastry bags

plastic containers with lids

plastic wrap

Xacto knife

The skills you will acquire in this lesson are a rich and valuable experience in the art of royal icing piping, the backbone of English, Australian, New Zealand, and South African techniques. Each of these countries adds a unique stamp to the art. Careful study and dedicated practice are essential for developing these advanced skills.

Runouts or Flooding

This is one of the easiest and most versatile techniques in the art of cake decorating. The decorator outlines a traced image that is covered with plastic wrap and uses a medium-stiff icing. The outline icing is thinned with a little water or pasteurized egg white and placed in a paper cone or a squeezer bottle. The tip of the bottle is placed in the center of the outlined design and pressure is applied to the bottle to release the soft icing. The bottle is then lifted from the surface and a toothpick or paintbrush is used to move it to the perimeter of the design. Once outlined and flooded, the design is air dried for 2 to 24 hours. The design is then carefully removed from the plastic wrap and placed on a plaque, rolled iced cake, or iced cookie.

This technique can be used to create beautiful monograms, colorful characters, and writing transfer designs (see Lesson 5 on Writing).

Bridge and Extension Work

This is a classic Australian-style cake-decorating technique. A rolled iced cake is carefully measured into sections, typically at the bottom. A bridge is constructed of overpiped lines in a crescent or scallop shape. The idea is to create a support structure that stands out from the cake. Lines of icing are then piped through the #0 or smaller tip. The piping starts from a marking near the center of the cake and proceeds to the bottom bridge. The piped lines are $\frac{1}{16}$ to $\frac{1}{8}$ in. (1.5 to 3 mm) apart.

Simple Lace Designs

This is also an easy technique that can be used in conjunction with bridge and extension work or alone on a rolled iced or royal iced cake. A pattern is traced and placed under plastic wrap. The design is carefully outlined with medium-stiff royal icing with the #0 tip. Once air dried, the lace pieces are carefully removed and attached to the cake with dots of royal icing.

Filigree Lace Designs

This technique is typically associated with South African cake art. Because of the size of these large, showy lace pieces, the lace is first piped with the #0, #1, or

#2 tip and then repiped or outlined again for reinforcement. A pattern is traced and placed under plastic wrap, and the design is piped with medium-stiff royal icing. Once air dried, the pieces are carefully removed from the plastic wrap and attached to a rolled or royal iced cake with dots of royal icing.

Filigree lace can also be done simply and in conjunction with cornelli lace, and it can be outlined once instead of twice. The size of the lace piece determines its need for reinforcement. The addition of pyramid piping around the filigree gives a stunning effect.

Ring Design with Trelliswork or Drop String Work

This style of royal icing was popular during the middle to the late nineteenth century. Ernest Schülbé, a cake artist during that time, developed elaborate trellis, string, and net designs. These designs were typically seen on cakes for the English royal family. Joseph A. Lambeth, the father of modern cake decorating, also developed elaborate cake decorating styles during the early twentieth century, notably lattice, cushion lattice, bias relief, and freehand sculptured designs.

Rings ¾ to 1 in. (1.9 to 2.54 cm) in diameter are piped with the #5, #6, or #7 round metal tip onto plastic wrap, air dried for several hours, then carefully removed with an offset metal spatula and attached at the shoulders of a royal iced cake. Large shells are piped around the cake's edge first and then the rings are attached between the shells, which hold them in place.

Lines of icing are piped directly over the attached rings with the #0 metal tip. This encases the rings. The rings are then overpiped with the tip used to create them, giving a polished look. Drop strings (or trelliswork) are piped under the rings for a spectacular effect.

Lattice

Lattice work in royal icing can be simple or complex. Lines of icing are piped with a round or star tip in one direction and then lines are piped across them to form a lattice pattern. This can be piped directly on a cake, plaque, or iced cookie. This style alone is beautiful, but when paired with cushion lattice, it is extraordinary.

Cushion Lattice

This is Lambeth's signature design. Using a star tip, a puff of icing in an oval shape is formed with a good deal of pressure. Lines of icing are then piped across it, starting with a large round tip and ending with a smaller round tip. The key to success is proper drying time between each set of crisscross lines.

New Skill: Runouts or Flooding

Quick Prep

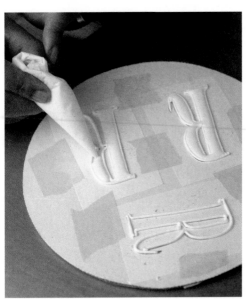

½ recipe Egg White Royal Icing (page 273)
6 oz (170 g) Flood Icing (page 274)
#2 or #3 round metal tip
metal spatula
paper cones
cardboard circles or squares
plastic wrap
masking tape
metal bowls
rounded toothpicks

Place 1 oz (28 g) Egg White Royal Icing in a small or medium-size paper cone fitted with the #2 or #3 round metal tip. This will be used to outline the runouts. Fill a medium to large-size paper cone or small squeeze bottle (with a cover and a small opening at the top) with 4 to 5 oz (114 to 140 g) Flood Icing. Select a runout pattern from Appendix 1 on Runouts, Flooding, and Monograms. Place the pattern on a flat surface and tape the ends. Cover the pattern tightly with plastic wrap and secure the ends with masking tape.

Position the tip at a 45-degree angle to the pattern and trace it with the tip just barely above the surface. If outlining a large monogram or a pattern with long lines or curves, touch the pattern surface with the tip and then raise it about 1 in. (2.54 cm) above the surface, letting the icing fall to the pattern (see Illustration 11.1).

To fill in the outline, position the squeeze bottle or cornet with the flood icing in the center of the design. Apply light pressure and allow the icing to flow into the outline. The icing should not spread more than ½ in. (1.3 cm) from the perimeter of the design. Stop and remove the cone. With a toothpick, move the icing to the outline. Work quickly, because the icing sets quickly.

Always work from the outside sections of a pattern toward the center. Never flood two adjoining sections at the same time. Flood widely separated sections and let the icing set before flooding adjacent sections. Flood Icing sets in 15 to 20 minutes. When a flooded section is set, go back and fill in the empty sections next to it. Let the completed flooded sections dry overnight. Carefully remove the masking tape or cut around the runouts with a sharp knife or Xacto knife. Carefully remove the runout and peel back the plastic wrap. Attach the runout to an iced cake, plaque, or iced cookie.

Illustration 11.1
Steps in outlining and flooding a monogram (from bottom and working clockwise)—the monogram is outlined with white royal icing. The second illustration shows the process of flooding the monogram with flood icing. The last illustration shows the complete flooded monogram.

New Skill: Bridge, Extension Work, and Hailspotting

Quick Prep

½ recipe Egg White Royal Icing (page 273)
3 oz (85 g) Flood Icing (page 274)
8-in. (20.3 cm) round Styrofoam covered with rolled fondant and attached to a 10-in. (25.4 cm) foil-covered round cardboard
paper cones
#2, #3 #5, #6, or #7 round metal tips and a PME 0 stainless-steel tip
metal spatula

Decorator's Hint

A PME 0 stainless-steel tip is the Rolls-Royce of piping tips. These tips are seamless and so pipe a perfect line. They are the tips of choice for piping fine or intricate royal icing work.

small metal bowls
rounded toothpicks
adding machine paper or strips of parchment paper
ruler
masking tape
stickpins

MARKING THE CAKE

To mark a cake, wrap a strip of adding machine paper around the circumference of the cake. Measure the paper carefully so the ends meet around the cake but do not overlap. Fold strip in half 4 times to create 16 equal sections.

Use the following chart to determine the width of the paper strip. Cut off any excess width.

CAKE HEIGHT	HEIGHT OF STRIP
3 in. (7.6 cm)	1¼ in. (3.2 cm)
4 in. (10.2 cm)	1½ in. (3.8 cm)
5 in. (12.7 cm)	1¾ in. (4.4 cm)

Position a rounded cookie cutter or a large glass at one end of the folded strip and draw a curve from one edge of the strip to the other (see Illustration 11.2). Carefully cut on the curved line. When the cut strip is unfolded, it will have a scalloped edge.

Attach the paper around the cake, about ¼ in. (6 mm) above the bottom, with the scalloped edge down and the straight edge up. Secure the paper to the cake with masking tape or stickpins.

Score the top edge of the paper with a quilting wheel; this is where the extension work will begin. Then score the scalloped bottom of the paper; this is where the bridge work will begin. Remove the paper from the cake.

MAKING THE BRIDGE

Pipe a snail's trail (also called a bead or oval border) around the bottom of the cake with the #5, #6, or #7 round metal tip. For the bridgework, use the #2 or #3 round tip. Pipe the first row of the scalloped bridge following the mark made by the quilting wheel. Once you have gone completely around the cake, pipe the next row above and parallel to the first. Build the piped lines upward 5 to 7 times (see the progression of the bridge in Illustration 11.3).

To smooth the bridge, brush 1 oz (28 g) Flood Icing over it to cover any cracks and spaces between the piped lines. Let dry 1 hour or overnight.

EXTENSION WORK

Rebeat 1 oz (28 g) Egg White Royal Icing by hand in a small ramekin, or use a metal offset spatula to smash the icing against a flat surface to get rid of lumps. Cut a small paper cone, fit it with a PME 0 metal tip, and load the rebeaten icing.

Starting at the top of the scored line, position the tip and touch the cake. Apply a burst of pressure at the start, creating a dot, then squeeze and pull the tip upward. Hold the string for a brief moment to dry slightly (see Illustration 11.3). Then bring the tip to the bottom of the bridge and break off the icing, or

Illustration 11.2
Making a paper pattern of scallops.

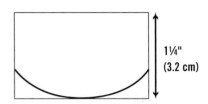

1¼"
(3.2 cm)

(a) This illustration shows a strip of adding machine paper that was folded four times (the width of the cake) equaling 16 sections. The height of the strip is 1¼ in. (3.2 cm) high—based on the height of the cake which is 3 in. (7.6 cm) high. A rounded object is placed at the based of the strip and a crescent line is drawn from the left to the right of the strip.

(b) This illustration shows the scalloped strip which was cut in illustration 11.2 (a). The strip is placed around the cake and taped with masking tape. The strip is raised ¼ in (6 mm) high from the base of the cake.

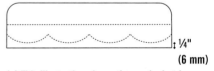

¼"
(6 mm)

(c) This illustration shows the marked strip against the cake. The top of the strip is scored with a quilting wheel as a starting point to the string work. The bottom of the strip shows the scalloped scoring with a quilting wheel. This is where the bridge work foundation begins and where the string work ends.

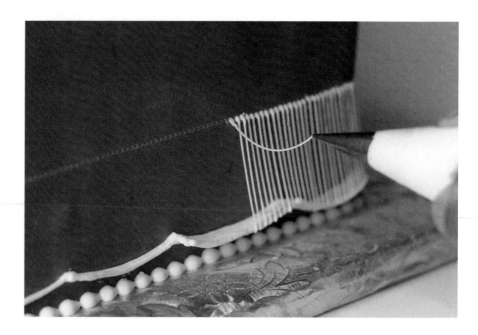

Illustration 11.3
Extension work. Hold the piped string briefly to air dry before breaking it off at the bridge.

move the tip slightly under the bridge to break off. It is important to predict the length of the string by measuring the distance from the top of the line to the bottom of the bridge.

The strings should be ¹⁄₁₆ to ⅛ in. (1.5 to 3 mm) apart. Continue until you have completed the stringwork.

HAILSPOTTING

Hailspots are similar to Swiss dots, but much smaller. The icing consistency for both techniques is the same. Place 1 oz (28 g) Flood Icing in a small paper cone without a tip. With scissors, snip a tiny hole at the end of the cone. Position the paper cone's tip at the top of the stringwork and squeeze. Only the icing should touch the stringwork. Carefully space the dots on the line. Do this to every other line (see Illustration 11.4).

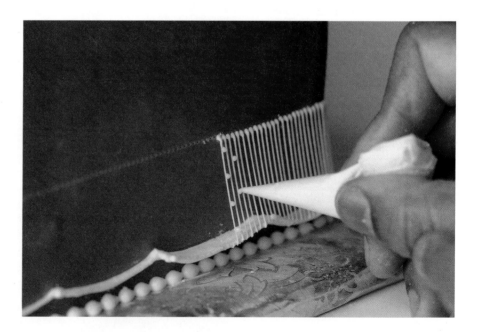

Illustration 11.4
Hailspotting.

New Skill: Simple Lace Designs

Quick Prep

> 5 oz (140 g) Egg White Royal Icing (page 273)
> cardboard circles or squares
> plastic wrap
> Xacto knife
> metal spatula
> paper cones
> PME 0 tip
> lace pattern design

Select a simple lace pattern design from Appendix 1 and carefully trace or copy it. Place the pattern on a sturdy piece of cardboard and tape down the ends. Place a piece of plastic wrap directly over the pattern and tape it securely with masking tape.

Load 1 oz (28 g) Egg White Royal Icing into a paper cone fitted with the PME 0 tip. Position the tip at a 45-degree angle to the pattern, with the tip slightly above the surface. Apply light to medium pressure as you trace the lace pattern. To end a stroke, stop the pressure, lower the tip to the surface, and drag it slightly. Go on to the next lace pattern and continue until all the lace pieces are done. Let the pieces dry completely. Small lace pieces need 20 minutes to 2 hours to dry. The kitchen or classroom environment will dictate how quickly the laces dry.

There are two ways to remove the lace from the plastic wrap. You can slide a small metal offset spatula under the lace. This works about 90 percent of time, but breakage is possible. The other way is to cut out a small area of the lace pieces with an Xacto knife. Carefully pick up the plastic wrap with some of the lace pieces on it. Place the lace on a plain cardboard round or square. Pull the plastic wrap to the end of the cardboard with your writing hand. As you pull on the plastic wrap, the lace will begin to release itself as each piece reaches the edge of the cardboard. Carefully collect the fragile pieces with a large metal spatula.

To attach the fragile lace pieces to a rolled iced cake, place a dot of royal icing at the left and right sides of the lace or at the center of the lace. Hold the lace between your thumb and index finger, with the thumb on the bottom and the finger on the top. Carefully attach the lace to the cake and hold it in place for 5 to 10 seconds. Do not apply any pressure or the lace will break and collapse in your hand. Continue attaching the lace pieces to the cake (see Illustration 11.5).

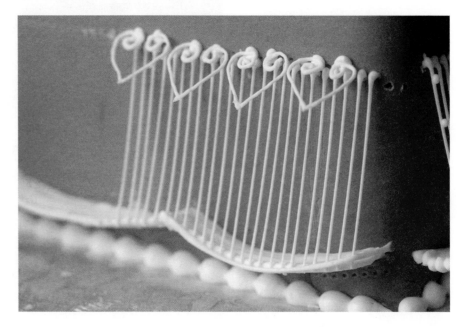

Illustration 11.5
A simple lace design can be attached to either bridge or extension work.

Decorator's Hint
The plastic wrap should be taut and free of wrinkles.

New Skill: Filigree Lace Designs

Quick Prep

5 oz (140 g) Egg White Royal Icing (page 273)
cardboard circles or squares
plastic wrap
Xacto knife
metal spatula
paper cones
PME 0 and #1 or #2 round metal tips
filigree lace patterns

Select a filigree lace pattern from Appendix 1 and carefully trace or copy it. Place the pattern on a sturdy cardboard and tape down the ends. Place a piece of plastic wrap directly over the pattern and tape it securely with masking tape.

FILIGREE WITH SCROLLS

Load two paper cones with 1 oz (28 g) each of Egg White Royal Icing. Fit one cone with the #1 tip and the other with the #2 round tip. Tape and secure a filigree pattern with scrolls from Appendix 1. Pipe the scrolls first, as this is the easiest skill, using the cone with the #1 tip. Then pipe the perimeter of the scrolls. The scrolls do not need to be dry before outlining them with the #2 round tip. Because this lace is larger, the #0 tip might be too fragile.

Make sure the outline of the filigree touches the edge of the scrolls, or when the filigree is removed, the outline will lift separately from the scrolls (see Illustration 11.6).

FILIGREE WITH CORNELLI LACE

Load two paper cones with 1 oz (28 g) each of Egg White Royal Icing. Fit one cone with the PME 0 tip and the other with either a #1 or #2 round metal tip.

> ### Decorator's Hint
>
> Because these lace pieces are much larger, put fewer pattern pieces on one cardboard. This gives you room to move around the pattern when piping. The more intricate the lace piece, the more room you will need on the cardboard.

Illustration 11.6
Filigree with scrolls.

(The #1 tip will give a more delicate appearance to the filigree than the #2.) Carefully outline all the filigree lace pieces. Use the PME 0 tip to pipe the inside of the filigree with the cornelli lace technique (see Lesson 7).

The cornelli lace must touch the filigree outline or it will not attach. Fill in the rest of the filigree and let dry. Carefully remove the lace with an offset spatula or pull it near the edge of the cardboard surface to remove it from the plastic wrap. Attach the filigree the same way as you would a simple lace design. However, you may need to hold the lace in place for 10 to 15 seconds with a little more than a dot of Egg White Royal Icing.

FILIGREE LACE WITH PYRAMID PIPING

This simple technique makes filigree lace look dazzling. It is done with the PME 0 tip and piped on the perimeter of the filigree lace.

Position the tip at a 45-degree angle at one edge of the filigree. Pipe three small dots very close to one another. Position the tip just above and between the first two dots and pipe another two small dots. Finally, position the tip above and between these two dots and pipe one small dot. Slightly drag the tip to the surface to end the dot. The next set of pyramid dots should be about ⅛ in. (3 mm) apart. Continue this technique until the lace is complete. Let dry completely. When the filigree is removed, the pyramid dots will attach to the filigree.

New Skill: Ring Design with Trellis Work

Quick Prep

16 oz (454 g) Egg White Royal Icing (page 273)
8-in. (20.3 cm) round Styrofoam attached to a 10-in. (25.4 cm) round cardboard
cardboard circles or squares
Xacto knife
metal spatula
medium-size paper cones
12-in. (30 cm) flex or disposable pastry bags
coupler
PME 0, #5 round metal tip, and #18 star tips

NUMBER OF RINGS NEEDED	SIZE OF CAKE
30 to 35	6 in. (15.2 cm)
40 to 45	7 in. (17.8 cm)
50 to 55	8 in. (20.3 cm)
60 to 65	9 in. (22.9 cm)
70 to 75	10 in. (25.4 cm)
80 to 85	11 in. (27.9 cm)
90 to 95	12 in. (30 cm)

PREPARING THE RINGS

Select a ring design pattern from Appendix 1. Carefully trace or copy enough of the pattern to decorate the cake. Place the pattern on a sturdy cardboard piece and tape down the ends. You may need more than one cardboard to accommodate

Decorator's Hint

Another option is to outline the scrolls with the PME 0 tip and then overpipe them with the #0 tip. This is the classic way to create a larger filigree, but it may not be practical when time is a factor. Keep this technique in mind, however, because it forms a much more delicate filigree and is desirable for competition pieces.

Decorator's Hint

Pyramid piping is not limited to filigree lace pieces. Use this technique directly on a rolled iced cake when you want delicate piping without the fuss of piping simple lace.

Decorator's Hint

Try using an un-iced 8-in. (20.3 cm) round Styrofoam instead of an iced round. The process for icing an 8-in. (20.3 cm) round Styrofoam in Meringue Powder Royal Icing takes 2 to 3 days.

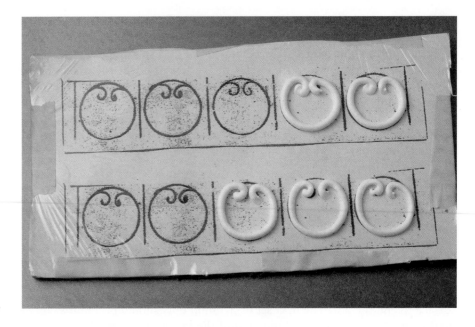

Illustration 11.7
Piping rings from a pattern.

the number of rings needed for this project. Place a piece of plastic wrap directly over the pattern and tape it securely with masking tape.

Place 2 oz (57 g) Egg White Royal Icing in a medium-size paper cone with the #5 round tip. Position the tip between the angles of 45 and 90 degrees. Touch the left or right inner curve of the ring. Raise the tip about ¼ in. (6 mm) from the surface and allow the icing to form into the shape of the ring. To end the ring, touch the surface and slightly drag the tip. Pipe the rest of the rings and let dry at least 1 to 2 hours or overnight (see Illustration 11.7).

ASSEMBLING THE RINGS

Carefully remove the rings from the plastic wrap and place them in a shallow container. Rebeat any leftover icing. Load a pastry bag or medium-size paper cone with 5 to 6 oz (140 to 170 g) rebeaten icing. Place the Styrofoam on your work surface and use a #18 star tip to pipe large shells (see Lesson 1). Be sure the shells are together, as their job is to hold the rings in place.

Pipe the shells on the inside edge of the Styrofoam. Before the shells begin to dry, carefully place the rings, curved ends in, between each shell. After placing five or six rings, check that the rings are evenly and properly spaced between the shells. Continue attaching the rings until all the spaces between the shells are occupied.

PIPING STRING ON THE RINGS

This is the most exciting part of ring design. Piped strings encase the rings, giving them a nautical look. Load a medium-size paper cone with 1 oz (28 g) Egg White Royal Icing and the PME 0 tip. You may wish to stand when piping this part of the exercise.

The first set of strings begins at the top center of the rings. The strings are carefully piped toward the surface of the cake top, then picked up from the center to the outside edge of the cake.

To begin, position the tip at a 45-degree angle at the center point of any given ring. Lightly touch the surface of the ring, apply pressure to the cone to begin the icing flow, and raise the tip 1 to 2 in. (2.54 to 5.1 cm). Pipe the strings in a counterclockwise direction if right-handed or clockwise if left-handed. Let

Decorator's Hint

The rings can be piped from a brand-new 12-in. (30 cm) flex pastry bag or plastic disposable bag. With either type, the tip should be held at a 90-degree angle when piping the rings. These pastry bags can hold 8 to 10 oz (228 to 283 g) Egg White Royal Icing.

the strings drop to the second, third, fourth rings, and so forth. After eight to twelve rings, you may need to stop to prevent the strings from breaking. To stop, carefully touch the surface of one of the rings. Stop the pressure and pull away.

Turn the cake and continue to pipe strings where you left off, stopping after every eight to twelve rings. Once you have gone completely around the cake, end the first round of strings by touching the surface of the ring where you began.

Begin the second round of strings by moving the tip toward the surface of the cake top, about ⅛ in. (3 mm) from the first. Repeat the process for piping strings for as many rounds as you choose (see Illustration 11.8).

When you get closer to the surface of the cake, the rings are more difficult to pipe continuously. You may need to put an object under one side of the cake to tilt it toward you or away from you, giving you a better angle. At this point, you will need to connect one ring at a time. When you get as close as you can to the inside of the cake's surface, position the tip back at the top center of the rings and continue piping rings toward the cake's outside edge. Again, when you get close to the outside edge, you will need to connect one ring at a time.

Illustration 11.8
Piping strings on the rings.

OVERPIPING THE RINGS

This is the trickiest part of this lesson. Each ring is to be overpiped with the same tip used to pipe the rings. The overpiping gives a neater and cleaner appearance to the design. The difficult part is tilting the cake away from you or picking up the cake in one hand and tilting it as you overpipe each ring.

Place 2 oz (57 g) Egg White Royal Icing in a medium-size paper cone fitted with the #5 round tip. Place an object under the cake at the 6 o'clock position, raising the front of the cake to an angle between 45 and 80 degrees. Position the tip at the inside end of one of the rings. To do this, carefully lean over the cake, being careful not to break the rings. Apply a burst of pressure and carefully lift the icing and let it rest over the ring. Move your hands and the icing toward the outside edge of the cake and carefully touch the ring to end the piping. Continue piping until all the rings are overpiped.

This skill is not easy and requires a lot of practice. If the cake were real, this would be the only way of accomplishing the task. When you are practicing with Styrofoam, you can lift the cake with one hand and tilt it inward and outward as you overpipe the rings.

TRELLIS (DROP STRING)

This is a beautiful extension to the ring design cake. The trelliswork can vary to each individual's taste. Following are three examples:

1. Each or every other ring is connected with a trellis. This motif extends completely around the cake. The next row of trellis is the un-trellis rings. Two rows of trellis piping, trellis and un-trellis, are considered one set. The second set of trelliswork drops slightly lower than the first but follows the same pattern.

Three sets are usually needed to complete the trelliswork, but you may opt for just two (see Illustrations 11.9 and 11.10).

2. Groups of five rings are attached to create a long trellis. Attach the rings all the way around the cake and let the trellis dry for 10 minutes. Go to the center point of the first trellis and actually touch the trellis with the icing from the PME 0 tip. Pull the string up and move over to the center point of the next trellis. Lightly touch the trellis with the icing. Continue with this technique until you have gone completely around the cake. Let dry for 10 minutes. Go to the center point of the second row of trellis and pipe a third row, following the same pattern (see Illustration 11.9).

3. Every other ring is connected with trelliswork, similar to the first option. However, instead of piping a connecting trellis between the empty rings, pipe a second row of trellis exactly where you started but slightly lower than the first row. Continue with a third row of trellis (see Illustration 11.10).

Review drop string piping in Lesson 4.

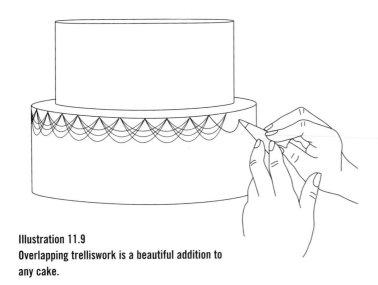

Illustration 11.9
Overlapping trelliswork is a beautiful addition to any cake.

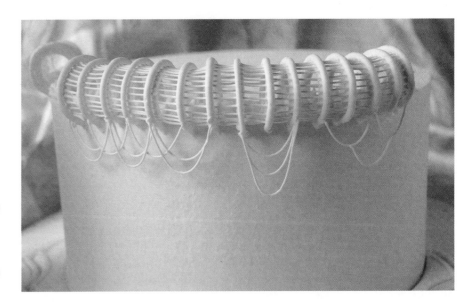

Illustration 11.10
Trelliswork (from left to right): Two sets of trellis connect every other ring, a long trellis is connected to the rings and then additional trellis connects the first trellis row, every other ring is connected with a trellis, and two additional rows of trellis piped just under the previous rows.

New Skill: Lattice

Quick Prep

8 oz (228 g) Egg White Royal Icing (page 273)
square cardboards
plastic wrap
#3, #4, or #5 round metal tips
medium-size paper cones
metal spatula

Load 2 oz (57 g) Egg White Royal Icing into a paper cone with either a #3, #4, or #5 round metal tip.

Illustration 11.11
Latticework.

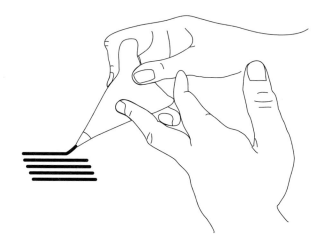

(a) First, pipe all lines in one direction.

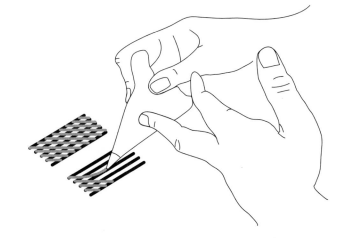

(b) Pipe the crossover lines, using the first line as the common line.

Position the tip at a 45-degree angle on a cardboard. Pipe a series of straight lines about ⅛ in. (33mm) apart. Pipe each line by applying a burst of pressure and raising the tip above the surface. Let the icing drop to the surface. Continue until all of the lines are piped in one direction (see Illustration 11.11a).

Turn the cardboard until the crossover lines run toward your body. Go to the tip of the second line and extend the piping to the first line. Go to the tip of the third line and connect it to the first line (see Illustration 11.11b). Continue this pattern until you reach the last line, which becomes the common line. Alternatively, turn the pattern ½ turn and repeat the directions.

Finish the exercise and then repeat it. Then practice piping a lattice design on a cake. (See Illustration 11.12 for an example of latticework on a cake.)

Illustration 11.12
Left: the first row of latticework lines.
Right: completed latticework.

New Skill: Cushion Lattice

Quick Prep

16 oz (454 g) Egg White Royal Icing (page 273)
#18, #20, or #199 star tips
#5, #3, and #1 round tips
8-in. (20.3 cm) round Styrofoam attached to a 10-in.
 (25.4 cm) round cardboard
metal spatulas
scissors or paring knife
medium or large parchment cones
12-in. (30 cm) brand-new flex pastry bag with coupler

Decorator's Hint

Wrap adding machine paper around the cake to obtain its circumference. Measure the length of the adding paper against a ruler and divide by six. Mark the adding machine paper with the results and remeasure the cake. Place a stickpin or pencil mark at the dividing points.

Decorator's Hint

When working with Egg White Royal Icing or Meringue Powder Royal Icing, do not use a pastry bag that once had Buttercream Icing in it. Any particle of grease will break down the icing. Washing icing tips, including the mixer bowl and paddle attachment in hot sudsy water cleans them enough to use with this icing, but it is impossible to remove all traces of grease from plastic spatulas or flex bags. For the same reason, use a brand-new rubber spatula whenever you are working with Egg White Royal Icing.

Attach the Styrofoam to the cardboard round with a little Egg White Royal Icing. Cut the edge of the Styrofoam with scissors, about ½ in. (1.3 cm) toward the cake's center and ½ in. (1.3 cm) on the top. This is called *beveling*. Measure the circumference of the cake into six equal sections.

Load a pastry bag with a coupler, the #18 or #199 star tip, and 8 oz (228 g) Egg White Royal Icing. Position the tip at a 45-degree angle to one of the measured points and in the cavity of the beveled surface. Apply a burst of pressure and build up a 1-in. (3.2 cm) oval by moving the tip in a zigzag motion. The oval should look like a garland—that is, smaller at one end and gradually building in the center. Ease off the pressure and let the oval narrow again. (See Lesson 1 to review garlands.)

Go on to the next measured point and make the next oval. Continue until all six ovals are piped. Let dry for at least 3 to 5 hours or overnight.

FIRST SET

Load 2 oz (57 g) Egg White Royal Icing with the #5 round metal tip in a medium-large paper cone. Position the tip at the left side of one of the ovals. Pipe lines at an angle, similar to piping lattice. Once you reach the right side of the oval, pipe lines in the opposite direction. Go on to the next oval and repeat the crisscross lines. Continue until you have gone completely around the cake.

Using the same tip, repeat the crisscross lines directly over the piped lines. Do this to the rest of the ovals. This completes the first set. Let dry 2 to 3 hours.

SECOND SET

Load 1 oz (28 g) Egg White Royal Icing into a paper cone with the #3 round metal tip. Position the tip at the left side of one of the ovals. Follow the pattern of lines piped with the #5 round tip. Pipe over these lines in the same direction as the first set. Go on to the next oval and do the same. Continue until all the ovals have a half-set of lines piped with the #3 tip.

Pipe another half-set of lines with the #3 round tip. The second set is complete. Let dry for several hours.

THIRD SET

Pipe crisscross lines with the #1 round tip with 1 oz (28 g) Egg White Royal Icing loaded in a paper cone. Pipe a full set to complete the cushion lattice (see Illustration 11.3).

The cushion lattice is complete (see Illustration 11.13). You can add decorative piping around it, such as scrolls or plunger flowers, to make the puffs more decorative. You may also wish to add another full set of crisscross lines with a PME 0 tip for a more refined cushion lattice.

Illustration 11.13
Cushion lattice.

END-OF-LESSON REVIEW

1. What is another name for *runouts?*

2. What is the difference between piped consistency and runout consistency?

3. What ingredients are used to soften Egg White Royal Icing to runout consistency?

4. What country is most noted for bridge and extension work?

5. What is the purpose of the bridge in extension work?

6. Why is the bridge flooded before adding the extension work?

7. What are the tiny dots on the extension work called? Why are they important?

8. What is another name for *trellis?*

9. Why must care be taken when piping and removing simple and filigree lace?

10. Who is the person most noted for creating lattice and cushion lattice designs?

PERFORMANCE TEST

Select and perform three of the following four exercises:

1. Roll ice and decorate a 6-in. (15.2 cm) round cake with Australian bridgework and hailspotting.

2. Pipe 1 dozen simple lace pieces and 6 filigree laces with scrolls in Egg White Royal Icing.

3. Pipe a lattice exercise on an 8-in. (20.3 cm) square cardboard in Meringue Powder Royal Icing.

4. Pipe 6 cushion lattices on a 6-in. (15.2 cm) round Styrofoam cake.

ROLLED ICING DESIGN SKILLS

Ruffling, Drapery, Smocking, Braiding, and Appliqué

You will need the following items to complete this lesson:

commercial rolled fondant or Rolled Modeling Paste (page 276

Quick Gumpaste (page 274)

skewers

rounded toothpicks

gel food colors

Styrofoams

#0, #1, #2, and #3 round metal tips

PME 0 tips

small and medium-size paper cones

small parchment cones

Xacto knife

#1 or #3 sable paintbrush

cornstarch

white vegetable shortening

plastic zippered bags

ruler

nonstick rolling pin

pasteurized egg whites

round cardboard

pastry brush

Rolled icing skills are essential decorative skills that add dimension and beauty to a cake iced in buttercream, marzipan, royal icing, or rolled fondant. An iced cake draped with rolled fondant, modeling chocolate, or a piece of icing made to look like ruffled fabric is simply glorious. Using braids of icing that look like woven ribbon or adding pieces of rolled icing shaped with cookie cutters is the difference between a cake decorator and a cake designer.

These are designer skills that are used often, especially for special events such as birthday parties, weddings, and holidays. Often, these highly decorative cakes are visual showpieces more than edible delights. In modest amounts, rolled icing can appeal to the eye and appetite.

A cake with these lavish designs can command a large amount of money. It will pay, therefore, to give special care and attention to this lesson.

New Skill: Ruffling

Quick Prep

8 oz (228 g) commercial rolled fondant
nonstick rolling pin
rounded toothpicks
cornstarch
gel food colors
ruler

Ruffles look like pretty frills at the bottom of a girl's dress and are easy to make from commercial rolled fondant. They are a simple way to dress up a cake.

For greater strength, you can make ruffles out of gumpaste (see Lesson 14) or Rolled Fondant Modeling Paste (page 276).

Measure out 4 oz (114 g) commercial rolled fondant and add food colors if you like. Sprinkle a work surface with cornstarch and roll out the fondant into a rectangle, about 4 by 8 in. (10.2 by 20.3 cm) and ⅛ in. (3 mm) thick. Trim the paste with an Xacto knife.

Cut the rectangle lengthwise into four equal strips, each 1 in. (2.54 cm) wide. Place three of the strips under a piece of plastic wrap to prevent drying.

Lightly dust the work surface with cornstarch and place the fourth strip on it so the length runs horizontally. Place a rounded toothpick about ½ in. (1.3 cm) on the paste. With the middle finger of your writing hand, apply medium to heavy pressure as your rotate the toothpick back and forth. This ruffles the

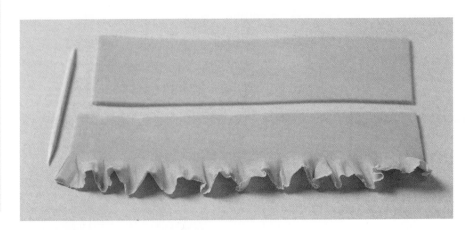

Illustration 12.1
A rounded toothpick is rotated back and forth underneath the paste to create a ruffle.

paste. Continue moving the toothpick down the strip in a back and forth motion until the entire length of the strip is ruffled (see Illustration 12.1). Ruffle the remaining three strips of fondant.

The ruffled paste can be attached to an iced cake with a little water or pasteurized egg white. It can be set in a crescent (scallop) shape or attached in a straight line at the bottom of the cake.

New Skill: Classical Drapery

Quick Prep

12 oz (340 g) commercial rolled fondant or Rolled Fondant Modeling Paste (page 276)
8 by 3 in. (20.3 by 7.6 cm) round Styrofoam attached to a 10-in. (25.4 cm) round cardboard
nonstick rolling pin
cornstarch
white vegetable shortening
#1 or #3 sable paintbrush
1 oz (28 g) pasteurized egg whites

This magnificent drapery work creates a beautifully tailored cake. Pieces of rolled icing are stuck together and made to resemble fabric pleats. The cake is carefully measured and these icing pleats are formed around the top edge for a perfect finish.

First, measure the circumference of the Styrofoam with adding machine paper and divide the paper into the desired number of sections. Remeasure the cake with the divided paper and use the creased sections to mark the Styrofoam with a pencil.

Rub a little white vegetable shortening on the work surface. Roll out the 4 oz (114 g) rolled icing on the shortening, which helps the icing adhere to the surface and allows the paste to be rolled thin. The shortening also keeps the paste intact and stable when strips are cut.

Roll and trim the fondant to a rectangle. Cut the rectangle into two or three strips, about 1½ by 6 in. (3.8 by 15.2 cm) and ⅛ in. (3 mm) thick. Turn the strips over to the fat side and brush the bottom of each with a little egg white. Fold the dry side of each strip to the wet side, developing a pillow or gathered effect (see Illustration 12.2).

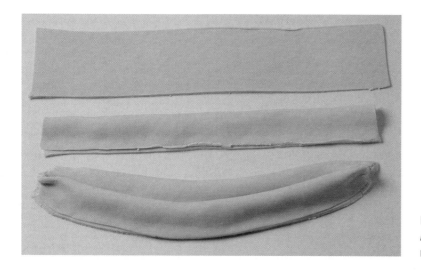

Illustration 12.2
A gathered effect when folding fondant is necessary in drapery work.

Brush a little egg white on one of the folded strips, just above the seam. Place another folded strip on the wet seam. Brush egg white on the seam of the second folded strip and add the third.

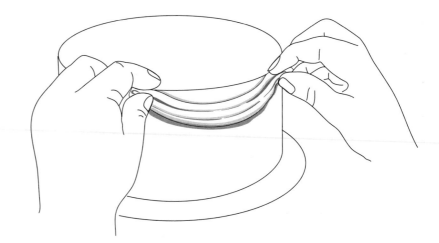

Illustration 12.3
Example of classic drapery.

Wet the area of the Styrofoam where the drapery will appear. One at a time, carefully pick up the folded strips by the ends. Shape the strips to the wet surface on the Styrofoam (see Illustration 12.3). Break off any extended pieces with your fingers and secure the ends of the folded strips to the Styrofoam. Make three more folded strips and attach them to the cake where the last three strips ended. The drapery should have a curved or crescent-shaped appearance.

For a decorative finish, make rounded balls from the modeling paste and attach them as clusters of three between each of the drapery seams. Alternatively, add two ribbon streamers made from the modeling paste. (See modeling chocolate streamers in Lesson 10.)

New Skill: Freehand Drapery

Quick Prep

> 16 oz (454 g) commercial rolled fondant or Rolled Fondant
>   Modeling Paste (page 276)
> nonstick rolling pin
> Xacto knife
> cornstarch
> ruler
> 8 by 4-in. (20.3 by 10.2 cm) round Styrofoam attached to a
>   10-in. (25.4 cm) round cardboard
> pastry brush

Freehand drapery is not as structured as classical drapery, but it is equally beautiful. A large piece of paste is cut and formed by hand and then added to an iced cake in a free-form style. The results are breathtaking!

Knead 8 oz (228 g) commercial rolled fondant until it is pliable. Sprinkle the work surface lightly with cornstarch and roll out the paste into a rectangle, about 6 by 9 in. (15.2 by 22.9 cm) and ⅛ in. (3 mm) thick.

With a pastry brush and a little water, brush the area of the Styrofoam where the drapery will be placed. Fold under the top and bottom edges of the paste, about ½ in. (1.3 cm) in to form a finished edge of your drape (see Illustration 12.4).

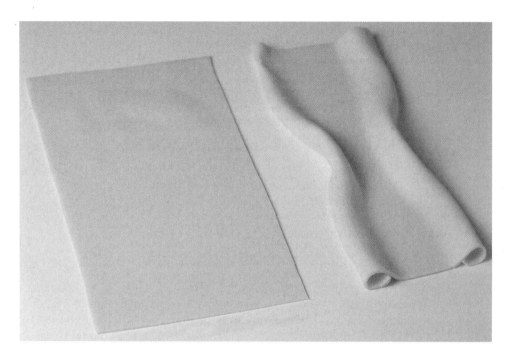

Illustration 12.4
To create freehand drapery, take a rectangular piece of rolled fondant (left) and tuck the top and bottom edges under the paste (right). Pick up the paste the move it around to form a drape.

Place both thumbs at the bottom of the tucked paste, the index fingers at the midpoint, and the middle fingers at the top edge. Gently pick up the paste and move it up and down until it drapes. Carefully attach the drape to the damp area on the Styrofoam (see Illustration 12.5). Taper the ends of the paste and tear off any excess.

Make another freehand drape with the remaining fondant and attach it to the Styrofoam.

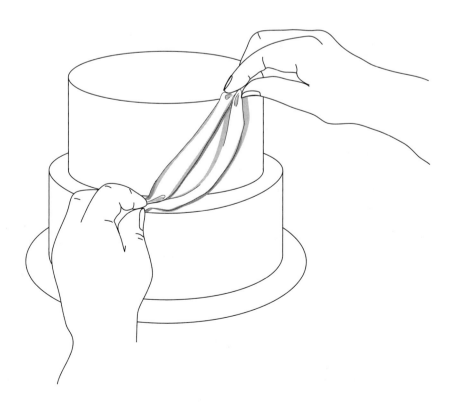

Illustration 12.5
Freehand drapery can be shaped in any way you choose. It is attached to a wet area of the Styrofoam surface.

New Skill: Appliqué

Quick Prep

8 oz (228 g) commercial rolled fondant or Rolled Fondant
    Modeling Paste (page 276)
nonstick rolling pin
Xacto knife
cornstarch
8-in. (20.3 cm) foil-covered round or square cardboard
pastry brush
assorted metal cookie cutters
plastic zippered bag
gel food colors
toothpicks

Appliqué is quite easy and is considered by many to be a cookie cutter technique. The appeal of this style is the structured look of the layers of icing.

Knead the paste and divide it into three or four pieces. Color each piece as desired. Lightly dust the work surface with cornstarch and roll out one piece of the colored paste to about ⅛ in. (3 mm) thick. No specific shape is required.

With cookie cutters, cut out as many shapes as you like. Place the cutouts in a plastic zippered bag. Roll out the remaining colored paste pieces and cut out as many shapes as desired.

Composing the collage is the fun aspect of appliqué. Stick the cutouts together with a little water. (See design suggestions in Illustration 12.6.)

Illustration 12.6
There is no limit to creativity in appliqué.

New Skill: Braiding

Quick Prep

> 4 oz (114 g) Rolled Fondant Modeling Paste (page 276) or
>   Quick Gumpaste (page 274)
> white vegetable shortening
> gel food colors
> toothpicks
> nonstick rolling pin
> ruler
> plastic zippered bag
> plastic wrap

Braiding is a technique usually associated with beautiful intricate breads or stunning hair designs. However, it is also used in sugarcraft to create beautiful designs that can be attached to a cake. Strips of modeling paste are woven together to form a decorative design that can enhance the beauty of a cake in a number of ways. The braided strips can be tied around a cake like ribbons or act as ribbon streamers under a pretty bow. This section shows you how to do two- and three-strand braiding with strips of rolled icing in different colors.

First, measure out four 1-oz (28 g) sections of paste and color each differently. Wrap each section in plastic wrap and place in a plastic zippered bag to prevent drying.

TWO-STRAND BRAIDS

Rub the work area with a little white vegetable shortening. Cut off ½ oz (14 g) each of two of the colored paste sections. Roll the sections separately on the shortening to about ⅛ in. (3 mm) thick. Trim each section to about 2 by 10 in. (5.1 by 25.4 cm).

Cut one strip from each of the two colors, trimming one shorter than the other. One strip should be about ¼ by 7 in. (3 mm by 17.8 cm) and the other strip should be about ¼ by 10 in. (3 mm by 25.4 cm). Place both strips on the work surface and cover the rest of the paste with plastic wrap and then a damp towel.

Stick the two strips together at the top edge with a dab of water or egg white, then slightly pull them apart. The shorter strip will remain stationary as you carefully wrap and fold the longer strip around it.

Begin by passing the long strip over the stationary strip (see Illustration 12.7). Carefully fold the strip at an angle, then crease and fold it under the stationary strip. Continue to fold and crease the strip as you pass it under the stationary strip. Follow the pattern until the longer strip is used up.

Illustration 12.7
Left: A two-strand braid. Right: a three-strand braid.

THREE-STRAND BRAIDS

Roll out three strips of modeling paste or gumpaste to the same length, ¼ by 10 in. (3 mm by 25.4 cm). Color each strip a different color.

Seal together the top edges of the strips with a little water or egg white. Slightly pull all three strips apart. Fold the left-hand strip (the first) over the center strip (the second). Carefully fold and crease the first strip over the second. Fold the right-hand strip (the third) over the first strip; be careful as you crease and fold the strip.

Fold the second or center strip over the third strip. Notice the development of the pattern. Continue to fold and intertwine the strips until you get to the end (see Illustration 12.7).

New Skill: Smocking

Quick Prep

> 16 oz (454 g) commercial rolled fondant or Rolled Fondant
> Modeling Paste (page 276)
> 4 oz (114 g) Meringue Powder Royal Icing (page 273)
> skewers
> white vegetable shortening
> cornstarch
> gel food colors
> PME 0 tips
> small parchment cones

Smocking is a stitching technique traditionally used to hold the fullness of fabric together in women's garments. Smocking gathers the fabric, and pretty embroidery piping is then stitched to the fabric for a beautiful effect. This technique can also be used to adorn the sides of a cake. It is typically used in conjunction with ruffles, swags, drapery, and extension work.

The technique used in this Lesson is the "classic" way of creating smocking; however, this technique can also be achieved with a special rolling pin with ribs.

To start, rub vegetable shortening on the work surface. Roll out the modeling paste and cut it to about 8 by 4 in. (20.3 by 10.2 cm) and ⅛ in. (3 mm) thick. Pick up the paste and place it on a little cornstarch to prevent sticking.

BASIC GATHERS

To gather the "fabric," place the first skewer underneath the paste. Place the second skewer on top of the paste, next to the first skewer. Place the third skewer underneath the paste, next to the second skewer. The gathers are starting to form (see the top left of Illustration 12.8).

Continue placing skewers until all of the paste is gathered. Let the paste set for 15 to 20 minutes. Remove the skewers to reveal the gathers (see the middle left of Illustration 12.8).

You can attach the gathers to a plaque of the same size using water or egg whites.

GATHERS WITH EMBROIDERY

To embroider completed gathers, color three 1-oz (28 g) portions of royal icing and place each portion in a paper cone fitted with a PME 0 tip. This exercise can also be piped without tips; cut the very tip of the cones to the same small opening size as a 0 tip.

Decorator's Hint

The gathers should be carefully trimmed with an Xacto knife but apply only a minimum amount of pressure; otherwise the gathers can lose their shape or become distorted. If attaching the gathered panel to a cake, wet the area lightly with water and quickly stick on the panel. If covering an entire cake, you will need to construct several panels of gathers and then butt them together.

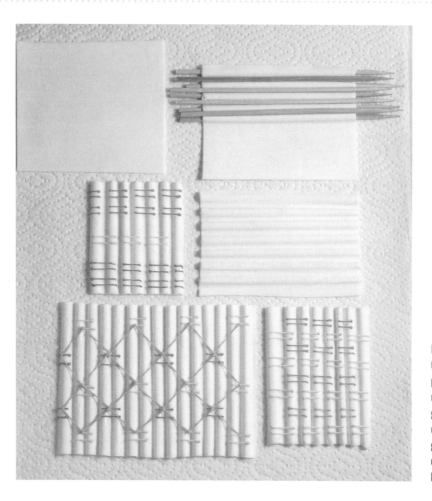

Illustration 12.8
Clockwise from top left: rolled out modeling paste; forming gathers by placing skewers underneath and over the modeling paste; the gathered paste after the skewers are removed; double-piped lines are alternated along the gathers; lines are piped to connected the double-piped lines; and another double-piped line pattern.

Panel 1

In the first pattern, the first two gathers are connected with a double piped line. The next two gathers are connected by a double piped line and so forth until you run out of gathers. This is the first row of piped stitches (see Illustration 12.9).

On the second row, the first gather is skipped and the second and third gathers are attached with a double piped line. Skip the fourth gather and attach the fifth and sixth gathers with a double piped line. Continue until there are no more gathers.

For the third and subsequent odd-numbered rows, repeat the style of the first row of stitches; for the fourth and subsequent even-numbered rows, repeat the pattern of the second row. Continue until the entire panel is embroidered (see Illustration 12.9).

Illustration 12.9
This pattern shows the double-pipe line smocking alternating the gathers.

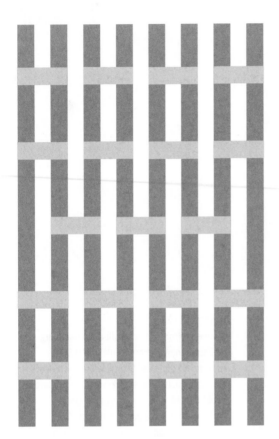

Illustration 12.10
This pattern shows two lines of double-piping followed by a third row of piping on alternate gathers. The final two rows are double-piped the same way as the first two rows.

Panel 2

In this panel, rows 1 and 2 are exactly the same. A double piped line is attached to every two gathers. On the third and centered row, a double piped line is attached to the second and third row. This pattern continues until the row is completed. The last two rows are piped exactly the same as rows 1 and 2 (see Illustration 12.9 and Illustration 12.10).

Panel 3

In this panel, the first two gathers are connected by a double stitch. The next two gathers are skipped. Then the fifth and sixth gathers are connected with a double stitch and then the next two are skipped. Follow this pattern through to the end of the row.

In the second row, the first two gathers are skipped and the third and fourth gathers are double stitched. The next two gathers are skipped and the seventh and eighth gathers are stitched. Follow this pattern through to the end of the row.

The next row is exactly the same as the first, and the last row is exactly the same as the second.

To complete the pattern, connect the stitching by piping a line from the center point of row 1 to the center point of row 2. Then pipe a line from the center point of row 2 back to row 1 at gathers 5 and 6. Pipe a connecting line from gathers 5 and 6 to row 2 at gathers 7 and 8 and so forth until you run out of gathers.

For row 3, connect lines from row 3 back to row 2 and continue back and forth until you complete all the gathers. For row 4, connect lines to row 3 and continue back and forth until you run out of gathers (see the bottom left of Illustration 12.9 and Illustration 12.11).

Illustration 12.11
This pattern shows alternate double-piping of gathers. The gathers are then connected by piping a line from one row to another.

END-OF-LESSON REVIEW

1. When ruffling commercial fondant or modeling paste, why is it important to work on a cornstarched surface?

2. What is the difference between classical drapery and freehand drapery?

3. What technique is used when various cookie-cutter shapes are placed together in a formal or free-form layered pattern?

4. Name two braiding techniques.

5. How can braiding be used on an iced cake?

PERFORMANCE TEST

Perform the following exercises:

1. Perform classical draping on an 8 by 3 in. (20.3 cm by 7.6 cm) round Styrofoam, either un-iced or iced with rolled fondant, and attached to a 10-in. (25.4 cm) round foil-covered cardboard. You can include elements of ruffling, braiding, or appliqué.

2. Perform smocked panels of your choice around an 8 by 3 in. (20.3 cm by 7.6 cm) round Styrofoam, either un-iced or iced with rolled fondant, and attached to a 10-in. (25.4 cm) round foil-covered cardboard. You can include elements of ruffling, braiding, or appliqué.

PASTILLAGE CONSTRUCTION

Place Cards, Gift Cards, Greeting Cards, Wheel Cart

You will need the following items to complete this lesson:

Pastillage (page 276)

support beams

Egg White Royal Icing (page 273)

Meringue Powder Royal Icing (page 273)

cornstarch

gel food colors

liquid whitener

#0, #1, #3, and #5 sable paintbrushes

palette

nonstick rolling pin

Xacto knife

ruler

fine sandpaper

Pastillage is a sugar medium that extends the pastry chef's art. Like chocolate showpieces and pulled and blown sugar, pastillage is generally used for three-dimensional constructions. This classically white sugar dough can be rolled, cut, air dried, and assembled to represent a small replica of a building, cake stand, doll furniture, a couple's silhouette, or locomotive train.

Pastillage can also be used simply as a place card at a formal dining setting, a beautiful greeting card, a small floral cart carrying a bunch of flowers, or a baby rattle. The possibilities for this construction medium are endless.

Recipes for pastillage vary widely. The straightforward approach involves adding 10x confectioner's sugar or cornstarch to leftover royal icing, making a thick paste. Complicated recipes call for many more ingredients.

Pastillage is similar to gumpaste in that it is generally not eaten. The consistency of both pastes is similar; thus, three-dimensional structures can be made out of gumpaste as well. However, pastillage dries much more quickly, is lighter in weight, and is a pristine white.

Classic pastillage pastes have little or no stretch and, thus, are unsuitable for making edible sugar flowers. More modern recipes offer a lot of stretch, which gives the pastry student or decorator more options.

New Skill: Place Cards, Gift Cards, Greeting Cards, and a Wheel Cart

Quick Prep

1 recipe Pastillage (page 276)
cornstarch
nonstick rolling pin
Xacto knife
ruler
pastillage patterns (including place cards, greeting cards, and floral cart)
support beams
2 oz (57 g) Meringue Powder Royal Icing (page 273)
#1 or #3 sable paintbrush
#10 round tip
4-in. (10.2 cm) piece of fine sandpaper

ROLL AND CUT

Trace and cut all the indicated pastillage patterns (see Appendix 1), including the support beams for the place cards and wheel cart. Divide the soft pastillage in two. Wrap one half in plastic wrap and place in an airtight container to prevent drying. Sprinkle the work area with 1 oz (28 g) cornstarch. Lightly knead the soft pastillage into the cornstarch until the paste absorbs all of the starch. Add more cornstarch until the paste is no longer sticky and has elasticity.

Clean the work surface and then sprinkle with more cornstarch. Place the pastillage on the cornstarch and roll into a rectangle about ⅛ in. (3 mm) thick. (This is suitable for most cutouts.) For the support beams, roll the paste a little thicker—between ⅛ and ¼ in. (3 and 6 mm) thick.

Place the patterns on the paste and cut carefully and accurately with an Xacto knife. You can use a round cookie cutter the same size as the pattern for the cart wheels. Use the #10 round tip to make the holes in the wheel and the holes in the gift card. For the place and greeting cards, you could use similar cookie cutters, if available.

Carefully move the cutouts to a clean area and let them dry completely—at least 2 hours. Turn over the pieces and let dry for at least another 2 hours or overnight. The dry pastillage pieces are strong, but remember they are still sugar and must be handled with care.

Carefully sand the edges of each piece with fine sandpaper. To sand the inside holes of the wheel, tear the sandpaper in half and fold one half to a sharp point. Insert the sharp end inside the holes and sand carefully.

Vegetable shortening is never used with pastillage. To rejuvenate dried paste, knead in a piece of fresh pastillage paste.

DECORATING

On the place and gift cards, pipe the names of people you would give a present to or invite to a dinner party. You can tie the gift card to the gift by passing either a gold or silver ribbon through the hole. Review Lesson 5 on writing and Lesson 7 on transfer designs.

Once piped and dried, gild the names with gold. Mix ½ tsp (2.5 ml) gold powder with a few drops of lemon extract in a small container. Carefully paint the writing on the plaques with the #1 sable paintbrush. Let dry completely.

Once dry, attach a support beam to the back of the place card so it can be displayed upright. To do this, turn the card over and pipe a small line of royal icing at a 45-degree angle on the support beam. Press the beam to the back of the card at the center bottom. Allow to dry for 10 minutes in this position. Carefully turn the card over to display it in an upright position (see Illustration 13.1).

You can design your own greeting card by transferring a pattern onto a plaque. These designs can be brush embroidered or painted with gel food color (see Lesson 17). Assemble the card by piping a line of royal icing on the inside edge of the greeting card's back. Brush the excess icing with either a #1 or #3 sable paintbrush dipped in little egg white. Allow the card to dry for several hours before moving it. Once the card is dry, you can gild the edges or petal dust

Decorator's Hint

Pastillage paste stretches as you cut it. Thus, you must anticipate when you are nearing the end of a seam and saw through the paste with an up-and-down motion instead of pulling the Xacto knife through the paste. Reshape the cut pieces with a metal spatula or a ruler to maintain the integrity of the shapes.

Illustration 13-1
Place cards.

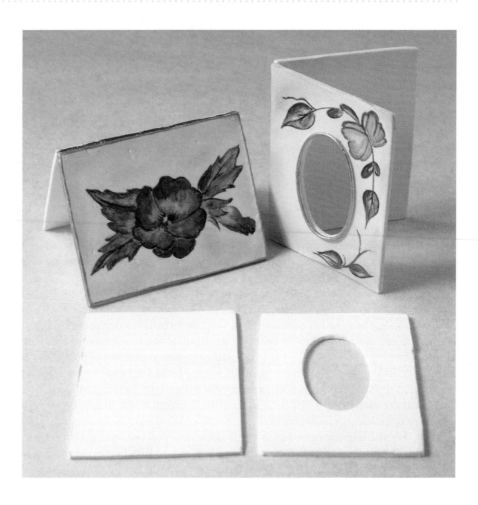

**Illustration 13.2
Greeting cards.**

the front of the card for an even warmer appearance (see Illustration 13.2). The card can be decorated with a beautiful floral spray and placed on an iced cake or set on a beautiful tray as a centerpiece at a formal gathering.

For the wheel cart, attach the beams to the cart's bench with royal icing. Add support beams just inside the cart's front (or narrow point) and about 1 in. (2.54 cm) in from the back of the bench (just inside its edge) on each side where the wheels are to be placed. Let dry for several hours. Be sure to attach the wide ends of the beams to the cart (see Illustration 13.3).

When the cart is dry, reverse it so it stands on its narrow end. To attach the wheels, pipe a dot of royal icing on the back of each wheel near the center. Press the wheels to the bench's edge and support beam. Let dry. For the wheel's bolts, cut out ¼-in. (6 mm) thick rounded pieces with the #10 round tip. Attach to the center of the wheel with a dot of royal icing. When dried, the wheel is complete. (See Illustration 13.3)

Illustration 13.3
The components of a wheel cart.

END-OF-LESSON REVIEW

1. What is pastillage used for?

2. Why use pastillage instead of gumpaste?

3. Can pastillage be colored with food color?

4. Can edible flowers be made from pastillage?

5. Is pastillage considered a high-end skill? Why or why not?

PERFORMANCE TEST

Perform the following exercises using pastillage:

1. Cut three place cards and decorate them with three names.

2. Cut two greeting cards and decorate them with brush embroidery or freehand embroidery.

3. Cut one wheel cart and assemble.

GUMPASTE FLOWERS

Basic Floral Skills

You will need the following supplies to complete this lesson:

Quick Gumpaste (page 274)

cell pad

ball or dogbone tool

Xacto knife

modeling stick (sharpened dowel)

24- and 28-gauge florist wires

cotton thread

Styrofoam to dry flowers

yellow cornmeal

florist tape

silicone leaf press

gel food colors

petal dust colors

rose, ivy, and hibiscus leaf cutters

#0, #1, and #3 sable paintbrushes

vegetable shortening

cornstarch

egg whites

toothpicks

parchment paper

masking tape

skewers

fine sandpaper

nonstick rolling pin

Welcome to the beautiful art of gumpaste flowers. Sugar flowers made in this medium are considered the top of the line, and to many cake decorators and designers they are the definitive art in sugarcraft.

In many countries, gumpaste is called petal paste, modeling paste, or flower paste. In the United States, the term *gumpaste* is used to indicate a material made from a gum derivative that gives the paste elasticity and strength. Two main molecular compounds are used in making gumpaste. The chief compound used in most paste is gum tragacanth; the other is tylose or tylose CMC. Both vegetable gums are polysaccharides that can absorb large quantities of water. These swell and produce thickness. Some are from cellulose gums—natural sources from trees, bushes, and shrubs—and are chemically modified to improve characteristics or properties like plasticity or elasticity.

Gum tragacanth—gum trag for short—is a water-soluble carbohydrate gum containing the polysaccharides tragacanth and bassorin. The source of gum tragacanth is the desert highland of northern and western Iran. The gum is harvested by making an incision on the upper part of the taproot in which the gum is collected. It is then processed into several forms. For cake decorating purposes, it is made into a powder. Gum tragacanth is used in many everyday commercial products, from cosmetics and toothpaste to jellies and salad dressings. It is also used in syrups, mayonnaise, sauces, liqueurs, candy, ice cream, and popsicles.

Tylose CMC is a balloonlike outgrowth of a type of plant cell, and CMC stands for carboxymethyl cellulose. This polysaccharide is the chief constituent of all plant tissues and fibers. Tylose is found in some dairy products and dental adhesives.

Tylose or tylose CMC are popular food additives in the making of gumpaste because only half the amount is needed to obtain the same strength and elasticity as gumpaste made with gum tragacanth. Tylose is also less expensive than gum tragacanth. Furthermore, it is available as a white powder, making it possible to achieve a white paste; gum tragacanth is beige in color, so gumpaste made with it is not truly white. Gum trag also has an off-putting taste if too much is used, while tylose does not have a noticeable taste. Both compounds are available at cake decorating supply stores.

This lesson covers small gumpaste blossoms, buds, and foilage. The approach taken here yields what is known as pulled flowers, meaning flowers created without metal or plastic cutters. The gumpaste is shaped by hand and with an Xacto knife and a modeling stick; it is pined and pulled to achieve the desired results. We will make some leaves without cutters and some with cutters.

New Skill: Pulled Blossoms and Buds

Quick Prep

1 recipe Quick Gumpaste (page 274)
28-gauge florist wires, 4 to 5 in. (10.2 to 12.7 cm) long
moss-green florist tape
vegetable shortening
cornstarch
cell pad
dogbone tool
silicone leaf press
 Xacto knife
modeling stick (sharpened dowel), 5 to 6 in.
    (12.7 cm to 15.2 cm) long

1 oz (28 g) egg whites
gel food colors
toothpicks
full sheet of parchment paper
masking tape
white cotton thread
2 wooden skewers
assortment of petal dust colors
#1 sable paintbrush (wet)
#3 and #5 sable paintbrushes (dry)
2-in. (5.1 cm) piece of fine sandpaper
nonstick rolling pin
small Styrofoam to dry flowers
2 oz (57 g) yellow cornmeal

Line your workstation with parchment paper, taping down the corners with masking tape. Measure out 1 oz (28 g) egg whites, 2 Tbsp (30 ml) cornstarch, and 1 oz (28 g) white vegetable shortening. Have on hand a modeling stick, an Xacto knife, and 28-gauge green or white florist wires.

Illustration 14.1
The bud and steps to creating a basic five-petal blossom.

BASIC FIVE-PETAL BLOSSOM WITH BUD

Measure out 1 oz (28 g) gumpaste and color it with gel food colors, if desired. You can also leave the paste natural white and then petal dust the dry flowers with powdered food colors. Set aside a pea-sized amount of paste. Cover the remainder with plastic wrap and place it in an airtight container.

Place the pea-sized bit of paste in your nonwriting hand. With the middle finger of your writing hand, rotate the paste into a round ball. Rotate one end of the ball to form a cone (see Illustration 14.1). Dip the modeling stick into a little cornstarch and then rotate the tip of the stick into the rounded edge of the cone. About ⅛ in. (3 mm) of the stick should be in the cone.

Hold the modeling stick and cone at a 180-degree angle and place the Xacto knife at the base of the cone at a 45-degree angle. Cut five slits in the base of the cone, about ¼ in. (6 mm) deep and equally spaced. Remove the paste from the modeling stick and open the slits. These are called *florets*. The bottom of the flower is called the *trumpet*.

Hold the trumpet part of the flower in your nonwriting hand. Position your thumb under one of the florets and your index finger on top, or visa versa. Pinch the floret with medium pressure to flatten the petal. Use your thumb to press around the petal to give it a more natural and rounded shape (see Illustration 14.2). Repeat the same technique until all of the florets are pressed into rounded petals. Press the tip of the modeling stick into the center of the flower to make a small cavity.

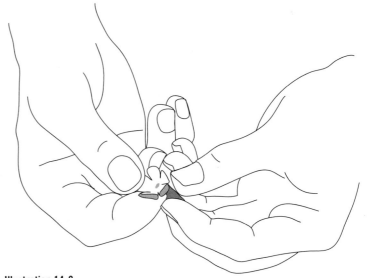

Illustration 14-2
Pinch the floret to flatten the petal. Then use your thumb to press around the petal to give it a more natural shape.

Make a small hook at one end of a 28-gauge florist wire. Dip the hook part into a little egg white, wiping off any excess. Thread the unhooked part into the cavity of the flower and pull the wire through the trumpet. When the hook reaches the cavity, rotate the trumpet until the hook is eased through the cavity. Apply light to medium pressure at the trumpet to secure the wire to the paste. Stick the wired flower into the Styrofoam to allow the flower to dry. Drying time can be as little as 2 hours.

BUD

To create a bud, rotate a pea-sized amount of gumpaste into a round ball. Dip a wire (hooked or unhooked) in egg white and insert it inside the ball of paste. Secure the paste to the wire by pinching and pulling down on it. Score five lines, equally spaced, around the top of the paste at a 45-degree angle. This flattens the paste by means of pressure. Rotate the center of the paste with your middle and index fingers until it looks like a bud (see Illustration 14.1). Place the bud on Styrofoam and let it dry. Drying time can be as little as 2 hours.

To petal dust the flower and bud, measure a tiny amount of powdered color as well as a small amount of moss-green petal dust. If you choose a dark color, place a small amount of cornstarch in the center of your artist's tray. Use the cornstarch to dilute the color to a softer or lighter shade.

For the flower, brush a lighter shade of the color on each of the petals with the #3 sable paintbrush. Do not cover the entire petal with color; leave some of the paste's original color showing. This adds depth to the flower. Petal dust each of the petals. Using a darker shade of the color or a contrasting color, brush the tip of each petal. This adds contrast and shadows. Brush a little moss-green color inside the cavity of the flower and at the very bottom.

For the bud, brush the darkest tone of the color underneath, extending it to the center of the bud. Brush moss-green color over the dark color to dilute it to a more natural tone. You can also add a touch of the dark color to the center of the bud, which gives the illusion that the bud is flowering.

FOUR-PETAL BLOSSOM WITH BUD

This four-petal flower resembles the *bouvardia*, an Australian wildflower. It is white and waxy, and the only color is a little moss-green petal dust at the bottom of the trumpet.

Measure ½ oz (14 g) gumpaste, remove a pea-sized bit, and cover the balance of the paste in plastic wrap. Position the pea-sized paste in the palm of your nonwriting hand. Place the middle finger of your writing hand on top of the paste and rotate until a rounded ball forms. Shape the paste at one end of the ball to form a cone.

Dip the pointed end of a modeling stick in cornstarch and insert it in the large end of the cone to a depth of about ⅛ in. (3 mm). Cut four slits into the rounded end of the paste, about ¼-in. (6 mm) deep. Remove the stick and open the florets.

Just as you did for the five-petal blossom, shape the florets by placing your thumb under one of them and your index finger on top, or vise versa. Press the paste lightly to flatten it and then turn your thumb and index finger to the left and right sides of the petal. Lightly pinch the petal on the side, then pinch the petal at the tip, pulling lightly, to form the shape of the petal. Do the same to the three remaining florets.

Make a small cavity in the center of the flower with the modeling stick. Make a hook in the end of a 28-gauge wire, dip the wire in a little egg white, and wipe off any excess. Thread the wire through the flower from the unhooked end.

When the hook reaches the center cavity, turn the trumpet end of the flower as you ease the hook through the flower. Pinch the trumpet lightly to attach the wire to the flower (see Illustration 14.3). Stick the wired flower into a piece of Styrofoam to dry. Drying time can be as little as 2 hours.

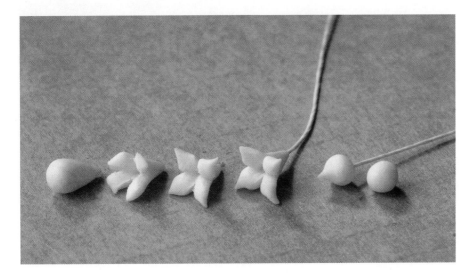

Illustration 14.3
The steps to creating a basic four-petal blossom (left) with bud (right).

BUD

Measure a pea-sized amount of gumpaste and rotate it into a round ball. Dip the unhooked end of a 28-gauge wire into egg white and stick it halfway inside the small ball of paste. Pinch the spot where the wire is inserted to secure it. Using your thumb and index finger, pinch the top center of the paste. Slightly pull the pinch out to form an onion shape (see Illustration 14.3). Stick the wired bud into a piece of Styrofoam to dry.

To petal dust the four-petal blossom, brush a little moss-green petal dust on the trumpet part of the flower. For the bud, brush the moss-green petal dust underneath and up to the middle. Both flower and bud are complete.

FORGET-ME-NOT

The technique for the five-petal forget-me-not is the same as that for the five-petal basic pulled blossom. Divide 1 oz (28 g) gumpaste from your stock in half. Color the halves with different shades of blue and violet gel food color. Wrap both halves in plastic to prevent drying.

To make the flower, form a pea-sized bit of bluish/violet gumpaste into a round ball. Shape one end of the ball into a cone. Dip a modeling stick into cornstarch and place it in the large part of the paste. Cut five slits, equally spaced, around the paste. Follow the same procedures for making the five-petal flower (page 195). Wire the completed flower and allow it to dry. Make more flowers using the other shade of bluish/violet-colored paste. Create the bud with the same technique as for the basic five-petal pulled blossom bud (page 195). Allow to dry. Drying time can be as little as 2 hours.

To petal dust the flower, brush a deeper shade of violet or purple petal dust on each petal, but do not completely cover them. Brush the trumpet of each forget-me-not with a deeper shade of petal dust.

Mix a small amount of lemon-yellow gel food color with a little liquid whitener. Brush the inside of some of the flowers with the yellow color, leaving the center unpainted. Using untinted liquid whitener, brush the inside of the remaining flowers, leaving the center unpainted.

Illustration 14.4
The steps to creating a forget-me-not (left) with bud (right).

For the bud, brush the bottom with a deeper shade of purple. You may also paint the bud's center with a yellow gel color and liquid whitener mixture or with untinted liquid whitener (see Illustration 14.4).

CHERRY BLOSSOM

The stamens of this beautiful five-petal pulled blossom are made from cotton thread, and the petals are shaped with and thinned by a skewer smoothed with fine sandpaper. Color 1 oz (28 g) gumpaste a soft pink color. Wrap in plastic until ready to use.

Making the Stamens

Wrap cotton thread 10 times around your index and middle fingers together. Cut the excess thread and carefully remove the ring of thread from your fingers.

Make a hook at one end of each of the 28-gauge white or green wires. Place each hooked end on opposing sides of the ring—that is, at the 12 o'clock and 6 o'clock positions. Close both hooks to secure the wires to the thread. Carefully pick up the two wires and cut the thread down the middle, making two sets of stamens (see Illustration 14.5).

Tape the end of the thread and hook part of each wire with florist tape to secure the thread to the wire. The thread should be no longer than ½ in. (1.3 cm). Trim with scissors if necessary.

Petal dust the thread with daffodil-yellow petal dust. Dip the ends of the thread in egg whites and then in cosmos (pinkish) petal dust to form pollen (see Illustration 14.5). Set aside.

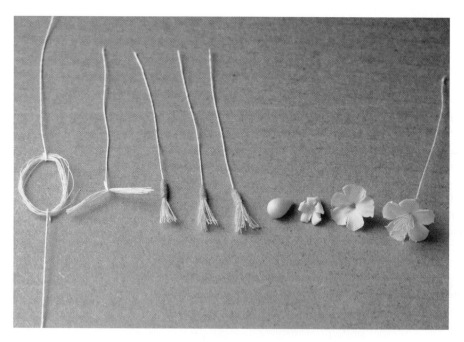

Illustration 14.5
The steps to creating a cherry blossom, from the stamen to the completed blossom.

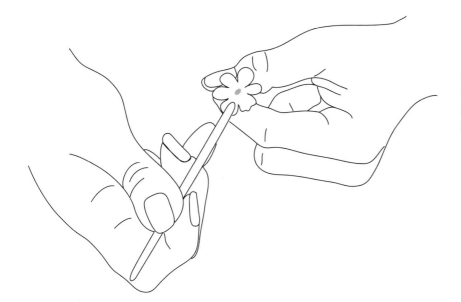

Illustration 14.6
Use a modeling stick to stretch the petals of the cherry blossom. Pull the stick across the floret to give it a rounded shape.

Special Modeling Stick

Cut the pointed end of one of the skewers with a pair of heavy-duty scissors, making it 5 to 6 in. (12.7 to 15.2 cm) long. Use the sandpaper to soften both ends of the skewer, rounding the ends and removing the hard edge. You will use this tool to soften, stretch, and mark lines on petals.

The Blossom

Shape a pea-sized bit of pink paste into a cone. Insert the modeling stick into the paste and make five equally spaced slits, using the same technique as for the basic five-petal blossom.

Put a little cornstarch on your index finger and carefully place the unshaped flower on it. Hold the trumpet part of the flower with your thumb. With your writing hand, place the modeling stick on top of one of the florets. Starting at the center of the floret, rotate the stick back and forth with your thumb and index finger, stretching the petal. Then pull the stick across the petal to round its edges (see Illustration 14.6). Shape each petal using this technique.

Insert the wire with stamens through the center of the flower. Brush egg white on the florist tape before it enters the cavity of the flower and carefully rotate the trumpet with your index finger and thumb to secure it to the wire (see Illustration 14.5).

To petal dust the cherry blossom, brush cosmos (pinkish) petal dust on the inside edge of each petal. Brush moss-green petal dust on the trumpet end.

HYACINTH

This six-petal blossom comes in various shades of blue, deep purple, pink, and white. After the flowers are made, they can be petal dusted any of these shades. The technique for making the pulled blossom is similar to the four-petal blossom, adding two additional petals.

Color 1 oz (28 g) gumpaste or, alternatively, leave it natural white. Shape a pea-sized bit of paste from the stock into a cone. Follow the procedures for making the four-petal flower, but when cutting slits into the base of the bud, be sure to cut six instead of four. Carefully open the florets and press the serrated side of the cone and serrated tool inside the cavity to score the florets. This forms the unique throat of the petals. Rotate the tool on the work surface so it scores each

Illustration 14.7
From left to right: The steps to creating a hyacinth blossom.

of the six florets. Remove the tool from the paste. Gently press each petal slightly flat, then pinch them to a point and curve the point down to resemble a hyacinth (see Illustration 14.7).

To petal dust the hyacinth, apply a deeper shade of color to the inside edge of each petal; the color should be darker than the base color of the flower. If you made a white flower, petal dust the center of the flower and the base of the trumpet with a little moss-green petal dust.

MIMOSA

This brightly colored bloom is a favorite of cake decorators. It is easy to make, and it is often seen on cakes for men, as its form is not too delicate.

Color 1 oz (14 g) gumpaste with lemon-yellow gel food color. Shape a pea-sized bit of this into a round ball. Dip the end of a 28-gauge wire in egg white and insert it into the ball. Stick the flower on a piece of Styrofoam to allow drying. Continue making flowers until all of the paste is used. Let dry at least 2 to 4 hours or overnight (see Illustration 14.8).

Illustration 14.8
From left to right: The steps to creating mimosa blossoms.

Pollen

To add pollen to a flower, place 2 oz (57 g) yellow cornmeal in a small shallow container. Add ¼ to ½ tsp (1.7 to 2.5 ml) daffodil-yellow petal dust color to the cornmeal for a brighter color.

Dip each flower in egg white and then in the yellow cornmeal. Arrange the flowers in a cluster of five or seven and tape with florist tape.

Foliage

Some leaves are rolled and cut freehand, without a plastic or metal cutter, and some are made using these tools. Here we practice both methods.

Freehand

Color 2 oz (57 g) gumpaste mint, leaf, moss, or forest green and wrap it in plastic. Remove ¼ oz (7 g) green paste and shape it into a round ball. Place the ball on a work surface and roll it into a log about 1½ in. (3.8 cm) long.

Brush a little egg white on a 28- or 26-gauge green or white florist wire and insert the wire into the log of paste to a depth of about ½ in. (1.3 cm). Pinch the end of the paste to secure it to the wire.

Rub a little solid vegetable shortening on the work surface and place the wired gumpaste on it. Press a nonstick rolling pin in the center of the paste to slightly flatten it. Thin the left and right sides of the paste with a modeling stick, leaving a ridge in the center. Part of the center ridge contains the inserted wire. With a modeling stick, thin the ridge above the inserted wire (see Illustration 14.9).

Return the wired paste to the work surface and place the end of the wire at the 12 o'clock position. Position an Xacto knife at the end of the paste to the left of the wire at a 45-degree angle. Drag the knife across the paste, making an oval shape from the back to the front. Stop the curve at the 6 o'clock position. Reposition the knife at a 45-degree angle at the end of the paste to the right of the wire. Drag the knife, making a curve that meets the left curve at the center point of the leaf. Remove the excess paste and lift the leaf from the wire. This technique can be used to make many types of leaves, petals, and sepals (see Illustration 14.9).

These leaf prototypes can be transformed into many types of foliage, including leaf blades, ferns, embossed leaves, and all-purpose leaves.

Fern

Rub a little vegetable shortening on the work surface. Place the leaf on the surface with the wire end at the 12 o'clock position. Starting at the tip of the right side of the leaf, make tiny cuts, slightly angled and about ⅛- to ¼-in. (3 to 6 mm) deep. Go down to the base of the leaf. Repeat on the left side of the leaf (see Illustration 14-9).

Illustration 14.9
Creating freehand leaves and
leaves made with cutters.

Leaf Blade

Place the leaf on a cell pad with the wire at the 12 o'clock position. Position a veining tool at a 45-degree angle starting at the center of the leaf's base. Drag the veiner with medium pressure from the base to the tip of the leaf. Then position the veiner about ⅛ in. (3 mm) to the left of the center vein. Drag the tool to make another vein, this time at a slight angle, from the base to the tip of the leaf. Score another vein to the left of the center vein. Now, score two veins to the right of the center vein. The leaf blade is complete.

Embossed Leaves

Place the wired leaf in the bottom of a two-part silicone leaf press. Apply medium to hard pressure to the top press. Raise the top press and carefully remove the leaf. The sides of the leaf can be softened with a ball or dogbone tool and a cell pad (see Lesson 10).

Cutter Leaves

This technique is the easiest and most widely used. With cutters, you can make any kind of leaf, and the technique for cutting and wiring is simple.

Divide 2 oz (57 g) gumpaste in half. Color each half a different shade of green (moss, leaf, forest, or mint). Wrap each half in plastic.

Roll ½ oz (14 g) green paste into a ball. Shape the ball into a log about 3 in. (7.6 cm) long. Rub the work surface with solid vegetable shortening and place the log on it. With a nonstick rolling pin, press the center of the length of the log, rocking the pin back and forth to flatten the log. Roll the paste from the center to one side, preferably toward yourself. Roll it petal thin at one side of the center and gradually thicken it on the other side. The center should be no thicker than ⅛ in. (3 mm).

Rub cornstarch on a clean area of the work surface. Place the flattened strip of gumpaste on the cornstarch. Cut out leaf shapes with the rose leaf, ivy, and hibiscus leaf cutters, positioning the cutters so the base of the leaf is on the thick part of the strip and the tip is on the thin part. Cut as many leaves as possible and place them under plastic wrap.

Repeat this technique with the rest of the green gumpaste.

Wiring and Embossing

To wire cut leaves, dip the tip of a 28-gauge wire into egg white and insert it into the thick part of the leaf to about ¼-in. (6 mm) deep. Let dry until all the leaves are wired.

Place each leaf in a silicone leaf press and firmly press the top and bottom presses to give it texture. Soften each leaf by placing it on a cell pad and applying light to medium pressure with the dogbone tool around the edges.

Coloring

Adding petal dust to leaves helps bring them to life. Divide a small portion of green petal dust into three parts. Add a little cornstarch to one portion for a lighter tone, daffodil yellow to another portion for an autumn leaf, and leave the third portion as is. Have some burgundy or cosmos (pinkish) petal dust on your palette.

Brush the center of each leaf with the lighter green. Blend the color beyond the center of the leaf, but do not go near the edge. Turn the leaf over and do the same thing. Brush the center of the leaf with the darkest green. This accents the veins and is used last at the very edge of the leaf. Turn the leaf over and do the same thing.

Add a little color—the green-yellow mixture or the cosmos—to the upper left corner of the leaf, where the sun would hit. Then brush the darkest green or burgundy color at the very edge. This gives the illusion that the sun has slightly scorched the edge of the leaf.

The color of each leaf can vary. Some leaves can be made deeper by using burgundy first and then adding dark green for the center and pink at the upper edge. Use real leaves as models or guides when you practice.

Shine

To give a natural shine to your leaves, pass them over a boiling kettle and allow the steam to coat them front and back. Pass each leaf several times to coat it. Allow the leaves to air dry.

Floral Corsage Sprays

Designing floral sprays is an art unto itself. It requires observation, the ability to create a pleasing line, and a focal point. Here we create a corsage. In Lesson 15, we explore sprays.

Corsage

Simple corsages include 8 to 12 leaves, a variety of blossoms and buds totaling 40 to 45 flowers, and 8 mimosa bunches. Decorating the corsage with fabric ribbons adds elegance to the presentation. Corsages and sprays require that smaller sprays be built into larger ones.

Look at the photograph that shows the placement of each bunch of flowers, foliage, and ribbon. To begin, add two or three blossoms, one or two buds, and one bunch of five mimosas to a leaf. The buds should be the highest point on top of the leaf and the blossoms closer to the bottom of the leaf. The mimosas are on top of the blossoms. Adjust each blossom and bud so that no two flowers are on the same plane. Tape the corsage with florist tape to hold it together (see Illustration 14.10).

Practice making three more sets of these minor corsages. Once you feel comfortable making them, make two major corsages by adding five blossoms, three buds, and two mimosa sprays per leaf.

Illustration 14.10
Suggested placement of blossoms for minor corsages.

Pulling It Together

Place one major corsage spray on the work surface and set a minor corsage spray on each side of it. Be sure the center spray is ½ to 1 in. (1.3 to 2.54 cm) higher than the two minor sprays. Carefully tape the three corsage sprays together with florist tape.

Make another corsage spray with one major spray and two minor sprays. Tape securely. Now you have two sprays. Put the sprays together, one spray pointing to the 12 o'clock position and the other to the 6 o'clock position. Tape them as closely together as possible without injuring the flowers. Carefully pull the taped flowers apart to reveal the beautiful spray. Tape sprays of ribbon together for a beautiful finish (see Illustration 14.11).

Illustration 14.11
A beautifully arranged corsage.

END-OF-LESSON REVIEW

1. Why is the term *pulled blossom* used to describe the making of various types of foliage, cherry blossoms, hyacinths, forget-me-nots, and four- and five-petal blossoms?

2. What material is used to make stamens for cherry blossoms?

3. What food product is used to make pollen for mimosas?

4. What sugarcraft product is used to give the pollen depth of color?

5. Describe the technique used to add sheen to leaves.

PERFORMANCE TEST

Make the following gumpaste blossoms and foliage:

1. Fifteen blossoms, including four- and five-petal blossoms with buds, cherry blossoms, and hyacinths. Color each blossom and bud with petal dust.

2. Fifteen mimosas.

3. Three pulled leaves, any variety. Petal dust each leaf.

4. Six cutter leaves, any variety. Petal dust each leaf and give it sheen.

ADVANCED GUMPASTE FLOWERS

Classic Rose, Full-blown or Open Rose, Carnation, Hibiscus, Tiger Lily, Arum (Calla) Lily, Anthurium Lily, Azalea, Cymbidium Orchid, and Closed Tulip

You will need the following supplies to complete this lesson:

Quick Gumpaste (page 274)

cell pad

ball or dogbone tool

veining tool

nonstick rolling pin

Xacto knife

modeling stick (sharpened dowel)

24- and 28-gauge florist wires

cotton thread

florist tape

silicone leaf press and flower formers (or cornhusk)

gel food colors

petal dust colors

gumpaste floral cutters: rose, calyx carnation, round scalloped shapes, hibiscus, tiger lily, azalea, cymbidium orchid, calla, anthurium lily

#0, #1, #3, and #5 sable paintbrushes

rounded toothpicks

plastic wrap

cornstarch

white vegetable shortening

egg whites

white plastic stamens

cornmeal

angular tweezers

These advanced gumpaste flowers are the hallmark of the cake decorating industry. Learning them can dramatically improve your business and add significant professionalism and style to your iced cakes. These flowers, skillfully produced, will give you and your prospective clients a wide range of choices in both design and price.

Purchasing real or lifelike silk flowers is the first step in gaining a better understanding of what the blooms really look like—their shape, their color, their shading. The next step is translating this understanding into gumpaste, gel food color, and petal dust. To aid this study, this lesson divides the flowers into groups.

New Skill: Classic Rose, Full-blown or Open Rose, Carnation, and Azalea

Quick Prep

1 recipe Quick Gumpaste (page 274)
gel food colors
rounded toothpicks
#1, #3, and #5 sable paintbrushes
petal dust in various shades
rose and calyx gumpaste cutters
azalea gumpaste cutter
carnation gumpaste cutter or small rounded scalloped
    cookie cutter
white cotton thread
plastic wrap
nonstick rolling pin
cornstarch
white vegetable shortening
1 oz (28 g) egg whites
Xacto knife
ball or dogbone tool
cell pad
white plastic stamens
florist tape
24-gauge white or green florist wires
modeling stick (sharpened dowel)

CLASSIC ROSE

Measure out 6 to 8 oz (170 to 228 g) Quick Gumpaste. The balance will be used for the open rose, carnation, and azalea. Color the paste a pastel shade using gel colors.

Shape about ¼ oz (7 g) paste into a round ball and then into a cone. Place the cone onto the pattern in Illustration 15.1 to determine what size rose to make. The cone should fit within the pattern you choose. Make several of these cones as flower bases.

Make a hook at the end of either a 24-gauge white or green florist wire. Dip the end of the hook into egg whites and then ease it into the large end of the cone to a depth of about ½ in. (1.3 cm). Secure the paste to the wire by pinching it. Repeat with two more cones. Let dry at least several hours or overnight.

Rub a little white vegetable shortening on the work area. With a nonstick rolling pin, roll out about 2 oz (57 g) of the remaining gumpaste until you can

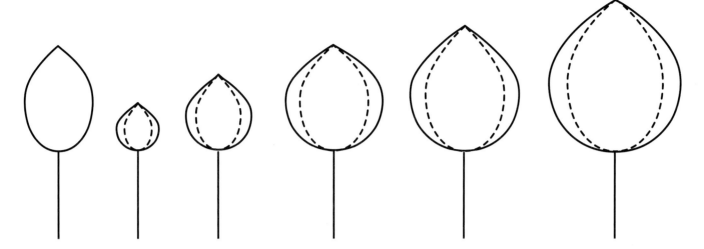

Illustration 15.1
Classic rose pattern in different sizes. The rose base should fit within the stitched lines.

see through it. Carefully pick up the paste and put it on a surface that is lightly sprinkled with cornstarch. Cut out four petals using the pattern you selected for the rose base or a metal or plastic cutter of similar size. Place the cutouts on a cell pad and lightly soften the edges with a ball or dogbone tool. Keep the other petals covered with plastic wrap to prevent them from drying.

Pick up a rose base and lightly brush it with egg white. Pick up one of the petals, holding it in one hand with the wired base in your other hand. Bring the petal bottom one-third the distance from the top of the petal and press it to the base. Tuck the left side of the petal to the base and overlap the right side of the petal, leaving a tiny opening at the top. Slightly pull the right side back with your thumb for a nice detail (see Illustration 15.2).

Decorator's Hint

Note that the first petal should be higher than the base when you attach it. Otherwise, it will not be large enough to overlap the top of the base.

Illustration 15.2
Classic rose (from left to right): a ball of gumpaste, the ball shaped into a cone, hooked florist wire, the hooked end of the florist wire inserted about ½-in. (1.3 cm) deep into the base of the cone, a rose petal, the first petal attached to the cone base, the second petal slightly higher than the first, a half-rose, the calyx, and the completed classic rose.

Decorator's Hint

When attaching the second set of petals, start the fifth petal at any seam or slightly to the left or right of any seam. This avoids the seam getting in the way of the overlapping petals.

Decorator's Hint

When attaching large petals to the rose base, you may have to turn the rose upside down to dry. After 15 to 20 minutes, turn the rose right side up and pinch the petals for a final touch.

Decorator's Hint

When making the stamens for a full-blown rose, wrap your index and middle fingers 30 times instead of the 10 times for the cherry blossom stamens. This will make two sets of stamens.

Brush the first petal and base lightly with egg white. Place the second petal over the seam of the first and slightly higher. Before attaching the next petal, brush the right side of the second petal about one-third the distance, if right-handed. If left-handed, brush the left side of the second petal. Attach the third petal to the brushed side of the second, overlapping by about one-third. Brush the third petal with egg white one-third the distance to the right of the petal, if right handed. Attach the fourth petal to the newly brushed side, with the right side inside the second petal and overlapping it. This is a rosebud (see Illustration 15.2).

With the same cutter, cut five more petals. Soften the edge of each petal and cover with plastic wrap to prevent drying.

Lightly brush the sides of the rosebud with egg white. Attach a fifth petal to the seam of any of the overlapped petals. This petal should be slightly taller or the same size as the previous petals. Brush and overlap each of the remaining four petals. Once all are attached, pinch the center of each petal for roselike detailing. This is a half-rose. Let this dry for 24 hours before attaching the final petals (see Illustration 15.2).

Place the dry half-rose inside the next rose base pattern to determine the next pattern or cutter to use. This last series of petals will cover the half-rose from top to bottom to make a full rose.

Roll out the paste and cut five more petals, softening each with a ball or dogbone tool. Because of their larger size, let these petals dry slightly before attaching them to the half-rose. Lightly brush the half-rose base with egg white. Attach each petal as you did the last five of the half-rose. They should be the same height as or slightly taller than the previous petals.

To complete the rose, roll out about ½ oz (14 g) moss-green or mint-green gumpaste. Cut out the calyx with a medium-size calyx cutter. Ease the calyx on the wire first, and then brush each sepal with egg white and ease the calyx onto the back of the rose. Put a small pea-sized bit of green paste on the back of the calyx and shape it onto the wire to complete the rose (see Illustration 15.2).

To color the rose, select petal dusts that offer both luster and contrast. For example, for a pink rose use mainly cosmos (pinkish) petal dust and contrast it with violet or purple petal dust.

Brush the center of the rose with cosmos petal dust. Next, brush the inside of each petal with cosmos petal dust. Finally, add violet or purple petal dust to the edge of each petal, including the center bud, for a beautiful contrast.

FULL-BLOWN OR OPEN ROSE

Make the stamens that will be the center of this beautiful flower. The procedure is the same as for cherry blossom stamens (see Lesson 14). Use the balance of the pinkish paste from the classic rose to complete the full-blown rose.

Brush the stamens cosmos petal dust to tint them a deep pink (see Illustration 15.3), then brush the tips with egg white. Add a pollen detail by dipping the tips in burgundy or red wine petal dust.

For the center of a full-blown rose, shape about ⅛ oz (3.5 g) paste into a round ball and ease it onto the wired stamens. Brush the florist tape while holding together the ends of the thread and the wire hook with egg white. Ease the ball of paste onto the florist tape and about 1/16 in. (1.5 mm) beyond. It should just cover the bottom of the stamens. Pinch the bottom of the ball of paste to secure it to the wire, completing the rose's center. Let dry for at least several hours or overnight (see Illustration 15.3).

Place the rose center in the rose base pattern to determine which size pattern or cutter to use. Roll out the pink paste and cut three petals. Soften the edges of each petal and cover them with plastic wrap to prevent drying.

Illustration 15.3
Full-blown rose (from left to right): To make the stamens, hook florist wire around a wrapped ring of cotton thread; cut across the center of the thread ring; tape the thread to the florist wire and petal dust the cotton thread to give it color; a ball of gumpaste; the ball of paste inserted into the florist wire and secured at the base of the stamens; the rose base with the first three petals attached.

Brush the base of the full-blown rose with egg white and place the first petal on the base. The tip of the petal should be about ¼-in. (6 mm) taller than the tip of the stamens. Shape the bottom of the petal to the rose's base. Brush egg white on the side of the petal (the right side, if right-handed; the left side, if left-handed) and attach the second petal to the first. Brush egg white on the side of the second petal and attach the third petal, sticking the right side inside the first so the first overlaps the third. This is the same technique used on the classic rose. Open and pinch the petals as you did for the classic rose (see Illustration 15.3). Let dry for 1 hour.

With the same cutter, cut out another five petals. Attach these petals as you did for the classic rose. Pinch each petal and let dry for at least several hours or overnight.

With a larger cutter, cut out the final five petals and attach them the same way as the last round of petals. Attach a calyx under the full-blown rose. Apply cosmos and violet or burgundy petal dust to complete the flower.

CARNATION

Measure out 4 oz (114 g) paste. Color 3 oz (85 g) of the paste a pastel tone. Alternatively, leave it white. Color the remaining 1 oz (28 g) mint or moss green. Wrap the paste in plastic to prevent drying.

To make the carnation bases, roll a pea-sized amount of paste into a tiny ball. Dip the end of a 24-gauge white or green wire in egg white and ease the ball onto the wire. Place your thumb and middle finger on the wired ball of paste and rotate it back and forth, applying pressure at the end of the paste to secure it to the wire. The completed base should look like a cotton swab and be no longer than ¼ to ½ in. (6mm to 1.3 cm). Make several bases.

Choose carnation cutters ¾ to 1 in. (1.9 to 2.54 cm) in size, or rounded scalloped cookie cutters that are the same size. These also make beautiful carnations.

Roll out the colored or neutral paste onto vegetable shortening until it is petal thin. Transfer the paste onto cornstarch. Cut out three petals with the carnation or cookie cutter and cover two of them with plastic wrap. Place the third petal on a little cornstarch and cut little slits in each of the scallops, about ¼-in. (6 mm) deep.

Place ½ in. (1.3 cm) of a rounded toothpick on the petal. Use either your index or middle finger to rotate the toothpick back and forth to ruffle the petal (see Illustration 15.4). Do this on each of the scallops. Ruffle the other two petals and cover them again with plastic to keep them moist.

Brush the carnation base with egg white and ease the wire through the center of one of the petals. Sandwich the base in the center of the petal (see Illustration 15.5). Brush egg white up the petal's center and overlap the left side. Put a little egg white on the overlapped side and overlap the right side of the petal. Gently gather the petal, applying light pressure at the trumpet while carefully shaping the flower. This is the first floret (see Illustration 15.5).

Brush egg white under the first floret and ease the second petal onto it as you did the first. Sandwich the floret and overlap the petal. Gently gather the petal to make the floret fuller. Repeat with the third petal; however, reverse this petal so the ruffles are on the underside. Egg wash, sandwich, and overlap the petal. Gently gather until the ruffles are full and lush. Use a toothpick to fluff the ruffles (see Illustration 15.5).

For a classic calyx, shape ¼ oz (7 g) green paste into a cone. Put the modeling stick in a little cornstarch and insert it in the wide end of the cone. Roll the modeling stick with the paste on the work surface to widen the interior of the paste. Reverse the wide end and place it on the work surface, making a wide-brimmed hat. Pinch the brim to make it smaller. Roll a rounded toothpick on the wide part of the hat, making it as thin as possible. Place a small rose calyx cutter over the brim and cut out the calyx. Insert a modeling stick into the cavity and widen it by pressing each of the sepals against the stick.

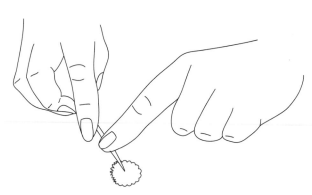

Illustration 15.4
To ruffle the carnation petal, rotate a rounded toothpick back and forth along it.

Illustration 15.5
Carnation (clockwise from left): The carnation base wire is eased through the first petal, the base is sandwiched between the petal halves, the petal is gently overlapped, the first floret, a second petal is added to the carnation, the calyx, and the completed carnation.

To complete the flower, ease the carnation into the calyx. Brush the interior of the calyx with egg white and place the carnation trumpet inside the calyx. Place a rounded toothpick ¼ in. (6 mm) from the bottom of the calyx and apply pressure to it as you turn the wire. This creates a little bud under the calyx. Pinch the end of the bud to secure it to the wire (see Illustration 15.5).

To color the carnation, brush the center of the carnation with a deep shade. Carefully brush the same color over each ruffle.

AZALEAS

Measure out the balance of the gumpaste—about 4 oz (114 g). Color half of the paste and keep the rest as a reserve. The paste can be white or colored red, burgundy, or yellow.

Prepare the stamens for the center of the azalea. Eleven stamens are needed to make up the flower. You will need to use plastic stamens, as sewing thread is too weak for so little. Prepare six stamens and secure them on a hooked 24-gauge wire. When they are folded, you will have twelve stamens. Cut off one or leave it at twelve. Tape the stamens securely with florist's tape. Pull one of the centered stamens to make it higher than the rest. This is the pistil, or dominant stamen.

Shape ½ oz (14 g) gumpaste into a cone (see Illustration 15.6a). Dip a modeling stick into cornstarch and insert it into the head of the cone. Roll the modeling stick within the cone (see Illustration 15.6b), applying pressure to open the paste to form a shape like a wide-brimmed hat (see Illustrations 15.6c, 15.6d, and 15.6e), as you did for the classic carnation calyx.

Decorator's Hint

For a quick carnation calyx, roll out green paste petal thin and cut with a small or miniature rose calyx cutter. Ease the calyx onto the carnation. Brush the sepals with egg white and secure the calyx to the back of the carnation. Next, roll a tiny ball of green paste and ease it onto the wire. Secure it to the end of the calyx and pinch it to secure it to the wire.

Illustration 15.6
Creating the azalea flower.

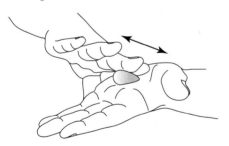

(a) Shape the gumpaste into a cone.

(b) Roll a modeling stick within the head of the cone.

(c) Use pressure to form a wide-brimmed hat.

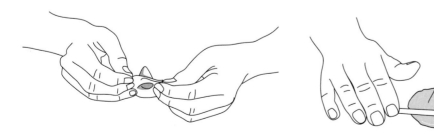

(d and e) Use your fingers or the modeling stock to flatten the brim of the hat.

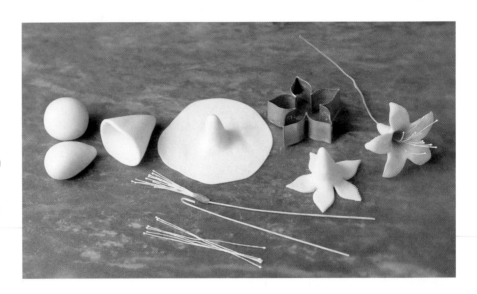

Illustration 15.7
Azalea (from bottom left to right): plastic stamens, florist wire, the stamens attached to the florist wire, a ball of gumpaste shaped into a cone, the cone opened using a modeling stick, the cone shaped like a wide-brimmed hat, an azalea cutter, the gumpaste hat after the azalea cutter is used, and the completed azalea.

Decorator's Hint

Some azalea variations are very ruffled. To emphasize the ruffles, use a ball or dogbone tool on the cell pad to ruffle the petals when they are just cut.

Place the azalea cutter over the wide-brimmed hat and cut out the flower. Press each of the petals on a flower former to form lines and carefully soften the edge of each petal with a ball or dogbone tool. Brush egg white on the florist's tape of the stamens and insert wire through the azalea's center. Apply pressure to secure the trumpet of the flower to the wire.

To color the flower, lightly brush the azalea's center with a soft burgundy petal dust. Use a toothpick to add gel food color burgundy dots on one or two of the petals. These should be deep inside the flower and extend to the middle of the petal (see Illustration 15.7).

New Skill: Arum or Calla Lily, Anthurium Lily, Closed Tulip

Quick Prep

1 recipe Quick Gumpaste (page 274)
gel food colors
rounded toothpicks
#1, #3, and #5 sable paintbrushes
petal dust in various shades
arum/calla lily cutters
anthurium lily cutter or pattern
medium-size tulip cutter or pattern
flower former or corn husk, tulip press, and leaf press
plastic wrap
nonstick rolling pin
cornstarch
white vegetable shortening
1 oz (28 g) egg whites
Xacto knife
ball or dogbone tool
cell pad
4 oz (114 g) cornmeal
florist tape
24-gauge white or green florist wires
modeling stick (sharpened dowel)

ARUM OR CALLA LILY

Measure out 8 oz (228 g) paste. Color 5 oz (140 g) of the paste a bright lemon yellow. Keep the balance of the paste white or choose a pastel or deep color for the lily. Wrap the paste in plastic to prevent drying.

For the spadix (base) of the flower, measure out ¼ oz (7 g) yellow paste and shape it into a 2-in. (5.1 cm) cylinder or elongated cone. Place the cone against the pattern to ensure the correct size. Dip ¼ in. (6 mm) of a 24-gauge wire into egg white and ease the wire into the pointed end of the cone to a depth of about ½ in. (1.3 cm). Pinch the end of the paste to secure it to the wire. Make several more bases and allow them to dry for at least several hours or overnight.

For a pollen effect, dip the spadix in egg white and coat it with cornmeal (see Illustration 15.8). Let dry for 2 hours.

For the spathe (petal) of the flower, roll out the other part of the measured gumpaste on vegetable shortening until it is petal thin. Place this on a work surface dusted with cornstarch. Cut out a petal with a metal or plastic cutter. Press a flower former or cornhusk onto the petal to form lines. Place the petal on a cell pad and soften the edges with a ball or dogbone tool (see Illustration 15.8).

To assemble, brush the bottom of the petal with a little egg white and place the cone at the bottom center. The bottom of the cone should be just inside the petal's edge. Lap the right side of the petal over the cone. Brush a little egg white on the overlapped side and lap the left side of the petal over the right. Slightly open the petal and fold the sides back for a more natural shape (see Illustration 15.8).

To color the lily, brush daffodil-yellow petal dust in the center of the flower, slightly under the spadix and extending up toward the tip. The color should fade

Decorator's Hint

Some of the yellow paste can be used for the spadix for the anthurium lily.

Illustration 15.8
Arum lily (bottom row): a ball of gumpaste for the spadix, florist wire, the spadix with florist wire inserted ½-in. (1.3 cm) deep, and the spadix rolled in cornmeal to give the effect of pollen. (Middle row): the spathe, or petal, for the lily and the spathe after the edges are softened. (Top row): the spathe is wrapped around the base of the spadix and the completed arum lily.

out ½ to 1 in. (1.3 to 2.54 cm) before the top edge. Brush yellow petal dust around the flower's trumpet and back. Then brush moss-green petal dust over the same area and blend the green color with the yellow petal dust. Make the color more concentrated near the bottom of the flower.

ANTHURIUM LILY

For the spathe (petal), measure out 3 oz (85 g) gumpaste. You can leave it white or color it a bright or deep red, burgundy, forest green, or bright yellow. Wrap the paste in plastic to prevent drying.

For the spadix (base), form some of the yellow paste you made for the arum lily into an elongated cone. Dip a 24-gauge wire in egg white and insert it at the wide end. Pinch to secure the paste to the wire. Allow to dry for several hours or overnight. When dried, brush the base in egg white and dip it in the cornmeal for pollen. Let dry for several more hours.

Roll out the paste you set aside for the spathe onto vegetable shortening until petal thin. If you don't have a cutter for this flower, trace the pattern from one in Appendix 1. Cut out the pattern, place it on the rolled-out paste, and carefully cut out the pattern with an Xacto knife. Cut out two more petals and cover them with plastic wrap to prevent drying.

Add texture and detail to the petals by placing them inside a silicone leaf press. For a waxy look, brush the front of the petals with egg whites and let dry for 1 hour.

Decorator's Hint

The arum or calla lily is quite bright and colorful. The flower can be petal dusted with yellow in the center and burgundy around the bottom trumpet and up the back, followed with moss green. The flower can also be petal dusted with gold, orange, or forest green.

Illustration 15.9
Anthurium lily (from bottom to top): a gumpaste ball (used to form the spadix), florist wire, the spadix with the florist wire inserted, the spadix is rolled in cornmeal to look like pollen, the spathe for the lily, a leaf press (used to give texture to the spathe), and the wire from the spadix pierces the spathe to begin to assemble the lily.

To assemble, place a petal brushed with egg white near the edge of a piece of Styrofoam. Using the wire from the cone, pierce the bottom of the petal about ½ in. (1.3 cm) from the base of the flower (see Illustration 15.9). Push the wire through the bottom of the petal until the base of the cone makes contact. The wire should extend through the Styrofoam and out the side for easy removal. Let dry for 24 hours.

Carefully push the wire through the Styrofoam and remove the dry flower. Brush the back of the flower with egg white and let dry for several hours with the tip of the wire just piercing the Styrofoam.

No petal dusting is necessary on a waxy flower.

CLOSED TULIP WITH BUD

Measure out the balance of the prepared gumpaste, about 5 oz (140 g). You can leave it uncolored for white tulips or color it a bright yellow, purple, or cranberry red.

To make the base, shape ¼ oz (7 g) into a cone like that for a rose. Dip a hooked 24-gauge wire in egg white and ease it into the bottom of the paste. Secure the bottom of the paste to the wire and let dry for ½ hour. Score three equal lines around the cone from bottom to tip with a veining tool or a rounded toothpick. The scored base is a tulip bud, or you can use the scores as a guide for placing tulip petals. Make several buds and let dry for several hours or overnight.

For the petals, select a tulip pattern or cutter, if available. Closed tulips can be made in an oval shape or have a scalloped top with rounded edges and a shaped bottom. To create the petals, roll out some of the colored paste on vegetable shortening. Place a pattern over the paste and cut out six petals; alternatively, transfer the paste onto cornstarch and cut out six petals. Cover the petals with plastic wrap until ready to use.

Add texture to each petal by firmly pressing it in a tulip press. You can soften the edges of the petals with a dogbone tool, if you like.

Brush a dried tulip bud with egg white and place the first petal at a seam. The petal should be at least ½-in. (1.3 cm) taller than the tip of the bud. Secure the petal to the base and use the base to shape the bottom of the tulip. Lightly cup the tip of the petal forward. Overlap the second petal about one-third the distance of the first petal. Attach the second petal with a little egg white. Repeat with the third petal, making sure it fits inside the first petal. Let dry for a ½ hour.

To attach the last three petals, lightly brush the tulip with egg white and attach the first petal at an overlapped seam. Attach the next petal with egg white one-third the distance of the previous petal. Follow this with the last petal, making sure to tuck it inside the fourth. Shape the top of each petal and allow the flower to dry thoroughly.

When the tulip is dry, brush it with daffodil-yellow petal dust, starting at the bottom and allowing the color to fade toward the top. Brush the edge of each petal with yellow or orange petal dust. Finally, brush green petal dust at the bottom of the flower, allowing the color to fade as it is brushed upward. See Illustration 15.10 for the stages of creating a closed tulip.

For the bud, brush the bottom of the flower with yellow petal dust, allowing the color to fade as it is brushed upward. Brush moss-green color at the bottom of the flower and complete the bud by brushing the base of the bud with chocolate-brown petal dust.

Decorator's Hint

Instead of brushing egg white on the back of the flower, make gum glue by mixing 1 part gum arabic with 6 parts water. Shake this mixture in a small container and let stand for several hours in the refrigerator. Reshake the container before using and keep refrigerated between uses. Gum glue gives a shiny appearance to any flower or surface.

Illustration 15.10
Closed tulip (counterclockwise from bottom right): gumpaste to roll out for tulip petals, a tulip petal, the tulip petal after texture is added from a tulip press, gumpaste to create the tulip base, florist wire, the cone base with florist wire inserted, the tulip base with scored lines (for placing the petals), the first petal applied to the base at the scored seam, the closed tulip with all petals attached, and the completed closed tulip brushed with petal dust.

New Skill: Hibiscus, Tiger Lily and buds, Cymbidium Orchid, and Flower Arranging

Quick Prep

1 recipe Quick Gumpaste (page 274)
gel food colors
rounded toothpicks
#1, #3, and #5 sable paintbrushes
petal dust in various shades
hibiscus cutters
tiger lily cutter or freehand cutter
cymbidium orchid cutter
flower former or cornhusk, leaf press
plastic wrap
nonstick rolling pin
cornstarch
white vegetable shortening
1 oz (28 g) egg whites
Xacto knife
ball or dogbone tool
angled tweezers
veining tool
cell pad
4 oz (114 g) cornmeal
florist tape
24-gauge white or green florist wires
28-gauge white florist wires
20 white plastic stamens
modeling stick (sharpened dowel)

HIBISCUS

Measure out 5 oz (140 g) paste. Color 2 oz (57 g) of the pastel a light pink, yellow, violet, or lavender color. Color the remaining 3 oz (85 g) a deeper shade of the same color. The lighter shade of color is for the flower's center, called the *pistil*. The deeper shade of color is for the petals.

To make the pistil, shape ½ oz (14 g) of the lighter paste into a log about 2-in. (5.1 cm) long. Roll the paste in the center with the back of a paintbrush or a modeling stick to form a waist (see Illustration 15.11). Measure the paste against the pattern to be sure the size is appropriate (see Appendix 1 for Hibiscus pattern, p. 296). Dip 1 in. (2.54 cm) of 24-gauge wire into the egg white and ease it up the pistil and through the waist. Pinch the paste to secure it to the wire. With angled tweezers, make five ridges at the bottom of the pistil. Distribute the ridges evenly, making them between ¼- and ½-in. (3 to 6 mm) long (see Illustration 15.11).

Make the stigma by placing five ¼-in. (3 mm) stamens on top of the pistil. The stamens should have heads, which you will pollinate later with cornmeal. Cut five plastic stamens and place them symmetrically around the top of the pistil. Cut the remaining stamens (without heads) into ¼-in. (3 mm) pieces for a total of 30 to 40 stamens. Randomly attach the stamens at a 45-degree angle to the upper portion of the pistil, above the waist (see Illustration 15.11). Let dry for several hours or overnight.

For the petals, roll ½ oz (14 g) of the darker paste into a log about 3-in. (7.6 cm) long. Dip a 24-gauge wire in egg white and insert it about ½-in. (1.3 cm) into the end of the log. Pinch the log to secure it to the wire. Place the wired log on the vegetable shortening work surface and flatten the center of the log with a rolling pin. Roll the paste on either side of the centered wire with a modeling stick (see Illustration 15.12). This is the same procedure you used to make freehand foliage in Lesson 14.

Illustration 15.11 The stages to creating a hibiscus.

Illustration 15.12 Creating hibiscus petals.

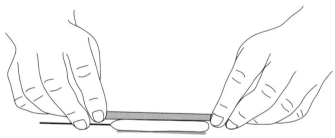

(a) With the florist wire inserted into the paste log, press a rolling pin in the center of the log and begin to flatten one side of the paste.

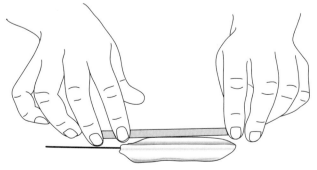

(b) Roll the paste on either side of the centered wire with a modeling stick to flatten it. It is now ready to be cut for the flower.

Place the wired paste on a lightly dusted cornstarch surface and cut out the petal with a hibiscus cutter. Remove the excess paste and wrap tightly in plastic. Firmly press the petal in a large leaf press. Remove the embossed petal and place it on a cell pad. Soften and ruffle the edges of the petal with a dogbone tool. Drape the petal over a rolling pin to dry in a natural curve (see Illustration 15.11). Using the same procedure, make four more petals. Let the five petals dry overnight on the rolling pin.

To color the hibiscus, brush the pistil with a slightly deeper shade of the paste color, extending the color up to the waist. Brush a little moss-green color over the bottom of the pistil and set aside. Brush the center of each petal with a deeper shade of petal dust than the paste color. Blend the color toward the sides of the flower but not as far as the edge. Brush the very edge of the flower with a contrasting color to add depth to the hibiscus. Brush a little moss green at the bottom of each petal.

When ready to assemble, arrange each petal between the ridges at the bottom of the pistil. Start with two to three petals, making sure the end of each is directly between two ridges. Tape the petals securely with florist tape. Add the balance of the petals to the pistil and retape the entire flower. Open the petals and turn one or two in the opposite direction for a more natural look (see Illustration 15.11).

TIGER LILY

Measure out 5 oz (140 g) of gumpaste. Leave 4½ oz (128 g) neutral or color it a pumpkin color, light orange, or mint green. This will be used for the petals. Color the remaining ½ oz (14 g) a light or mint-green color. This will be for the stamens and the pistil. Wrap the paste in plastic to prevent drying.

Six stamens and one pistil are needed to complete the center of the flower. To make the stamens, roll a pea-sized amount of green paste into a tiny ball. Brush the length of a 28-gauge white florist wire about 4.5 to 5 inches (11.43 to 12.70 cm) long with egg white and thread the ball to the center of the wire (see Illustration 15.13). Place the wire and ball on the work surface and roll the ball back and forth with your middle finger, stretching the paste against the wire. Continue to roll the paste, using more fingers as it stretches. When the paste extends beyond the reach of your fingers, place the paste and wire between your hands and rub them back and forth to stretch the paste along the length of the wire. Continue to roll the paste until it extends beyond the wire. The paste will be extremely thin against the wire. Break off any excess and slightly curve the wired paste for a natural form (see Illustration 15.13). This is the first stamen. Make six more.

To create the pistil, roll out a seventh stamen, leaving a tiny piece of paste at the end of it and making it slightly longer than the other stamens. Shape the pistil to a natural curve and let it dry overnight. Once dry, surround the pistil with the other six stamens and tape them together with florist tape. Open the stamens for a more natural look.

For the petals, roll ¼ oz (7 g) paste into a 3-in. (7.6 cm) log. Dip a 24-gauge wire in egg white and insert about ½-in. (1.3 cm) deep into one end of the log. Pinch to secure the paste to the wire. Roll out the log and cut out the petal using the same technique as for the hibiscus or freehand foliage from Lesson 14. Press a cornhusk or leaf former onto the petal to create lines. Place the petal on a cell pad and score a line down the center with a veining tool. Lightly soften the edge of the petal with a dogbone tool, but be careful not to ruffle it. Drape the petal over a nonstick rolling pin and allow it to dry (see Illustration 15.13). Make five more petals plus one extra in case of breakage.

For the bud, roll ½ oz (14 g) paste into a large cone, 2½- to 3-in. (6.4 to 7.6 cm) long. Ease a 6-in. (15.2 cm) florist wire into the large end of the cone and pinch the paste to secure it to the wire. Let dry for 1 hour. Score six equal lines from the bottom to the tip of the paste with a veining tool.

Illustration 15.13
Tiger lily. The steps to create the petals for the flower (left) and the stamen and pistil (right).

Brush each petal with petal dust in a deeper shade of the paste color. Blend the color toward the edge of each petal. For a white lily, use a soft leaf green or mint green to color the petals. Petal dust the edge of each petal as well. The base of each petal should be moss green. For sheen, brush the stamens with a little super pearl petal dust. Petal dust the top of the pistil with chocolate brown or moss green. Petal dust the bud with the same color used for the petals, allowing it to fade toward the tip of the bud. Brush the bottom of the bud with moss-green petal dust. For the dots on each petal, use a toothpick and moss green food color. Dip the toothpick into the color first. Carefully add random dots from the base of each petal to the middle and gradually ease off.

To assemble the flower, attach the three largest petals to the center spray of stamens and tape securely. Add the three smaller petals at the seams and tape securely. Open the petals and stamens for a more natural look (see Illustration 15.13).

CYMBIDIUM ORCHID

Measure out the balance of the prepared paste, about 6 oz (170 g). Color 5 oz (140 g) a light yellow, moss green, pink, or natural white. Reserve 1 oz (28 g) for the lip of the flower, which is generally a lighter color.

For the sepals (petals), roll a ¼-oz (7 g) ball of gumpaste into a long sausage shape. Dip about ½ in. (1.3 cm) of 24-gauge wire into egg white and insert it into one end of the gumpaste log to a depth of about ½ in. (1.3 cm) and pinch one end to secure the paste to the wire. This is the same technique as for hibiscus and tiger lily petals. Cut out petals with an orchid petal cutter and emboss each front and back with a cornhusk or flower former to create lines. Carefully

Illustration 15.14
Cutting out the sepals, the lip and the column of the Cymbidium Orchid (from left to right). The sepals and lip are shaped and dried to form a natural curve.

Illustration 15.15
The steps to assembling an orchid.

Illustration 15.16
Creating a floral spray (from left to right): a ball of fondant used as the base of the spray; flowers, leaves, and buds that make up the spray; beginning to build the spray.

soften the petal on a cell pad, but don't ruffle it. Drape the petal over a rolling pin and allow it to dry. Make four more petals and one extra in case of breakage (see Illustration 15.4).

The lip of the flower should be a lighter shade than the petals. To accomplish this, mix half of the neutral paste with half of the colored paste used for the orchid. Once the color is even, roll ¼ oz (7 g) into a sausage shape. Dip a 24-gauge wire in egg white and insert it into the sausage as you did for the petals. Cut out the lip with the orchid lip cutter. (It is, as always, a good idea to make a spare in case of breakage.) Emboss the lip with a cornhusk to form lines and lightly soften the edge of the lip. Ruffle the three scallops—only in front of the lip—with a rounded toothpick. Carefully bend the ruffled lip backward and raise the two back scallops, pinching them toward the center of the lip. Drape the lip over a rolling pin and allow to dry (see Illustration 15.14).

While the lip is drying, complete its back by rolling a pea-sized bit of lighter-colored paste into a small sausage shape and pull the ends together to form an upside-down *U*. Brush the back of the drying lip with a little egg white and attach the *U* shape.

When the lip is dry, make the column of the flower by shaping a small ball, less than ⅛ oz (3.5 g) lighter-colored gumpaste into a cone. Dip a 24-gauge wire in egg white and ease it into the cone's narrow end. Hollow out the cone shape with a ball or dogbone tool, leaving a ridge at the top of the column. Attach a tiny ball of paste at the center top of the column with a little egg white. Let dry for several hours.

Complete the lip by attaching the column to its back and taping securely with florist's tape (see Illustration 15.15 for the steps to assembling the orchid).

To color the orchid, petal dust each sepal in a deeper shade of the paste color chosen. Brush the color up the sepal's center, leaving the edges neutral. Then brush the deepened shade of petal dust color to the edge of each sepal. Brush a little moss green at the base of each sepal. For the lip, use petal dust in a deeper shade of the paste color. Then, brush daffodil-yellow petal dust lightly, under the upside-down *U* shape and just above the ruffles. (This would apply to any lip in any color) Brush burgundy petal dust on the ruffled area only of the lip. Then paint the ruffled edge of the lip with burgundy paste or gel color to create depth. Using a rounded toothpick, paint little dots on the lip with burgundy gel colors, extending them from the *U* shape to the ruffled area of the lip.

Brush the upside-down *U* shape with egg white and sprinkle a little yellow cornmeal to create pollen details. Brush the center of the column with egg white and add cornmeal. Add dots of burgundy to the column's center as well.

To assemble the flower, tape two sepals to each side of the lip. Tape two more sepals slightly above the previous two. Last, tape the last sepal to the orchid, facing either inward or outward.

ARRANGING A ROUND SPRAY

Select flowers that will bring both lightness and fullness to the spray. Include one family of large flowers, medium-size flowers, and lots of blossoms, buds, and leaves. The flowers should not have to compete; rather, they should be harmoniously arranged. For example, a spray of orchids, roses, hibiscus, and lilies is way too much for a cake. This combination would do better in a large sugar vase as a centerpiece of a table.

To arrange a spray of roses, make a ball of 4 to 6 oz (114 to 170 g) commercial rolled fondant. Slightly flatten the ball and place it on the work surface. Cut the flowers' wires to 2-in. (5.1 cm) long. Space the larger roses equally around the ball of fondant and place one in the center. Add leaves between the roses and around the center. Add blossoms and buds above the leaves. Remember, no two flowers should be on the same plane. Next, add medium-size flowers such as carnations and azaleas to fill up the negative spaces. Add more blossoms, buds, and leaves to complete the spray (see Illustrations 15.16 and 15.17).

Illustration 15.17
A beautiful floral spray.

END-OF-LESSON REVIEW

1. What is the difference between a classic rose and a full-blown rose?

2. Why are plastic stamens used for the azalea flower?

3. How many petals make up a closed tulip?

4. What are the similarities and differences between an arum or calla lily and an anthurium lily?

5. What is another name for tiger lilies and cymbidium orchid petals?

6. What is the center petal of the orchid called?

7. How are dots applied to an azalea and the lip of an orchid?

8. What is used to form lines on a petal to give it texture?

PERFORMANCE TEST

Prepare a recipe of Quick Gumpaste and make six of following, including a hibiscus, tiger lily, or cymbidium orchid:

classic rose	3 carnations	3 closed tulips	2 anthurium lilies	tiger lily
full-blown rose	3 azaleas	2 arum (calla) lilies	hibiscus	cymbidium orchid

MINIATURE CAKES AND DECORATED COOKIES

You will need the following items to complete this lesson:

Butter Cookies (page 288)

Chocolate Rolled Fondant (page 272)

Marzipan (page 270)

half-sheet cakes (High-Yield Yellow Cake, page 277)

preserves

commercial rolled fondant

cookies

Glacé Icing for Cookies (page 268)

Glacé Icing for Petit Fours (page 269)

Meringue Powder Royal Icing (page 273)

raspberry preserves

sieved apricot jam

assorted mini-cookie cutters

serrated knife

offset metal spatula

simple syrup

water and granulated sugar

brandy or liquer

paper cones

squeezer bottles

nonstick rolling pin

corn syrup

pastry brush

melted chocolate

royal icing flowers

gel food colors

rounded toothpicks

metal tips: #18 star, PME 0 and #3 round tips

Petit fours are beautifully decorated bit-size cakes. They are often referred to as miniatures and are an important part of a Viennese table at lavish banquets and wedding receptions. These cakes can be iced with poured fondant, glacé icing, melted chocolate, marzipan, or rolled fondant. They come in four forms: petit four sec, glacé, *frais* and demi-sec. The sec are a variety of small cookies, such as financiers, madeleines, *palmiers*, and macaroons; the glacé are small decorated cakes with shiny poured icing; the *frais* is fruit tartlets, cream puffs, éclairs, and the demi-sec are sandwich filled dried cookies. Petit fours can be decorated with melted chocolate designs, royal icing piping, and/or royal icing flowers. For a high-end look, the bottom is dipped in tempered chocolate, or the sides are wrapped in transfer design paper or exquisite ribbons.

Iced and decorated cookies are important elements of any well-balanced, exquisite table. They are often packed in beautiful tiny boxes and given as wedding favors at receptions. For this purpose, these beautiful cookies can be decorated with royal icing flowers, and many are monogrammed and gilded with the couple's first, last, or shared initials.

New Skill: Petit Fours

Quick Prep

> 9 by 13 in. (13 by 22.9 cm) half-sheet cake [small quantity of High-Yield Yellow Cake (page 277) or Cherry/Cranberry Pound Cake (page 281)]
> 1 recipe Marzipan (page 270)
> Glacé Icing for Petit Fours (page 269)
> raspberry preserves
> sieved apricot jam
> assorted mini-cookie cutters: rounds, squares, ovals, hearts
> serrated knife
> offset metal spatula
> 4 oz (114 g) simple syrup
> 1:1 ratio of water and granulated sugar with 2 oz (57 g) of brandy or liqueur added
> paper cones

Decorator's Hint

1. If using a single rich layer, brush the top of the cake with simple syrup and then a thin layer of raspberry preserve. This will help glue the marzipan to the cake.

2. Traditionally, the cake is a dense almond cake, known as frangipane. The cake is cut into 1 in. (2.54 cm) or two to three thin layers, equaling 1 in. (2.54 cm).

Prepare the cake the day before and let it cool. Level it with a serrated knife and cut off rounded ends for an evenly rectangular cake.

Cut the cake in two and reserve one half. Carefully split the half-cake in two or three thin layers. Especially rich cakes—for example, the Cherry-Cranberry Pound Cake and the Almond-Walnut Pound Cake—need not be split.

To assemble, brush the bottom layer with simple syrup and then a thin layer of raspberry preserve. Place the second layer on top. Brush that layer with simple syrup and then a thin layer of raspberry preserve. Add the third layer. Brush the top layer with simple syrup and then a thin layer of sieved apricot preserve. This will help glue the marzipan to the cake.

Roll out the marzipan to ¼-in. (6 mm) thick and cut it to the approximate size of the cake. Roll the marzipan onto a rolling pin and unroll it onto the cake. Then roll the rolling pin over the marzipan to secure it. Trim the marzipan and the cake for a more attractive cut.

Measure the height of the cake. It should be ¾-in. to 1-in (1.9 to 2.54 cm) tall. If it is too tall, place plastic wrap over the cake, set a heavy weight on top to compress it, and refrigerate overnight. Whether or not the cake needs to be weighted, it can be wrapped in plastic and refrigerated until it is cut into small rounds, squares, or ovals. Once cut and iced, however, the petit fours should not be refrigerated, as condensation may change their appearance.

The next day, remove the weight and plastic wrap and measure the height of the cake. If the cake is still slightly taller than 1 in. (2.54 cm), you can get away with it. Cut the cake into the desired shapes with mini-cookie cutters and place them on a cooling rack over a large bowl.

Prepare the Glacé Icing for Petit Fours. Divide the icing among several bowls and color each bowl with a pastel food color. Cover with plastic wrap to prevent drying. Place one bowl of colored icing over a double boiler and stir as it begins to heat. The icing should be warm to the touch. Remove the icing from the double boiler, dry the bottom of the bowl, and place a large spoon in it. This will be used to ice the mini-cakes.

Begin by spooning a generous amount of the glacé icing over the mini-cakes, starting in the center of each cake and pouring in a widening circular motion. Check the sides of the cake to make sure the icing covers them. Keep a small offset metal spatula in your opposite hand and use it to help spread the icing on the sides of the cakes. Catch excess icing in the bowl under the cooling rack (see Illustration 16.1).

Allow the icing to set and dry before carefully removing the mini-cakes from the baking rack. When ready to do so, use a large offset metal spatula and scrape under the cake to prevent injury to the sides. Remove the cakes and place on parchment paper to begin decorating.

Decorator's Hint

Traditionally, commercial poured fondant is used to ice petit four glacé.

Illustration 16.1
Petit fours: Cut the cake into the desired shapes using mini-cookie cutters. To ice the petit four, place the mini-cake on a cooling rack over a bowl; ice the mini-cake by slowly and evenly pouring the icing at the center of the cake, catching excess icing in the bowl beneath the cooling rack.

Illustration 16.2
Iced and decorated petit fours.

Decorator's Hint

Attach icing flowers to petit fours with melted chocolate or royal icing. When attaching royal icing flowers to an iced cookie use royal icing.

The mini-cakes may be decorated with chocolate piping, royal icing, or royal icing flowers (see Illustration 16.2).

New Skill: Decorated Cookies

Quick Prep

1 recipe Butter Cookies (page 288)
1 recipe Glacé Icing for Cookies (page 268)
6 oz (170 g) White Rolled Fondant
6 oz (170 g) Chocolate Rolled Fondant (page 272)
6 oz (170 g) Meringue Powder Royal Icing (page 273)
6 4- to 6-in. (10.2 to 15.2 cm) squeezer bottles
paper cones
piping tips: #0 and #3 round
gel food colors
assorted cookie cutters
rounded toothpicks
nonstick rolling pin
3 fl oz (90 ml or 128 g) corn syrup
pastry brush

Divide the prepared butter cookie dough in two. Give half to a partner, if working in teams, or wrap it tightly in plastic and refrigerate for several days or freeze up to 3 months.

Roll out the dough to ⅛- to ¼-in. (3 to 6 mm) thick and cut out about 1½ dozen cookies. After baking, let cool on baking sheet.

GLACÉ ICED COOKIES

While the cookies are cooling, make up a double batch of Glacé Icing for Cookies. Measure out 3 to 4 oz (85 to 114 g) icing and set it aside for later use as outline icing. Divide the balance of the icing among four or five bowls.

Color each bowl of icing as desired and then add flavor to each using the icing color as your guide. Thus, match lemon extract, lemon juice, or banana flavoring to yellow icing and strawberry oil or kirsch (cherry brandy) to pink. The flavors should be subtle, not overwhelming. Pour the colored icing into individual squeeze bottles with caps to prevent drying or crusting over.

To outline the cookies, stiffen the reserved icing with several tablespoons of 10x confectioner's sugar to a medium-stiff consistency. This icing can be colored or left neutral, and it does not need to be flavored.

Place the #3 round tip in a paper cone and load the cone with 1 Tbsp (14 g) outline icing. Set aside. Select 10 baked cookies. The rest will be decorated later with rolled icing.

Starting just inside one cookie with the tip at a 45-degree angle, outline it with the #3 round tip (see Illustration 16.3). Outline all of the cookies.

Flooding

Remove the cap of one of the squeezer bottles. Place the tip of the bottle at the center of the cookie and begin to squeeze. Allow the icing to build up in the center but continue to squeeze until the icing approaches the outline. Stop and use a toothpick to move the icing to the outline. Work quickly, as the icing sets quickly (see Illustration 16.3).

Once the cookie is flooded, allow the icing to dry for 24 hours before doing any pipework. When the icing is dry, pipe out fine embroidery, a monogram gilded with gold, or a cameo molded from rolled fondant or modeling chocolate.

Single Webbing

This technique works best on rectangular cookies and requires two or more icing colors. This exercise calls for three icing colors. Starting at the left side of the cookie, squeeze a line of icing from the squeeze bottle, making it as straight as possible and about ¼-in. (6 mm) wide. Squeeze a second line of icing in a different color. Continue with the next line and a third color. Then repeat the first color, followed by the second and third. Use a toothpick to fill in spaces between the colors.

Position a toothpick at the upper left-hand corner of the cookie. Stick the toothpick into the icing and drag it to the right edge of the cookie. When you reach the right edge, move the toothpick slightly down and then drag it to the left edge of the cookie. Continue to drag the toothpick to the right and left until you run out of space. This is a single-webbed cookie (see Illustration 16.3).

Illustration 16.4 contains additional single webbing designs and a circular design using a toothpick. To achieve the circular design, rotate the toothpick in the circular motion—starting in the center and ending near the edge of the cookie.

Double Webbing

Take a just-iced single-webbed cookie and turn it one-quarter to the right. Position the toothpick at the left of the cookie and begin another single-web design. The resulting design will look even more intertwined (see Illustration 16.3).

Decorator's Hint
Meringue Powder Royal Icing can be used to outline the cookies.

Decorator's Hint
The flooding technique is described in Lesson 5 on Writing and in Lesson 11 on Advanced Royal Icing Piping and Design Skills.

Decorator's Hint
Alternatively, drag the toothpick from the top of the cookie to the bottom and reverse from the bottom to the top if the cookie is iced horizontally instead of vertically.

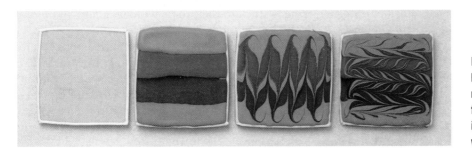

Illustration 16.3
Decorating cookies with glacé icing (from left to right): a cookie outlined with icing, the cookie flooded horizontally with different colors of icing, a single-webbed cookie, and a double-webbed cookie.

Illustration 16.4
Additional cookies using the single web and circular design technique.

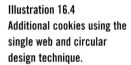

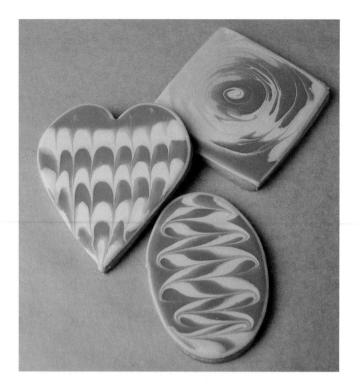

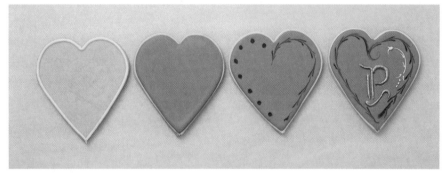

Illustration 16.5
Decorating a round or heart-shaped cookie with glacé icing (from left to right): a cookie outlined with icing, the cookie flooded with icing, small dots are piped around the edge of the cookie and a toothpick dragged from dot to dot to connect them, and a completed heart-shaped cookie with a gilded monogram.

Connecting Hearts

Flood a round or heart-shaped cookie. Before the icing begins to crust, squeeze small dots around the cookie's edge at ¼-in. (6 mm) intervals. Stick a toothpick into one of the dots and drag it to the next dot. Drag the toothpick through a third dot and continue dragging until all of the dots are connected. Notice the heart shapes connecting (see Illustration 16.5).

ROLLED ICED COOKIES

Cookies iced in modeling chocolate, rolled fondant, or marzipan do not need to be outlined in icing. The icing is stuck to the cookie with light corn syrup or a sieved apricot jam.

To begin, brush the cookies lightly with corn syrup or sieved apricot jam. Roll out modeling chocolate, rolled fondant, or marzipan to ⅛ to ¼ in. (3 to 6 mm) thick. Cut out the icing shapes with the same cookie cutter used for the butter cookies. Carefully place the icing shape on the cookie. The cookie is now ready to be decorated with royal icing pipework, flooded ovals, royal icing flowers, miniature marzipan fruits or vegetables, or beautiful chocolate roses (see Illustration 16.6).

Decorator's Hint

When rolling out rolled fondant, dust the work surface lightly with cornstarch. When rolling marzipan, dust the work surface lightly with 10x confectioner's sugar. When rolling out white modeling chocolate, dust the work surface with cornstarch, and for dark modeling chocolate or chocolate rolled fondant, use a scant amount of 10x confectioner's sugar.

Illustration 16.6
Decorated cookies, starting from the top left (clockwise): a rolled iced cookie with brush embroidery piping, a rolled iced cookie with a scalloped outline and a flooded monogram, a rolled iced cookie with cornelli lace around the edge of the cookie and a beautiful cameo, and a rolled iced cookie with a flooded monogram and satin stitch piping.

END-OF-LESSON REVIEW

1. What are petit fours sec? Give examples of this type of petit four.

2. What are petit fours glacé?

3. Briefly explain the procedures for icing petit fours.

4. What must be done before flooding a cookie with glacé icing?

5. Can an iced cookie be piped on just after it has been flooded?

6. How is rolled icing made to stick to cookies?

7. Can a cookie be piped on after it has been iced with rolled icing?

8. How are royal icing flowers attached to cookies or petit fours?

PERFORMANCE TEST

Perform the following exercises:

1. Decorate 12 petit fours with Glacé Icing for Petit Fours.

2. Decorate 6 cookies with Glacé Icing for Cookies.

3. Decorate 6 cookies with any combination of rolled icings.

CAKE BOARDS, COLOR CHARTS, PAINTING, AND MORE TECHNIQUES

You will need the following items to complete this lesson:

8-in. (20.3 cm) round and square cardboards

decorative foil

Xacto knife

masking tape

assorted gel or paste food colors

liquid whitener

artist tray

rounded toothpicks

small plastic mixing cups

paper cone

cornstarch

#2 pencil

Small Pansy Spray

fine sable paintbrushes, including #00, #0, #1, #3, and #5

PME 0 metal tip

triangular-cut parchment paper

3 oz (85 g) Quick Gumpaste (page 274)

cell pad

ball or dogbone tool

plunger cutters

3 oz (85 g) Meringue Powder Royal Icing (page 273)

Styrofoam cake with rolled icing

Crimper tools

In this lesson, you will learn the correct way to cover a round or square cardboard with decorative foil, how to combine food colors to make additional colors with the aid of a color chart, and to make simple sugar flowers, known as plunger flowers. These flowers can be used to decorate cakes, cookies, and petit fours.

This lesson also explores painting with food colors to create beautiful designs that can be added to an iced plaque or cake. Finally, it covers how to use crimper tools to give rolled iced cakes a decorative border.

New Skill: Covering a Cake Board

Quick Prep

8-in. (20.3 cm) square cardboard
8-in. (20.3 cm) round cardboard
decorative foil
masking tape
Xacto knife

A beautifully covered cake board is essential to cake decorating. Not only does it add to the beauty of the cake but it also provides a platform to which the decorator can add piped or hand-sculptured work, giving the illusion that the cake is larger than it actually is.

Deciding on the type of foil to cover a cake board is essential. If the cake is iced with buttercream, it is important to use a cake foil that is greaseproof. A

Illustration 17.1
Covering a cake board. Examples of square and round cake boards.

thin film of plastic is attached to the decorative foil to prevent spoiling the cake foil with the fat or oil from the buttercream.

When covering a cake board, the rule is simple. If the cardboard is round, a round piece of foil is needed. If it is square, a square piece of foil is key. If it is oval, an oval piece of foil is necessary. Never force a large piece of rectangular foil over a round cardboard. Its bulk will not allow the board to lie flat.

SQUARE CARDBOARD

Roll out decorative foil several inches larger than the cardboard. Cut the foil with an Xacto knife and trim it so it is about 2 in. (5.1 cm) larger on each side than the square cardboard.

Turn the cardboard over so the white side faces the nondecorative side of the foil. Fold the top edge of the foil over the board toward the center and tape it securely with masking tape. Fold the bottom edge of the foil toward the center of the cardboard and tape it securely with masking tape (see Illustration 17.1).

Turn the board one quarter to the right. Fold the left edge of the foil to the edge of the cardboard, forming a triangle. (See Illustration 17.1). Do the same for the right side of the cardboard. Tape the foil securely with masking tape on both sides. The board is complete (see Illustration 17.1).

ROUND CARDBOARD

Cut a round piece of decorative foil approximately 2 in. (5.1 cm) larger than the round cardboard. Pull the foil from the 12 o'clock position toward the center of the cardboard and tape it securely. Pull the foil from the 6 o'clock position toward the center of the cardboard and tape it securely. Repeat this for the 3 o'clock and 9 o'clock positions, taping each. The board and foil should have perfect tension (see Illustration 17.1).

Pull and gather the foil completely around the cardboard and tape each gathered section with masking tape. Overlap the taping to make a perfect fit. When the foiled board lies flat, it is complete (see Illustration 17.1).

New Skill: Color Chart

Quick Prep

gel or paste food colors
round toothpicks
liquid whitener
small plastic mixing cups

Mixing and matching food colors is essential in cake design. Often, through experimentation, the designer finds little tricks that are useful for coordinating color schemes.

One way to begin is by mixing colors together, along with liquid whitener. The whitener will develop the color so you can see its true tone. This is excellent practice. Take note of the color combinations you like so you can use them in the future. Once you know the color combination, simply add the color(s) directly to white buttercream, white rolled fondant, or gumpaste to achieve a perfect match.

If your colors are too bright, tone them down with a little violet or brown. If the colors are too dark, add more white icing or a little liquid whitener.

The first two columns of the color chart below comprise a recommended list of colors for the decorator or pastry chef to purchase at a local supply house. A color swatch chart is also provided as a guide (see Illustration 17.2).

To begin, we list the most frequently used combinations and their results.

Illustration 17-2
Color swatch chart.

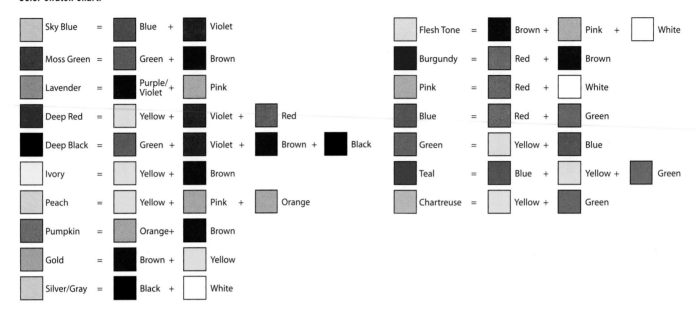

Sky Blue	=	Blue	+	Violet
Moss Green	=	Green	+	Brown
Lavender	=	Purple/Violet	+	Pink
Deep Red	=	Yellow	+	Violet + Red
Deep Black	=	Green	+	Violet + Brown + Black
Ivory	=	Yellow	+	Brown
Peach	=	Yellow	+	Pink + Orange
Pumpkin	=	Orange	+	Brown
Gold	=	Brown	+	Yellow
Silver/Gray	=	Black	+	White

Flesh Tone	=	Brown +	Pink	+	White
Burgundy	=	Red	+	Brown
Pink	=	Red	+	White
Blue	=	Red	+	Green
Green	=	Yellow	+	Blue
Teal	=	Blue	+	Yellow + Green
Chartreuse	=	Yellow	+	Green

COLOR CHART

COLOR(S)	+	COLOR	=	DESIRED COLOR
Royal or Sky Blue		Violet		Sky Blue (real)
Leaf Green		Chocolate Brown		Moss Green
Purple or Violet		Pink		Lavender
Egg Yellow, Violet		Red		Deep Red*
Forest or Leaf Green, Violet, Brown		Black		Deep Black**
Lemon Yellow		Warm Brown		Ivory
Lemon Yellow, Soft Pink		Sunset Orange		Peach
Sunset Orange		Warm Brown		Pumpkin
Chocolate Brown		Egg Yellow		Gold
Super Black		Liquid Whitener		Silver Gray
Warm Brown, Pink		Liquid Whitener		Flesh Tone
Super Red		Chocolate Brown		Burgundy
Christmas Red		Liquid Whitener		Pink
Christmas Red		Leaf Green		Blue
Lemon Yellow		Sky Blue		Green
Sky Blue, Yellow		Forest Green		Teal
Lemon Yellow		Leaf Green		Chartreuse

*Two types of reds are needed to achieve a really deep red color. These red food colors should be used in much larger proportions than the others.

**Use a great deal of black food color to achieve a deep black.

New Skill: Plunger Flowers

Quick Prep

> 3 oz (85 g) Quick Gumpaste (page 274)
> 1 oz (28 g) Meringue Powder Royal Icing (page 273)
> gel food colors
> cornstarch
> rounded toothpicks
> 1 set of plunger cutters (mini-scalloped)
> ball or dogbone tool
> cell pad
> PME 0 metal tip
> paper cone

Plunger flowers, or small blossoms, are basic to the work of busy decorators and pastry chefs. They are easy to make, and they can be made in advance and in an abundance of colors to match any cake. They can be kept for months or even years if packaged in a cardboard box and kept in a dry place.

Color gumpaste as desired or leave it the natural color. Rub vegetable shortening onto the work surface and roll out the paste until it is petal thin. Transfer the paste to a surface lightly dusted with cornstarch.

Press a plunger cutter into the paste and move it back and forth to separate the petals from the rest of the paste. When you lift the cutter, the petals will be attached to it. Place the cutter on a cell pad and press the plunger to release the cupped petals. Repeat this until you have made 24 five-petal flowers.

Position the small ball of the dogbone tool at the edge of one of the blossoms. Gently pull the ball tool toward the center of the flower (see Illustration 17.3). This thins the edge of the petal and further cups the flower. Go to the next petal and repeat the technique. Continue until the entire flower is complete.

To finish the flower, pipe a small dot of royal icing in the center with a PME 0 metal tip.

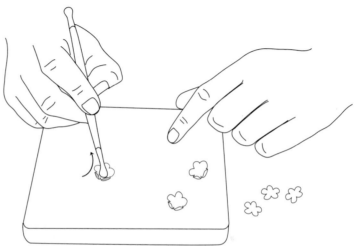

Illustration 17.3
To thin the edge of the petals and cup the flower, pull the ball tool from the petal's edge toward the center.

New Skill: Food Color Painting

Quick Prep

> 6-in. (15.2 cm) cardboard round
> gel food colors
> liquid whitener
> #0, #1, and #3 sable paintbrushes
> artist tray
> parchment paper
> #2 pencil
> Small Pansy Spray from patterns section

Painting is a challenge and a pleasant change from standard cake decorating practices. This beautiful art form can be easily incorporated into cake designs or competition pieces. It encourages creativity; you may amaze yourself with the outcome of your project!

Illustration 17.4
Food color painting (from top to bottom): the pattern, the pattern transferred to the cardboard, painting in progress, and the completed food color painting.

Select the Small Pansy Spray pattern from Appendix 1. Trace and transfer the pattern to the 6-in. (15.2 cm) round cardboard. Prepare a color tray with the colors you will need for the spray. The pansy itself can be a lemon or egg yellow, violet, purple, lavender, pinkish, or dusty rose. Include foliage colors, such as mint, leaf, or forest green. Shadow colors and highlight colors will complete the painting. The shadow color can be a chocolate brown, violet, black, or a deeper shade of any pastel color. For highlights, use full-strength liquid whitener. Add liquid whitener to gel food colors to achieve a pastel tone.

Squeeze a dot of gel color into the tray or on a small plastic paper plate. Squeeze a dot of liquid whitener next to the chosen color. Mix the two to achieve a pastel tone. Squeeze the green color for the leaves and a dot of liquid whitener next to the green. Mix a small portion of the green and white together and leave the rest unmixed. This will be the leaf color and the shadow color for the leaves.

For the highlighter, squeeze another dot of liquid whitener on another section of the tray along with a dot of the shadow color or the color to be used for the pansy. Three sable paintbrushes—fine, small, and medium—should also be nearby on the workstation. Prepare two small containers of water for cleaning the brushes and diluting food colors as needed.

Start with the leaves by dipping a fine brush into water and then into the shadow green color. Trace the pattern outline with the green color. Dip the brush in water to clean it and then outline the pansy with the appropriate shadow color (see Illustration 17.4).

With a small sable paintbrush, paint a deeper edge of the shadow-green color inside the leaves. Using a little water, brush the edge of the green to fade the color toward the center of the leaf. Paint a thicker border around the pansy with the shadow color, using the same technique as for the leaves. Brush the deeper color of the pansy with a little water to thin the edge of the shadow color.

Go back to the leaves. Thin a little of the mixed green color (green with liquid whitener) and begin to fade this color inside the leaf with the medium brush. Use very little water, which can dilute the color too much or make the painting too wet. Do this to all of the leaves.

For the pansy, begin to fade in the mixed color (chosen color and liquid whitener), using a little water with the medium brush. Use long strokes as you brush the color toward the center of the flower (see Illustration 17.4).

Go back to the leaves and paint in the veins with a deeper color or the shadow color for the pansy. Return to the pansy and fade in the highlight. Let the painting dry for 2 hours before adding the center to the pansy.

When the pansy is dry, paint a circle in the middle with a highlight color or a different bright color. With a deeper color, paint tiny stamens with a fine brush around the circle. The painting is complete (see Illustration 17.4).

New Skill: Crimping

Quick Prep

> 6-in. (15.2 cm) Styrofoam cake,
> round or square, iced with
> rolled icing
> selection of crimper tools

Crimping gives a quick and easy decorative finish that does not require piping. Tie a ribbon around the middle or bottom of the cake and you are done! Of course, piping in addition to crimping will raise the decorative value of the design.

To begin, select a crimper tool to give a decorative finish to the shoulder of the cake. Use the rubber band around the crimper tool to determine the size of the opening. Adjust the rubber band to the size you want. Press the tool about ⅛ in. (3 mm) into the cake shoulder. Squeeze the crimper together and then immediately release it. Carefully pull the tool out. The design is embossed on the cake.

Continue with this technique until the entire shoulder is crimped (see Illustration 17.5).

Illustration 17.5
Crimping tools (top) and the crimped edge of a cake (bottom).

END-OF-LESSON REVIEW

1. Why is it important to cover a cake board with decorative foil?

2. Compare the technique for covering a round board and a square or rectangular board. Why are different techniques necessary?

3. What is the name of a quick blossom often used by decorators that can be made up in abundance and in advance?

4. What two colors make up moss green?

5. What two colors make up ivory?

6. What neutral food color is used for highlights in painting or to give food colors a pastel shade?

7. What can you do if your food colors are too bright?

PERFORMANCE TEST

Perform the following exercises:

1. Select the Large Pansy Spray from the pattern section in Appendix 1 and paint it with food colors.

2. Cover a round or square cake with rolled icing and crimp the top edge with a variety of crimper tools.

CAKE AND CONFECTIONERY GALLERY

This lesson features a gallery of cakes and confectionery art. While some of the projects require a good deal of patience, they can all be accomplished using the skills you practiced in the last seventeen lessons, and they present an opportunity to show off your artistic flair and ability. Some of the projects are time-consuming and can be worked on for weeks.

These projects are good models for acquiring the skills necessary for success. Take your time and select projects that interest you, or use this lesson as a means of creating your own masterpieces.

Marbled Cake with Gumpaste Flowers

This single-tier cake is made with two colors that are not completely combined. The top of the cake is scalloped and completed with fine piping. A beautiful spray of gumpaste flowers adorns the cake as well.

   The bottom of the cake features the Victorian lace pattern (see Appendix 1). Pretty ribbons tied around the cake conceal the edge of the lace pattern, and simple plunger flowers complete the design (see Illustration 18.1).

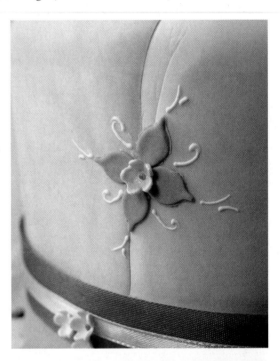

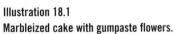

Illustration 18.1
Marbleized cake with gumpaste flowers.

Scalloped Heart Monogrammed Plaque

This distinctive plaque incorporates flooded round collars in slightly different sizes that are placed on a rolled iced board. The board is decorated using crimper cutters and small sprays of blossoms arranged around the collars. The collars are stacked in sizes ranging from 8 to 10 in. (20.3 to 25.4 cm). The monogram has three initials. These are piped on a heart-shaped scalloped plaque accentuated with cornelli lace. The edge of the heart is overpiped to give depth to the plaque.

A small spray of gumpaste flowers and lacy ribbons completes this plaque (see Illustration 18.2).

Illustration 18.2
Scalloped heart monogram plaque.

Swiss Dot Cake with Modeling Chocolate Roses

This simple yet refined cake is covered in a mixture of rolled fondant and marzipan. Swiss dots are piped randomly around the cake, and cornelli lace is piped inside the shoulder.

The cake is completed with three outstanding modeling chocolate roses with leaves (see Illustration 18.3).

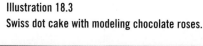

Illustration 18.3
Swiss dot cake with modeling chocolate roses.

The Nautical Cake

Two tiers make up this outstanding cake, piped in the old and new English tradition of cake art. The cake is completely iced in Meringue Powder Royal Icing. The old English skill used is the rings (see Lesson 11), which are piped in advanced and then attached to the cake. Tiny blossoms are encased in the rings, and stringwork is piped to connect each ring. Trelliswork or drop strings adorn the sides of the cake, to which the rings are connected.

The new English tradition is the flooded collars, which are piped separately and attached to the royal-iced cake board. Overpiping added to the collars gives the cake depth and dimension.

The cake is complete with a sweet sailboat on top (see Illustration 18.4).

Illustration 18.4
The nautical cake.

White Chocolate Roses and Ribbon Cake

This is a two-tier cake iced in egg-yellow rolled icing. Brush embroidery is piped and brushed along the sides of the cake and accentuated with embroidery piping. Flowing freehand drapery work gives the cake lushness, as do the rolled iced ribbons stitched on the cake edges with a quilting tool.

Pretty bead piping around the bottom of each tier and sumptuous white chocolate roses complete this cake (see Illustration 18.5).

Monogrammed and Extension Work Cake

This tiny masterpiece is an example of refined and stately work. Decorated in the Australian style, it features bridge and extension work around the bottom and a double bridge for side curtains. The lacy look of the piped lines comes from hailspotting. Beautiful cornelli lace and pyramid piping complete the fantasy.

A flooded monogram is added to the top of the cake, and dainty piping and straight lines give it depth. Plunger flowers complete the bottom of the cake (see Illustration 18.6).

Illustration 18.5
White chocolate roses and ribbon cake.

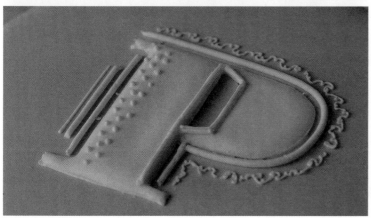

Illustration 18.6
Monogrammed and extension work cake.

Marzipan Still Life

A collection of marzipan fruit and veggies is arranged as a still life. These confections sit on a Tiffany cake stand in their own lovely world (see Illustration 18.7).

**Illustration 18.7
Marzipan still life.**

Forget-Me-Not and Bridgework Cake

This one-tier wedding cake is a beautiful tribute to a couple having a small, intimate ceremony. Lavishly piped in the Australian style with beautiful bridgework and exquisite embroidery and brushwork, this cake exhibits elegance, style, and a rich formality with taste and distinction (see Illustration 18.8).

**Illustration 18.8
Forget-me-not and bridgework cake.**

The cake is ornamented with a stunning spray of forget-me-nots, which embody trust, longevity, and undying love—the perfect sentiment for a wedding cake.

Barrel of Fruit

This work of art is a magnificent showpiece. Nearly full-size marzipan peaches, pears, oranges, apples, and a stunning pumpkin adorn this life-size barrel, which itself is made of gumpaste panels. The panels are painted with layers of food color paint mixed with gum glue for extraordinary shine. The panels are held together with side buckles.

A beautiful spray of variegated ivies and leaves completes the display (see Illustration 18.9).

Illustration 18.9
Barrel of fruit.

Barrel Construction

A 10 × 4-in. (25.4 × 10.2 cm) round Styrofoam is the center of the display. Cut out panels of gumpaste as shown in Illustration 18.10. (The pattern for the barrel is in Appendix 1.) Let the panels dry for 15 to 20 minutes before attaching it to the Styrofoam. Brush the panels with egg white or softened royal icing and attach them to the Styrofoam (see Illustration 18.10).

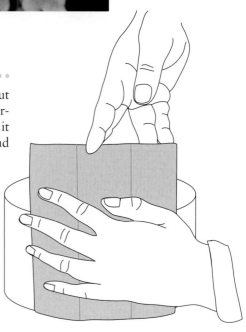

Illustration 18.10
Attach the panels to the Styrofoam with egg white or softened royal icing.

Two-tier Blue Lace Chocolate Cake

Cornelli lace in blue royal icing makes this two-tier chocolate cake a beautiful choice for either a wedding or an anniversary. Pyramid piping is stitched along the bottom edge of the second tier, and sky-blue ribbons add an elegant touch.

A heart-shaped ornament with cornelli lace is placed on top, and clusters of plunger flowers complete the cake (see Illustration 18.11).

Illustration 18.11
Two-tier blue lace chocolate cake.

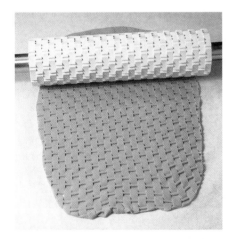

Illustration 18.12
The result of using a basketweave rolling pin.

Chocolate Basket with White Roses Cake

A basketweave rolling pin is used to give this cake its beautiful texture (see Illustration 18.12). White chocolate roses and leaves fill the basket along with beautiful ribbons and royal icing violets.

Making the Basket

Measure the circumference and height of the cake with adding machine paper. The top of the cake will be iced in rolled icing, but not textured with the rolling pin. Place a round cardboard with the diameter as the top of the cake on a piece

Illustration 18.13
Chocolate basket
with white roses
cake.

of commercial fondant rolled to ¼-in. (6 mm) thick. Carefully cut out the fondant and attach it to the top of the cake. Trim the fondant with scissors.

Roll out the fondant to be textured with the basketweave rolling pin to ¼- to ½-in. (6 mm to 1.3 cm) thick. Position the rolling pin at one end of the strip of fondant and roll it using a great deal of pressure. As you roll it, the fondant will stretch. Cut and trim the textured paste. Roll the paste into a log and attach it to the buttercream-iced cake (see Illustration 18.13).

Chocolate Bow and Ribbon Cake

This is a rich and lavish chocolate fantasy wrapped in perfect rolled chocolate fondant. A luscious bow is anchored in the front of the cake, surrounded by chocolate leaves and beautiful embroidery piping (see Illustration 18.5). The cake is completed with a spectacular top ornament of chocolate ribbons, which is a complement to the bridal table as a groom's cake (see Illustration 18.14a–c).

(b) Ribbon Bouquet.

 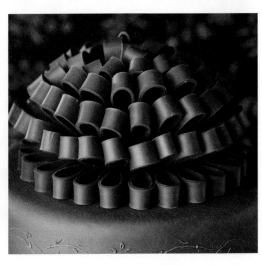

Illustration 18.14
(a) Chocolate bow.

Illustration 18.14 *(continued)*
(c) Completed ribbon cake.

Making the Ribbon Bouquet

Begin with a ball of modeling chocolate. Roll the chocolate thin. Use a ruler and an Xacto knife to carefully cut and measure strips ½-in. (1.3 cm) wide and 4-in. (10.2 cm) long. Shape 24-gauge florist wires into a *U*. Insert the *U* into a modeling chocolate strip to a depth of about ¼ in. (6 mm). Brush a little water over the wire to secure it and then bend the strip over into a closed *U* shape. Insert the wired ribbons into a large ball of Chocolate Molding Paste 3 to 4 in. (7.6 to 10.2 cm) in circumference (see Illustration 18.15).

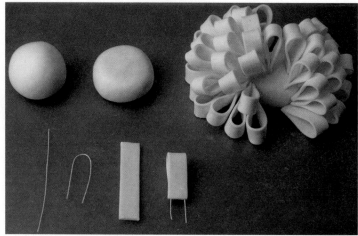

Illustration 18.15
Making a ribbon bouquet (counterclockwise from top left): balls of modeling paste, a strip of florist wire, florist wire in a *U* shape, a strip of rolled-out paste for a ribbon, the curved end of the *U*-shaped florist wire inserted into a strip of paste, and the ribbon bouquet in progress.

Illustration 18.16
Purple lace monogram cake.

Purple Lace Monogram Cake

This peach-colored royal icing cake is decorated with piped swags, scalloped dropped strings, and cornelli lace. The lace is piped in purple and accented inside the cake's edges. Exquisite purple lace ovals are piped off the cake and then attached for an airy and extended look. Clusters of small pearls added to the top edge of the cake complete the swags.

Finally, a large flooded monogram is anchored in the center, along with a small spray of purple and violet carnations (see Illustration 18.16).

Classic Drapery Cake with Floral Spray

Moss green and deep lavender together give this cake a rich textured look. The classic drapery work in a deep chartreuse/gooseberry color adds boldness as well as elegance and balance to this stately cake. Beautiful scalloped piping below the fabric trim is a delicate counterpoint, as are the clusters of blossoms and lavender pearls.

The back of the cake is gathered with a stunning bow and streamers that convey a Victorian mood. The cake board is beautifully decorated with a scalloped cutout in which the lavender cut-outs are marbleized (see Illustration 18.17).

The top and front of the cake are just as magnificent as the sides and board. A glorious spray of textured roses and tulips is richly and boldly colored, and the front of this masterpiece is adorned with tassels and three tapered tails (see Illustration 18.18).

Illustration 18.17
Classic drapery cake with floral spray.

Illustration 18.18

Blue and White Edifice Cake

This three-tier cake resembles an imposing monument. All three tiers are iced in a deep-blue rolled fondant. The top and bottom tiers feature panels of rolled fondant with scalloped tops. Tiny holes are made with the #5 round tip after the panels are attached to the iced cake, which is also accented with Swiss dots. (See Appendix 1 for the pattern.)

The middle tier is paneled with smocking. Beautiful stitching is added to the panels, and a ribbon ties it together.

Finally, the top ornament is made of three pastillage screens attached with royal icing and decorated with clusters of blossoms and fine vines (see Illustration 18.19).

Illustration 18.19
Blue and white edifice cake.

Black-and-White Polka Dot Cake

This one-tier wedding or anniversary cake resembles an elegant dress with lacy puffed shoulders and a wide dress with polka dots. This image is expressed in black and white. The puffed shoulders are filigree laces attached to the cake with royal icing. The black stitching on the filigree is simply pyramid piping. All the pieces are attached with a PME 0 tip.

The overpiped half-moons are piped with the #3 round tip and gradually ended with the #0 tip. The lace collar around the shoulder of the cake—almost like a necklace—is piped in white icing with a black royal icing overpipe. Cornelli lace is piped outside the collar for added elegance.

The bridge and extension work is extended to the cake board rather than built up traditionally near the bottom of the cake. The bridgework is intricately expressed in a beautiful scalloped pattern like a grand dress with ruffles and folds. Black hailspotting is piped on the extension work for class and distinction. The middle of the cake is tied with a black gumpaste ribbon and accented with embossing tools.

Finally, a butterfly couple is elegantly portrayed on the top of the cake, one anchored higher than the other (see Illustration 18.20). (See patterns in Appendix 1 for butterfly patterns and support beam.)

Illustration 18.20
Black-and-white polka dot cake.

Two-tier Appliqué Cake with Floral Spray

This two-tier cake has a southwestern flair and a floral spray in bold colors. The cake is iced in an egg-yellow rolled icing, and beautiful green ovals adorn each tier. Handsome calla lilies and roses set the tone, as do the burgundy and green appliqués.

The tiers are separated by spiked pillars surrounded by a cloud of yellow tulle (see Illustration 18.21).

Illustration 18.21
Two-tier appliqué cake with floral spray.

Decorated Cookies

This is a collection of beautiful cookies iced in glacé and rolled icings. Some of the cookies have piped stitching, brush embroidery, cameo, and monogrammed initials. Some feature several colors of flowing icing that was dragged with a toothpick for a decorative finish (see Illustration 18.22).

**Illustration 18.22
Decorated cookies.**

Petit Fours

These lovely petit fours are iced in a traditional glacé icing and adorned with Swiss dotting, royal icing rosettes, embroidery piping, Jordan almond monogram, and cornelli lace. They are decorated with fabric ribbons and set on a pastillage wheel cart (see Illustration 18.23).

**Illustration 18.23
Petit fours.**

Victorian Water Pitcher with Gumpaste Flowers

This spectacular showpiece, made from gumpaste and sprayed with a mixture of cocoa butter and coverture chocolate, is a lavish display of art and craft. The pitcher is decorated with beautiful brush embroidery, freehand embroidery, and piped lilies-of-the-valley. The bottom of the pitcher is elegantly draped with chocolate fondant, and the stunning flowers in the vase are handcrafted from gumpaste (see Illustration 18.24).

Illustration 18.24
Victorian water pitcher with gumpaste flowers.

Constructing the Vase

Divide a double recipe of Quick Gumpaste in half. Roll out one of the gumpaste halves until it is ¼-in. (6 mm) thick and wide and tall enough to fit half of the vase or water pitcher. Generously dust the pitcher with cornstarch and place the gumpaste directly on one side. Let rest for 20 to 30 minutes.

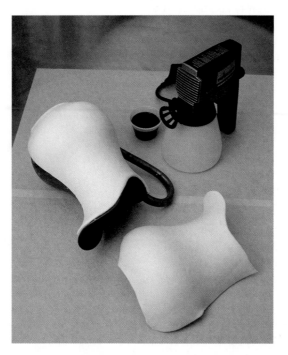

Illustration 18.25
Constructing the water pitcher (counterclockwise from the bottom): half of the paste pitcher after removal from actual pitcher, a sanded half of the paste pitcher, and spray gun.

Carefully trim the paste with an Xacto knife, keeping as true to the shape of the vase as you can. Let dry completely for 24 hours. Carefully remove the half-pitcher and turn the gumpaste over to dry on the inside for an additional 24 hours. Once both the inside and outside are completely dry, carefully sand the edges with fine sandpaper (see Illustration 18.25).

Repeat the procedure for the other side of the water pitcher. The handle can be made freehand and air dried for 24 to 48 hours.

Once all of the pieces are dried and sanded, attach the two halves with Meringue Powder Royal Icing and let dry. Sand the pitcher all over until it looks even. Attach the handle with royal icing. Let dry for 24 hours.

Spraying the Water Pitcher

Melt together 1 part cocoa butter to 2 parts coverture chocolate (ratio of 1:2) or 1 part cocoa butter to 1 part coverture chocolate (ratio 1:1) in a double boiler. Heat the mixture by carefully melting the cocoa butter and chocolate. Remove the mixture from the double boiler when three-quarters are melted. Continue to stir until all the pieces are melted. Check the temperature. The temperature should be 115°F (46°C). Now begin to temper the mixture, which is a process of cooling the mixture down to 95-96°F (35-36°C) by swirling the mixture around in the pan on top of the double boiler. Once at this temperature, the mixture is ready. Pour the mixture in the container of a Wagner Spray Gun. Be sure to read the spray gun directions before using it.

Line your work area with newspaper and a backdrop. Place the pitcher in the center and spray it with one even coat of the cocoa mixture. Let dry for 2 hours. Spray with a second coat and let dry for 24 hours.

Spray the water pitcher again with another coat of the cocoa liquid until it has a beautiful chocolate finish. Let dry for another 24 hours.

Note: Swirling the mixture around in the pan is necessary when cooling; otherwise, the mixture will dry grainy. Left over mixture can be re-heated, re-tempered, and re-used.

Antique Bell-Shaped Wedding Cake

This is a beautiful cake for an upscale wedding. Powder-blue rolled icings cover the bottom, middle drum, and top bell of the cake. All the tiers are decorated with classic brush embroidery work. In addition, the bottom tier is decorated with classic Australian bridgework and the finest freehand embroidery. The middle drum is decorated with cornelli lace, clusters of blossoms, and brush foliage work. The top tier is elegantly adorned with cushion lattice piped at the top of the crown and finished with ropes made using a clay gun. Lovely brushwork adorns the bell, and a Victorian lace fan is attached at the bottom of the bell with its edges over-piped for a standout look. (See pattern for Victorian lace band in Appendix 1.) Pretty blue ribbons and an Australian bow complete this masterpiece (see Illustration 18.26).

Illustration 18.26
Antique bell-shaped wedding cake.

RECIPES

Good recipes are the bread and butter of every good baker, decorator, and chef. Knowing a recipe intimately and making it many times gives these professionals confidence in achieving a wide range of goals.

If the skills are there but the product isn't correct, the baker can't complete his or her task.

You should become intimate with the recipes you love, but don't be afraid to add new ones to your repertoire.

Decorator's Buttercream Icing

	5 OR 6-QT MIXER	20-QT MIXER	Ingredients
YIELD:	5 lb (80 oz or 2.27 kg)	20 lb (320 oz or 9.07 kg)	
	1 lb (16 oz or 454g)	4 lb (64 oz or 1.81 kg)	Unsalted butter
	8 oz (230 g)	2 lb (32 oz or 0.91 kg)	Solid vegetable shortening
	1½ tsp (7.5 ml or 3 g)	2 Tbsp (30 ml or 1 oz)	Lemon, vanilla, or almond extract
	1 tsp (5 g)	4 tsp (20 g)	Salt
	3 lb (48 oz or 1.36 kg)	12 lb (5.44 kg)	10x confectioner's sugar
	3 Tbsp (¾ oz or 24 g)	4 oz (114 g)	Meringue powder
	4½ fl oz (133 ml or 128 g)	18 fl oz (532 ml or 510 g)	Water, milk, heavy cream, or clear liqueur

Note: Double the 20-qt quantity ingredients for a 60-qt mixer

- Cream the butter and shortening with a paddle-whip mixer for 3 minutes on medium-high speed. Stop and scrape bowl. Cream for an additional 60 seconds. Add flavoring and salt and mix until combined. Gradually add sugar, then meringue powder. The mixture will appear dry.

- Add the liquid and beat until the mixture is light and fluffy, 5 to 8 minutes. Once the buttercream is made, keep the bowl covered with a damp cloth or plastic wrap to prevent it from drying out.

- Store the icing in an airtight container and refrigerate for up to 2 weeks or freeze for up to 3 months.

French Vanilla Buttercream

	5 OR 6-QT MIXER	20-QT MIXER	
YIELD:	**2½ to 3 lb (1.13 to 1.36 kg)**	**10 to 10.5 lb (4.45 to 4.76 kg)**	**Ingredients**
	12 oz (340 g)	3 lb (48 oz or 1.35 kg)	Granulated sugar
	6 fl oz (180 ml or 170 g)	24 oz (710 ml or 680 g)	Whole milk
	1½ Tbsp (⅜ oz)	6 Tbsp (1.5 oz or 38 g)	All-purpose flour
	¼ tsp (1 .5 g)	1 Tbsp (15 g)	Salt
	1 Tbsp (15 ml or ½ oz)	2 fl oz (59 ml or 57 g)	Pure vanilla extract
	3 fl oz (90 ml or 85 g)	9 fl oz (270 ml or 266 g)	Heavy cream
	1¼ lb (57 kg or 568 g)	5 lb (80 oz or 2.27 kg)	Unsalted butter, cut into pieces

Note: Large-quantity recipe above can be multiplied 5 times for a 60-qt mixer.

- Make a custard by heating the sugar and milk over a double boiler until the sugar crystals dissolve. Remove from heat. Add the flour and salt and whisk until incorporated. Place over an ice bath until the custard is slightly cooled.

- Pour the custard mixture in the mixer bowl. Add the vanilla, cream, and butter. Using a paddle attachment, mix on low speed to fully incorporate the ingredients or until the mixture thickens.

- Mix on the next highest speed until mixture starts to look light and fluffy. This can take 7 to 10 minutes or longer for larger batches.

- Store the buttercream in an airtight container for 1 week in the refrigerator or store up to 2 months in the freezer.

Note: If the buttercream curdles, it will just take longer for the butter to warm up. Continue beating until the butter softens and the mixture looks light and fluffy.

Swiss Meringue Buttercream

	5 OR 6-QT MIXER	20-QT MIXER	Ingredients
YIELD:	2½ qt (2.37 L)	12.5 qt (11.9 L)	
	12 oz (355 ml or 340 g)	3¾ lb (60 oz or 1.8 L)	Egg whites
	1½ lb (24 oz)	7.5 lb (3.40 kg)	Granulated sugar
	3 lb (48 oz or 1.36 kg)	15 lb (6.80 kg)	Unsalted butter
	2 Tbsp (30 ml or 1 oz)	5 oz (148 ml or 140 g)	Lemon, almond, vanilla, or orange extract. Or, up to 3 oz (90 ml or 85 g) for 5 or 6 quart mixer or 15 oz (450 ml or 425 g) for 20-qt mixer) of light rum, framboise, kirsch, amaretto, or Poire Williams

Note: The larger quantity recipe above can be doubled or tripled for a 60 qt mixer.

- Lightly whisk the egg whites and sugar together over simmering water until the mixture is hot to touch or a candy thermometer reads 140°F.

- Pour the hot mixture into a room-temperature mixer bowl and whip with a wire whip on medium-high speed until doubled in volume. Mixing is complete when the meringue does not move around in the bowl when the mixer whip is stopped. Meanwhile, cut the butter into medium-size pieces. The butter should be slightly moist on the outside but cold inside.

- Remove the whip and attach the paddle. Divide the butter into 4 parts. Add the first part and mix on stir speed for 15 seconds. Add the second part and mix on slow speed for 15 seconds. Add the third and fourth parts. In 10-second increments, slowly raise the mixer speed from the lowest speed to medium-high.

- Continue beating until the mixture begins to look light and fluffy. Stop and scrape the bowl. Add the flavoring and beat on low speed for 45 seconds, then on medium-high speed for an additional 45 to 60 seconds. Store leftover buttercream in plastic containers with lids and refrigerate for up to 1 week or freeze for up to 3 months.

Note: In hot weather, you can replace some of the butter with high-ratio shortening, an emulsion that contains water. It is not as greasy as commercial vegetable shortening and does not leave an aftertaste on the back of your palate. High-ratio shortening can be used as a substitute in any recipe that calls for butter or margarine.

- For the smaller recipe, use 2 lb 10 oz (1.26 L) butter and 6 oz (170 g) high-ratio shortening. For the larger recipe, use 11 lb (4.99 kg) butter and 4 lb (1.81 kg) high-ratio shortening.

Amaretto Mocha Buttercream

	5 OR 6-QT MIXER	20-QT MIXER	Ingredients
YIELD:	2½ qt (2.37 L)	12.5 qt (11.9 L)	
	2½ qt (80 oz)	25 lb (12.5 qt or 11.9 L)	Unflavored Swiss Meringue Buttercream (page 262)
	4 Tbsp (½ oz or 13 g)	2.5 oz (71 g)	Instant espresso coffee
	3 oz (90 ml or 85 g)	15 oz (450 ml or 425 g)	Amaretto

Note: Larger quantity above can be doubled or tripled for 60-qt mixer.

- Place the Swiss Meringue Buttercream in the mixer bowl and mix on stir speed with the paddle attachment.

- In a separate small bowl, thoroughly mix the coffee and amaretto until the coffee is dissolved. Slowly pour the coffee mixture into the buttercream. Beat on medium-high speed for 2 to 3 minutes or until the coffee mixture is fully incorporated.

- Store leftover buttercream in a plastic container with a lid and refrigerate for up to 1 week or freeze for up to 3 months.

White Chocolate Buttercream

	5 OR 6-QT MIXER	20-QT MIXER	Ingredients
YIELD:	3 qt (2.83 L)	12 qt (11.35 L)	
	1 recipe	4 recipes	Unflavored Swiss Meringue Buttercream (page 262)
	16 oz (454 g)	4 lb (64 oz or 1.81 kg)	White Ganache, refrigerated (page 264)
	4 oz (120 ml or 114 g)	16 oz (473 ml or 454 g)	Godiva White Chocolate Liqueur

- Place the Swiss Meringue Buttercream in a mixer bowl and mix on stir speed. Add the white ganache, 4 oz (114 g) at a time, to the buttercream. Continue to add ganache until all of it is incorporated into the buttercream.

- Slowly add the liqueur. Beat until the icing is light and fluffy.

- Store leftover buttercream in a plastic container with a lid. Refrigerate for up to 1 week or freeze for up to 2 months.

Ganache

YIELD:	1.75 lb (28 oz or 793.8 g)	Ingredients
	12 fl oz (355 ml or 340 g)	Heavy cream
	1 lb (454 g)	Semisweet, bittersweet dark, or white chocolate, chopped or in disks
	Note: This recipe may be doubled or tripled.	

Preferable Technique

• In a heavy saucepan, boil the cream and then cool it down to 90°F (32°C).

• Meanwhile, temper* the chocolate. Once the chocolate has been tempered and brought up to 90°F (32°C), combine both the heavy cream and chocolate and mix in a mixer with paddle attachment or hand whisk until fully blended.

• The ganache is ready to be used as a glaze onto iced cakes. Pour remainder into a room temperature metal bowl with plastic wrap directly over the ganache and let it set at room temperature overnight to firm up. This is preferable when adding firm ganache to buttercream icings or enrobing chocolate.

• Refrigerated dark ganache will be too firm the next day to use. If refrigerated, let it set at room temperature until softened.

Quick Technique (not always reliable)

• In a heavy saucepan, boil the heavy cream. Cut off the heat and add the chocolate pieces. Let rest.

• Stir with a wooden spoon until the heavy cream and chocolate are fully incorporated and all of the chocolate pieces have melted. Whip with the wire whisk until fully blended.

• Pour into a room temperature metal bowl and cover with plastic wrap until ready to use, or use immediately if glazing cakes. The balance of the ganache can rest overnight to firm up if adding to buttercream icings.

*Tempering is a technique in which chocolate is stabilized through a melting and cooling process, thereby making it more malleable and glossy. This technique is important for candy making or chocolate decorations, but isn't for most recipes.

Commercial chocolate is already tempered; however, this condition changes when the chocolate is melted. Chocolate must be tempered because it contains cocoa butter— a fat that may form crystals after the chocolate is melted and cooled. If these crystals aren't stabilized through tempering, they can form dull gray streaks, known as *blooms*.

There are several ways to temper chocolate. A quick method is to melt ½ to ⅔ of the chocolate (preferably in a microwave) to 115° to 120°F (46° to 49°C) and then add the remaining ½ to ⅓ (disc or finely chopped) chocolate, stirring constantly until the chocolate mixture is smoothed and reaches 90°F (32°C) or stir the mixture using an immersion blender.

Italian Meringue Buttercream

	5 OR 6-QT MIXER	20-QT MIXER	Ingredients
YIELD:	35 oz (2.18 lb or 0.984 kg)	10.9 lb (4.90 kg)	
	1 lb (454 g)	5 lb (80 oz or 2.27 kg)	Granulated sugar
	8 fl oz (240 ml or 228 g)	40 fl oz (1.2 L)	Cold water
	6 oz (180 ml or 170g)	30 oz (887 ml or 851 g)	Egg whites
	1 lb (454 g)	5 lb (80 oz or 2.27 kg)	Unsalted butter, room temperature, cut into pieces
	1 Tbsp (15 ml or ½ oz)	5 Tbsp (74 ml or 2.5 oz)	Vanilla extract

- Bring the sugar and water to a boil in a medium-size pot. Clean down the sides of the pot with a pastry brush dipped in cold water to prevent crystallization of the sugar. When the sugar syrup comes to a boil, place a candy thermometer in it.

- When the syrup temperature reaches 215°F (102°C), begin to whisk the egg white on high speed for 5 minutes until stiff peaks form.

- Check the temperature of the sugar syrup temperature. When it reaches 238° to 240°F (114° to 116°C), or soft boil stage, remove the pot from the heat. Slowly pour the syrup in a steady stream down the side of the bowl while the whites are still whisking. Make sure the syrup does not touch the wire whisk.

- Continue whisking until the meringue cools. This could take 6 to 10 minutes.

- Add the butter, a piece at a time, while the mixer is still whisking. Add the vanilla and beat until light and fluffy.

- If the icing gets too soft, refrigerate it for 15 to 20 minutes and rebeat until it is light and fluffy.

- Store leftover icing in plastic containers with lids. Refrigerate for 3 to 5 days or freeze for up to 2 months.

Buttercream Icing For Piped Roses

	5 OR 6-QT MIXER	20-QT MIXER	Ingredients
YIELD:	2¼ qt (2.13 L)	11¼ qt (10.65 L)	
	1¼ lb (567 g)	6¼ lb (100 oz or 2.72 kg)	Unsalted butter
	4 oz (114 g)	20 oz (567 g)	Vegetable shortening
	1 Tbsp (15 ml or 14 g)	5 Tbsp (74 ml or 75 g)	Water, milk, lemon juice, or liqueur
	3 lb (48 oz or 1.36 kg)	15 lb (6.80 kg)	10x confectioner's sugar
	3 Tbsp (¾ oz or 24 g)	3.75 oz (106 g)	Meringue powder
	1 tsp (5 g)	5 tsp (25 g)	Salt

Note: Larger-quantity recipe may be doubled or tripled for 60-qt mixer.

- Follow the procedure for making Decorator's Buttercream Icing (page 260). If the icing is too stiff, take a portion of icing and place it in a small bowl. Add drops of water or milk to the small bowl of icing. If the icing is too soft, add extra confectioner's sugar.

Practice Buttercream Icing

	5 OR 6-QT MIXER	20-QT MIXER	Ingredients
YIELD:	26 oz (1.6 lb or 0.78 L)	9.75 lb (4.68 L)	
	8 oz (230 g)	3 lb (48 oz or 1.36 kg)	Vegetable or high-ratio shortening
	3 Tbsp (44 ml or 42.5 g)	9 oz (266 ml or 255 g)	Water
	1 lb (454 g)	6 lb (96 oz or 2.72 kg)	10x confectioner's sugar
	1 Tbsp (¼ oz or 8 g)	6 Tbsp (1.5 oz or 42.5 g)	Meringue powder

Note: Larger-quantity recipe may be quadrupled in 60-qt mixer.

- Follow the procedure for making Decorator's Buttercream Icing (page 260). Beat for 8 to 12 minutes. The recipe may be doubled as many times as needed. Store the icing in a plastic container with a lid. It does not need to be refrigerated.

Cream Cheese Buttercream

	5 OR 6-QT MIXER	20-QT MIXER	
YIELD:	1¼ qt (1.18 L)	6¼ qt (5.91 L)	Ingredients
	8 oz (228 g)	2.5 lb (40 oz or 1.13 kg)	Unsalted butter
	2 oz (57 g)	10 oz (283 g)	Solid vegetable shortening
	10 oz (283 g)	3.75 lb (60 oz or 1.40 kg)	Cream cheese (regular or mascarpone)
	1½ lb (680 g)	7.5 lb (3.40 kg)	10x confectioner's sugar
	2 Tbsp (30 ml or 28.35 g)	5 fl oz (148 ml or 140 g)	Heavy cream
	1 tsp (5 ml or 2 g)	5 tsp (25 ml or 17 g)	Vanilla extract
	1 Tbsp (15 ml or 12 g)	5 Tbsp (75 ml or 70.8 g)	Fresh lemon juice
	1 Tbsp (¼ oz or 10 g)	5 Tbsp (1.5 oz or 42 g)	Meringue powder

- Cream the butter, shortening, and cream cheese together for 3 minutes. Stop and scrape the bowl. Cream for an additional 60 seconds.

- Slowly add the sugar to the butter mixture. Add the cream, vanilla, lemon juice, and meringue powder. Beat for 1 minute on slow speed to incorporate the ingredients, and then beat on medium-high speed for 3 minutes.

- Stop and scrape the bowl. Beat for 2 to 3 more minutes. The buttercream should look light and fluffy. Do not overbeat, as the buttercream will become too soft for icing and piping.

- Store leftover buttercream in plastic containers with lids. Refrigerate for up to 1 week or freeze for up to 2 months.

Buttercream Icing for Flooding

YIELD:	15 oz (425.25 g)	Ingredients
	6 oz (170 g)	Decorator's Buttercream Icing (see page 260)
	6 fl oz (9 actual oz or 266 ml or 255 g)	Light corn syrup

- Mix the corn syrup into the buttercream icing with a rubber spatula until smooth. Divide the buttercream icing into two or three small containers and color as desired.

- This recipe may be doubled or tripled.

Note: This buttercream icing is thick and not quite the consistency of royal icing flood icing.

Measuring Corn Syrup, Molasses, Honey, and Glucose

Use a liquid measure cup to measure slow, sticky liquids to obtain the volume weight. If you use a scale to measure these liquids, muliply the weight by 1.5 to obtain the volume weight. For example: 6 fl oz × 1.5 equals 9 actual oz (255 g). This is the correct weight for liquid. The 6 fl oz is the volume weight measured in a liquid measuring cup, and the 9 oz (225 g) is the scale weight.

Chocolate Glaze for Piping

YIELD:	8 oz (228 g)	Ingredients
	8 oz (228 g)	Semisweet chocolate
	1 Tbsp (15 ml or 14 g)	Corn or canola oil

Note: This recipe may be doubled or tripled.

- Melt the chocolate over simmering water in a double boiler until it is ¾ melted. Remove from the double boiler and stir until all of the pieces are melted. Stir in oil. Let rest until the chocolate thickens a little.

- If the chocolate gets too thick, replace the bowl over the warm water, but leave the heat off. Stir the chocolate and check occasionally until the chocolate is the right consistency for piping.

Glacé Icing for Cookies

	5 OR 6-QT MIXER	
YIELD:	20 oz (567 g)	Ingredients
	1 lb (454 g)	10x confectioner's sugar
	3 fl oz (90 ml or 85 g)	Whole milk or water
	3 fl oz (4.5 actual oz or 133 ml or 128 g)	Light corn syrup
	Flavor options: 1 tsp (5 ml oz or 2 g)	Concentrated extract *or*
	1 Tbsp (15 ml or 14 g)	Alcohol or liqueur or 2 to 3 drops concentrated candy oil

Note: This recipe can be doubled or tripled. Store leftover icing in a plastic container with a lid in the refrigerator for up to 1 week.

- Mix together the sugar and milk until the mixture is creamy, about 3 minutes. Add the corn syrup and beat until incorporated.

- Divide the icing among 3 to 4 bowls. Color each with gel colors and then flavor as desired.

Glacé Icing for Petit Fours

5 OR 6-QT MIXER

YIELD:	20 oz (567 g)	Ingredients
	1 lb (454 g)	10x confectioner's sugar
	2 fl oz (59 ml or 57 g)	Whole milk or water
	4 fl oz (6 actual oz or 177 ml or 170 g)	Light corn syrup
	Flavor options: 1 tsp (5 ml or 2 g)	Concentrated extract *or*
	1 Tbsp (15 ml or 14 g)	Alcohol or liqueur or 2 to 3 drops concentrated candy oil

Note: The cooled icing may be reheated and reused. Left over icing can be placed in a lidded container and refrigerate for up to 3 days. The recipe may be doubled or tripled.

- Mix the sugar and milk or water together until the mixture is creamy, about 3 minutes. Add the corn syrup and beat until incorporated.

- Place the icing in a medium-size bowl and heat over simmering water until the icing warms and thickens. Stir with a wooden spoon or rubber spatula while the icing is heating. The icing should be warm, not hot, to the touch.

- Remove the icing from the heat. Add food color of choice and flavor the icing as desired. Spoon the icing over petit fours right away, allowing the excess to drip into a small bowl under a cooling rack.

Confectioner's Glaze (Gum Glue)

YIELD:	6 oz (170 g)	Ingredients
	6 oz (177 ml or 170 g)	Tap water
	2 Tbsp (½ oz or 16 g)	Gum arabic

Note: Use this on show pieces that require a high sheen.

- Measure water and gum arabic into a small bottle with a lid. Shake vigorously for 30 seconds. Let sit for 30 minutes and then shake vigorously again.

- Store in the refrigerator, as the glaze develops a sour smell if left at room temperature for more than 1 day. It will keep in the refrigerator for up to 2 weeks.

Marzipan

	5 OR 6-QT MIXER	20-QT MIXER	
YIELD:	2 lb (0.91 kg)	10 lb (4.54 kg)	Ingredients
	1 lb (454 g)	5 lb (80 oz or 2.27 kg)	Almond paste
	1 lb (454 g)	5 lb (80 oz or 2.27 kg)	10x confectioner's sugar
	3 fl oz (4.5 actual oz or 133 ml or 126 g)	15 fl oz (23 actual oz or 450 ml or 425 g)	Light corn syrup*
	1 tsp (5 ml or 2 g)	5 tsp (25 ml or 17 g)	Vanilla extract
	1 tsp (5 ml or 2 g)	5 tsp (25 ml or 17 g)	Light rum

- Cut up the almond paste with a bench scraper and place in a mixer bowl. Attach the paddle and mix on low speed until some of the oil is extracted from the paste, about 30 seconds.

- Add half of the sugar and continue to mix while slowly pouring in the corn syrup, vanilla, and rum. Mix until the dough comes together and sticks to the paddle. Remove the dough from the paddle.

- Sieve the remaining sugar onto the countertop. Knead all of the sugar into the dough. If the dough is still sticky, knead in a little more sugar. Continue kneading until the marzipan has a fine, smooth texture. It should feel soft but firm.

- Double-wrap the marzipan in plastic wrap, then place in a zippered bag and store in the refrigerator until ready to use. It can be kept in the refrigerator for several weeks and frozen for 3 to 5 months.

*Corn syrup is heavier than water, milk, or juice. Thus, 3 fl oz corn syrup measured in a liquid measuring cup has a different weight in ounces measured on an electronic scale.

Marzipan is the best medium to create a beautiful still life.

Marzipan Modeling Paste

YIELD:	16 oz (454 g)	Ingredients
	12 oz (340 g)	Marzipan (see above)
	4 oz (114 g)	Commercial rolled fondant
	Note: The recipe may be double or tripled.	

- Knead the marzipan and the fondant together until pliable. If the paste gets sticky, sprinkle a little confectioner's sugar on the work surface and knead it in. Double-wrap the paste in plastic wrap and then in a zippered bag. Refrigerate until ready to use. This paste keeps in the refrigerator for several weeks and in the freezer for 3 to 5 months.

Modeling Chocolate or Chocolate Plastic

YIELD: (TK)	Ingredients
1 lb (454 g)	Semisweet, bittersweet, white, or milk chocolate
5 fl oz (7.5 actual oz or 222 ml or 210 g)	Light corn syrup*
Note: The recipe may be doubled or tripled.	

- Finely chop the chocolate and place it in a bowl over simmering water. Stir to evenly melt the chocolate. When ¾ melted, remove from the heat. Continue stirring until all the pieces are melted.

- Use a rubber spatula to stir in the corn syrup. Continue to stir until the chocolate starts to leave the sides of the bowl. Dark chocolate does this in about 60 seconds. White or milk chocolate does it in 20 to 30 seconds.

- Scrape the chocolate mixture onto a piece of plastic wrap and spread it out to about ½-in. (1.3 cm) thick. Place another piece of plastic wrap directly on top of the chocolate. Refrigerate or let rest in a cool dry place for 24 hours.

- When it is aged, cut the chocolate into smaller pieces. Microwave the pieces for just a few seconds to take off the hard edge. Knead thoroughly with the heels of your hands until the chocolate has elasticity and a shiny coat. Wrap in plastic until ready to use.

- This chocolate paste keeps for several weeks without refrigeration, provided it is placed in a cool, dry area.

*For white or milk chocolate, use 1 oz (28 g) less than you used for dark chocolate. Thus, use 4 fl oz or 6 actual oz (168 g) corn syrup for 1 lb (454 g) white or milk chocolate.

Chocolate Rolled Fondant

YIELD:	24 oz (680.4 g)	Ingredients
	24 oz (680 g)	Commercial white rolled fondant
	6 Tbsp (1 oz or 48 g)	Dutch–processed cocoa powder
	1¼ Tbsp (⅝ oz or 20 g)	Solid vegetable shortening
	1 tsp (5 ml or 2 g)	Vermeer Dutch Chocolate Cream liqueur or Godiva liqueur

- Knead the fondant until pliable. Make a well in the center and place 2 Tbsp (16 g) of the cocoa powder in the well. Measure out 1 tsp (⅛ oz or 3 g) of the solid vegetable shortening and rub it in your hands lightly. Knead the shortening into the fondant and cocoa powder until the cocoa powder is evenly distributed.

- Make another well in the center in the fondant and add an additional 2 Tbsp (16 g) of the cocoa powder. Measure out another 1 tsp (⅛ oz or 3 g) of solid vegetable shortening and repeat the process of kneading the cocoa powder and shortening into the fondant. Repeat this a third time, using the remaining cocoa powder and an additional tsp (⅛ oz or 3 g) of solid vegetable shortening. Knead until the cocoa powder and shortening is evenly distributed.

- Make a fourth well in the center of the fondant. This time, add the liqueur. Rub the balance of the shortening into your hands. Knead it and the liqueur into the fondant until smooth and pliable. Wrap in plastic wrap until ready to use.

- This chocolate fondant can last for several weeks in an airtight container. It does not require refrigeration.

Egg White Royal Icing

	5 OR 6-QT MIXER	20-QT MIXER	
YIELD:	1 lb (454 g)	5.5 lb (2.49 kg)	Ingredients
	3 oz (90 ml or 85 g)	15 oz (450 ml or 425 g)	Fresh or pasteurized egg whites, room temperature
	1 lb (454 g)	5 lb (80 oz or 2.27 kg)	10x confectioner's sugar, sifted
	½ tsp (2.5 ml or 1 g)	2½ tsp (12.5 ml or 9 g)	Lemon extract

- Lightly whip the egg whites on medium speed, using a paddle, until they are frothy and form soft peaks. This takes about 3 minutes. Lower the speed and gradually add the sugar.

- Add the lemon extract and beat on medium-high speed for 5 to 8 minutes, or until the icing forms medium to stiff peaks. Cover the icing with plastic wrap until ready to use.

- Store the icing in a glass container with a lid and use within 1 day or refrigerate for up to 3 days.

Meringue Powder Royal Icing

	5 OR 6-QT MIXER	20-QT MIXER	
YIELD:	1.2 lb (0.54 kg)	6 lb (2.7 kg)	Ingredients
	1¼ oz (37 g)	6.25 oz (177 g)	Meringue powder
	4 oz (120 ml or 114 g)	20 oz (591 ml or 567 g)	Cold water
	1 lb (454 g)	5 lb (80 oz or 2.27 kg)	10x confectioner's sugar, sifted
	½ tsp (2.5 ml or 1 g)	2½ tsp (12.5 ml or 9 g)	Lemon extract

- Add the meringue powder to the water in a mixing bowl. Beat to soft peaks, about 3 minutes, on medium-high speed. Slowly add the sugar until it is incorporated.

- Add the lemon extract and beat for an additional 5 minutes on medium-high speed or until the icing forms medium to stiff peaks. Cover with plastic wrap until ready to use.

- This icing does not need to be refrigerated if kept in a cool dry place and used within 2 weeks. Rebeat before using.

Quick Gumpaste

YIELD:	1 lb (454 g)	Ingredients
	1 lb (454 g)	Commercial rolled fondant
	1 tsp (1.5 g)	Tylose,* Tylose C, or CMC
	½ tsp (1 g)	White vegetable shortening
	As needed	Cornstarch

- Knead the fondant until pliable. If it is sticky, knead in a little cornstarch.

- Make a well in the center of the rolled fondant. Add the Tylose. Rub the vegetable shortening into your palms and knead the paste for 3 to 5 minutes. Double-wrap the paste in plastic wrap and place in a zippered plastic bag or airtight container. Let rest in the refrigerator (or cool dry place) until ready to use. This paste can be used immediately but will perform better if allowed to rest for 24 hours.

- Recipe may be doubled but may be difficult to handle if tripled.

  *Tylose can be replaced with gum tragacanth. However, 1½ to 2 tsp (2 to 3 g) gum tragacanth is needed to equal 1 tsp (1.5 g) Tylose. The paste can be used immediately for some aspects of sugarcraft, but it performs better if allowed to rest for 24 hours.

Flood Icing

YIELD:	9 oz (255 g)	Ingredients
	8 oz (228 g)	Meringue Powder Royal Icing (page 273) or Egg White Royal Icing (page 273)
	1 to 2 fl oz (30 to 59 ml or 28.3 to 56.7 g)	Water or pasteurized egg whites

Note: Choosing egg whites to flood your icing will result in the product having a nice sheen when it is dried. With water, the product dries flat. The recipe may be doubled or tripled.

- Carefully stir the water or egg whites into the royal icing a little at a time. After adding half the liquid, check to see if you have a flow consistency. Add more liquid if necessary. Cover with plastic wrap to prevent drying.

- Keep the icing refrigerated in an airtight container. It will last for a few days.

How to Check for Flow Consistency

You have achieved a flow consistency if, after you draw a knife through the icing, the icing completely comes back together after you count to 10 seconds. If the icing comes together before 7 seconds, add a little more royal icing to thicken it. Check for consistency again. If the icing does not come together within 10 seconds, add a little more liquid.

Rolled Fondant

YIELD: 2 lb (908 g)

Ingredients

1 Tbsp (9 g)	Unflavored gelatin (about 1 envelope)
2 oz (60 ml or 57 g)	Cold water
1 tsp (5 ml or 2 g)	Lemon, almond, or orange extract
4 fl oz (6 actual oz or 177 ml or 168 g)	Light Corn syrup
1 Tbsp 15 ml or 14 g)	Glycerin
2 1bs (908 g)	10x confectioner's sugar
½ tsp (1 g)	Vegetable shortening

Note: The recipe may be doubled.

- In a small bowl, sprinkle the gelatin over the water. Let stand for 2 minutes to soften. Place the mixture over a pan of simmering water until the gelatin dissolves, or microwave for 30 seconds on high power. Do not overheat. Add the flavoring.

- Add the corn syrup and glycerin and stir until the mixture is smooth and clear. Gently reheat if necessary, or microwave for an additional 15 to 20 seconds on high power. Stir again.

- Sift 1½ lb (680 g) of the sugar into a large bowl. Make a well in the sugar and pour in the liquid mixture. Stir with a wooden spoon. The mixture will be sticky.

- Sift some of the remaining sugar onto a smooth work surface. Place the gelatin mixture on the work surface and knead in as much of the remaining sugar as the mixture will take. Knead the fondant, adding more sugar, if necessary, to form a smooth, pliable mass. The fondant should be firm but soft.

Rolled fondant is the choice foundation to create such a beautiful plaque.

- Rub the vegetable shortening into your palms and knead it into the fondant. This relieves stickiness in the fondant.

- Wrap the fondant tightly in plastic wrap and then in a zippered plastic bag. Place it in the refrigerator until ready to use. Rolled fondant works best if allowed to rest for 24 hours.

- Store fondant, wrapped, in the refrigerator for up to 2 months.

Pastillage

YIELD:	7½ oz (212 g)	Ingredients
	7 oz (198 g)	Egg White Royal Icing (page 273)
	2 tsp (3 g)	Tylose
	5 to 7 Tbsp (40 to 56 g)	Cornstarch

Note: This recipe may be doubled.

- Place the icing in a medium-size bowl. Make a well in the center and add the Tylose. Stir vigorously with a rubber spatula or wooden spoon until the mixture begins to tighten and thicken.

- Put the cornstarch on the work surface and the icing on the cornstarch. Knead the icing into the starch until the paste becomes elastic and pliable but is still soft. Wrap the paste in plastic wrap and place in a zippered plastic bag.

- When ready to use, sprinkle additional cornstarch on the work surface. Break off a piece of the paste and knead until it has no stickiness. Roll out the paste to the desired thickness and cut with cutters or an Xacto knife.

- This icing is not refrigerated and will last for up to 3 days.

Rolled Fondant Modeling Paste

YIELD:	16 oz (454 g)	Ingredients
	12 oz (340 g)	Commercial rolled fondant
	4 oz (114 g)	Quick Gumpaste (page 274)
	As needed	Cornstarch

Note: This recipe may be double or tripled.

- Knead the fondant and the gumpaste together until pliable. If the paste gets sticky, sprinkle a little cornstarch on the work surface and knead it in. Double-wrap the paste in plastic wrap and place in an airtight container until ready to use. Store in the refrigerator for up to 2 months.

High-Yield Yellow Cake

YIELD:	5 OR 6-QT MIXER	20-QT MIXER	
	4 8 × 2 in. (20.3 × 5 cm) cake pans or 3 10 × 2 in. (25.4 × 5 cm) cake pans or 2 12 × 2 in. (30 × 5 cm) cake pans	12 8 × 2 in. (20.3 × 5 cm) cake pans or 8 10 × 2 in. (25.4 × 5 cm) cake pans or 6 12 × 2 in. (30 × 5 cm) cake pans or 3 full-size sheet pans	**Ingredients**
	1 lb 6 oz (624 g)	5 lb (80 oz or 2.27 kg)	Cake flour
	2 lb (32 oz or 908 g)	6 lb (96 oz or 2.72 kg)	Granulated sugar
	2 Tbsp (24 g)	3 oz (85 g)	Baking powder
	1 tsp (5 g)	1 Tbsp (15 g)	Salt
	1 lb (454 g)	3 lb (48 oz or 1.36 kg)	Unsalted butter, very soft
	8 oz (240 ml or 227 g)	24 oz (710 ml or 680.4 g)	Whole milk
	16 oz (473 ml or 454 g)	48 oz (1.4 L or 1361 g)	Buttermilk
	2 tsp (10 ml or 2 g)	2 oz (60 ml or 57 g)	Vanilla extract
	20 oz (591 ml or 567 g)	60 oz (1.8 L oz or 1.71 kg)	Whole eggs (shelled)
	As needed	As needed	Vegetable spray

Multiply the 20-qt yield 3 or 4 times for a 60-qt mixer.

BAKING TIMES: 45 to 50 minutes for 8-in. (20.3 cm) cake pans
60 to 70 minutes for 10-in. (25.4 cm) cake pans
70 to 80 minutes for 12-in. (30 cm) cake pans

TEMPERATURE: 325°F (163°C)

- Preheat the oven to 325°F (163°C). Spray vegetable spray on the cake pans and line them with parchment paper.

- Measure the flour, sugar, baking powder, and salt into mixer bowl. Attach the paddle to the mixer and mix for 3 minutes to fully sieve and incorporate the dry ingredients.

- Add the butter and mix on low speed for 2 minutes. Then mix on the next highest speed for 3 minutes to fully incorporate the butter.

- Return to low speed and add the whole milk. Mix until incorporated, about 2 minutes, and then mix on the next highest speed for 1 minute.

- Whisk the buttermilk, vanilla, and whole eggs together in a separate large bowl. Return the mixer to low speed and add the buttermilk mixture in 4 stages. Mix on the next highest speed for 1 minute.

- Fill the cake pans about ⅔ full. Hit the pans against the counter to burst any air bubbles and clean the sides. Smooth the top of the batter with a small offset metal spatula.

- See table for baking times or bake until a toothpick inserted in the center comes out clean and the cake slightly shrinks from the sides of the cake pan.

- Let the cakes completely cool in the pans.

This great cake is delicious no matter what the design; however, it is a great complement with simplistic pipe work and beautiful chocolate roses

Applesauce Fruitcake with Lacing Sauce

5 OR 6-QT MIXER

YIELD: 10 × 4 in. (25.4 × 10.2 cm)
or 12 × 3 in. (30 × 7.6 cm) cake

	Ingredients
16 oz (454 g)	Pitted dates
8 oz (228 g)	Pitted prunes
8 oz (228 g)	Raisins
4 oz (114 g)	Maraschino cherries, halved
12 oz (340 g)	Pecans
12 oz (340 g)	Shelled walnuts
12 oz (340 g)	All-purpose flour
2 tsp (8 g)	Baking soda
1 tsp (3.5 g)	Baking powder
½ tsp (1 g)	Ground cloves
½ tsp (1 g)	Ground nutmeg
1 tsp (1.5 g)	Ground cinnamon
½ tsp (2.5 g)	Salt
4 oz (114 g)	Unsalted butter, room temperature
4 oz (114 g)	Light brown sugar
4 oz (114 g)	Granulated sugar
1 Tbsp (15 ml or 14 g)	Vanilla extract
2	Eggs
4 fl oz (118 ml or 114 g)	White grape juice
16 oz (454 g)	Applesauce
4 fl oz (118 ml or 114 g)	White rum or brandy
1 recipe	Lacing Sauce (page 279)
As needed	Oil or vegetable spray

A fruitcake would be the fitting choice for this cake, which is covered in marzipan and iced with royal icing. The precision piping and purity of the whiteness lends itself to a formal event.

- Preheat the oven to 275°F (135°C).

- Cut up the fruit and coarsely chop the nuts. Mix fruit and nuts together in a very large bowl.

- Sift the flour, baking soda, baking powder, spices, and salt together in a separate bowl. Set aside.

- Cream the butter and sugars together for 2 minutes. Add the vanilla. Add the eggs one at a time to the creamed mixture.

- Add the dry ingredients and grape juice until blended. Mix in the fruit and nut mixture and the applesauce. Stir in the rum or brandy.

- Lightly spray heavy brown paper with oil or vegetable spray and line the bottom and sides of the cake pan with it. Extend the paper along the sides of the pan so it is 2 to 3 in. (5 to 7.6 cm) higher than the height of the pan.

- Pour the batter into the pan and work it evenly into the corners. Raise the pan and let it drop to the countertop several times to burst any air bubbles. Level the top of the batter with an offset metal spatula.

- Bake for 3 to 3½ hours or until a toothpick inserted in the center comes out clean. Remove the cake from the pan, but leave it in the brown paper wrapping until ready to ice. When ready to ice, remove the cake from the paper wrapping.

- While still warm, puncture holes in the fruitcake with a skewer and pour 2 oz (60 ml or 57 g) of the lacing sauce over the fruitcake. Double-wrap the cake carefully with plastic wrap and store in a cool, dry place.

- Don't refrigerate! The cake is meant to age. After 1 week, carefully unwrap the cake and soak it with another 2 oz (60 ml or 57 g) of the lacing sauce. Double-wrap again. Repeat this process every week until all of the lacing sauce is used. This could take 6 to 8 weeks. After the last lacing, let the cake rest for another week or two. Then the cake can be completed.

- This cake can be decorated with marzipan and several coats of royal icing or a layer of rolled fondant.

Note: The longer the fruitcake rests, the better it tastes!

Lacing Sauce

YIELD: 16 to 18 fl oz (473 to 532 ml)	Ingredients
2 fl oz (59 ml or 57 g)	Maraschino cherry juice
4 fl oz (120 ml or 114 g)	White grape juice
4 fl oz (120 ml or 114 g)	Pineapple juice
1 tsp (5 ml or 1 g)	Vanilla extract
8 fl oz (236.58 ml or 228 g)	Light rum or brandy

- Mix all the ingredients together. The sauce is ready to use.

- Store the sauce in an airtight container and refrigerate for up to 2 months.

Chocolate Fudge Cake

5 OR 6-QT MIXER	20-QT MIXER	Ingredients
YIELD: 2 8-in. (20.3 cm) cake layers	12 8-in. (20.3 cm) cake layers	
10 oz (283 g)	3.75 lb (60 oz or 1.69 kg)	All-purpose flour
10 oz (283 g)	3.75 lb (60 oz or 1.69 kg)	Granulated sugar
6 oz (170 g)	2.25 lb (36 oz or 1.12 kg)	Dark brown sugar
3 oz (85 g)	18 oz (510 g)	Dutch-processed cocoa powder
2¼ tsp (9 g)	4.5 Tbsp (54 g)	Baking soda
1½ tsp (7.5 g)	3 Tbsp (45 g)	Salt
18 fl oz (532 ml or 510 g)	3.375 qt (108 fl oz or 3.24 L)	Buttermilk
8 oz (228 g)	3 lb (48 oz or 1.36 kg)	Unsalted butter, softened
2 large	12 large	Eggs
1½ tsp (7.5 ml or 3 g)	3 Tbsp (45 ml or 71 g)	Vanilla extract
6 oz (170 g)	2.25 lb (36 oz or 1021 g)	Semisweet or bittersweet fine dark chocolate, melted
As needed	As needed	Vegetable spray

BAKING TIME: 45 to 50 minutes   **TEMPERATURE: 350°F (176.68°C)**

- Heat the oven to 350°F (176.68°C). Vegetable spray and parchment line the cake pans.

- Measure all ingredients except the chocolate into a large mixer bowl. Blend for 30 seconds on low speed, scraping constantly.

- Add the melted chocolate to the bowl and beat 2 minutes on medium speed. Beat on high speed for another 2 minutes, scraping the bowl. Lumps may appear in the batter due to the temperature of the butter. This is fine.

- Pour the batter into the prepared pans and level it with an offset metal spatula.

- Bake according to the baking chart or until a toothpick inserted comes out clean. Cool the cake in the pans before turning out onto wire racks.

This creamy and delightful cake accentuates and best illustrates the lush and lavish chocolate elements of this design.

Cherry/Cranberry Pound Cake

	5 OR 6-QT MIXER	20-QT MIXER	
YIELD:	1 10 × 3 in. (25.4 × 7.6 cm) cake pan or 2 9 × 2 in. (22.9 × 5.1 cm) round cake pans	6 10 × 3 in. (25.4 × 7.6 cm) cake pans or 12 9 × 2 in. (22.9 × 5.1 cm) round cake pans	Ingredients
	1 lb (454 g)	6 lb (2.72 kg)	Cake flour
	1 lb (454 g)	6 lb (2.72 kg)	Granulated sugar
	1½ Tbsp (18 g)	9 Tbsp (108 g)	Baking powder
	1 tsp (5 g)	2 Tbsp (30 g)	Salt
	8 oz (228 g)	3 lb (48 oz or 1.36 kg)	Unsalted butter, softened
	8 oz (228 g)	3 lb (48 oz or 1.36 kg)	Cream cheese, softened
	8 oz (238.56 ml or 228 g)	48 oz (1.44 L)	Eggs (shelled)
	6 oz (177.4 ml or 170 g)	36 oz (1.08 L)	Buttermilk
	2 oz (57 g)	12 oz (354.88 ml)	Whole milk
	1½ tsp (7.5 ml or 3 g)	4.5 Tbsp (67.5 ml or 64 g)	Almond extract
	1½ tsp (7.5 ml or 3 g)	4.5 Tbsp (67.5 ml or 64 g)	Vanilla extract
	4 oz (114 g)	24 oz (680 g)	Dried cranberries
	4 oz (114 g)	24 oz (680 g)	Drained maraschino cherries, chopped
	As needed	As needed	Vegetable spray

Note: Recipe may be tripled for 60-qt mixer.

BAKING TIME: 80 to 85 minutes for 10 × 3 in. (25.4 × 7.6 cm) cake pans 60 minutes for 9 × 2 in. (22.9 × 5.1 cm) cake pans

TEMPERATURE: 350°F (176.68°C)

- Preheat the oven to 350°F (176.68°C). Vegetable spray and parchment line the cake pans.

- Mix the flour, sugar, baking powder, and salt in large bowl. Mix for 2 minutes on stir speed with the paddle attachment to sieve the ingredients.

- Add the butter and cream cheese and beat on low speed for 1 minute. Beat for 2 minutes on medium-high speed. Stop and scrape the bowl. Beat for an additional 60 seconds.

- Whisk the eggs, buttermilk, whole milk, and almond and vanilla extracts together. Add to the batter in 3 stages on low speed, then increase to medium speed for 3 minutes. Stop, scrape the bowl, and then beat for 60 seconds longer.

- Mix in the chopped fruit on low speed for 60 seconds.

- Pour the batter into the prepared pans and bake according to the time chart or until a toothpick inserted into the center comes out clean.

- Cool the cakes in the pans and then turn out onto a baking rack.

This rich and delicious pound cake is the perfect complement to a formal design such as this with exquisite piping and hand-shaped floral details.

Carrot Cake

5 OR 6-QT MIXER	20-QT MIXER	Ingredients
YIELD: 1 10 × 3 in. (25.4 × 7.6 cm) or 2 9 × 2 in. (22.9 × 5.1 cm) round cake pans	6 10 × 3 in. (25.4 × 7.6 cm) or 12 9 × 2 in. (22.9 × 5.1 cm) round cake pans	
9 oz (255 g)	3.375 lb (54 oz or 1530 g or 1.51 kg)	All-purpose flour
16 oz (454 g)	6 lb (2.72 kg)	Granulated sugar
2 tsp (8 g)	4 Tbsp (48 g)	Baking soda
2 tsp (10 g)	4 Tbsp (60 g)	Salt
2 tsp (3 g)	4 Tbsp (20 g)	Cinnamon
12 fl oz (354.88 ml or 340 g)	72 fl oz (2.16 L or 2041 g)	Vegetable, corn, or canola oil
4 large (about 270 ml or 7 oz or 199 g)	24 large (about 42 oz or 1.26 L)	Eggs (shelled)
10 oz (283 g)	3.75 lb (60 oz or 1.70 kg)	Grated carrots
5 oz (140 g)	30 oz (851 g)	Raisins
4 oz (114 g)	24 oz (680.4 g)	Chopped pecans
As needed	As needed	Vegetable spray

BAKING TIME: 90 minutes for 10 × 3 in. (25.4 × 7.6 cm) cake pans
55 to 60 minutes for 9 × 2 in. (22.9 × 5.1 cm) cake pans

TEMPERATURE: 350°F (176.68°C)

- Preheat the oven to 350°F (176.68°C). Vegetable spray and parchment line the cake pans.

- Mix together the flour, sugar, baking soda, salt, and cinnamon for 2 minutes with the paddle attachment to sieve the ingredients.

- Add the oil and mix for 1 minute on low speed. Beat for 2 minutes on medium speed. Stop and scrape the bowl. Beat for 60 seconds longer.

- Whisk the eggs thoroughly and add to the batter in two parts. Beat on medium-high speed for 3 minutes or until the batter turns light and golden. Stop and scrape the bowl. Beat for 60 seconds longer.

- Fold in the carrots, raisins, and pecans.

- Pour the batter into the prepared pans and bake according to the time chart or until a toothpick inserted in the center comes out clean. Cool the cakes in the pans for 15 to 20 minutes before turning them out onto a cooling rack.

A carrot cake complements the design elements of this cake perfectly.

Almond/Walnut Pound Cake

	5 OR 6-QT MIXER	20-QT MIXER	Ingredients
YIELD:	2 10 × 2 in. (25.4 × 5.1 cm) cake pans or 3 9 × 2 in. (22.9 × 5.1 cm) cake pans or 4 8 × 2 in. (20.3 × 5.1 cm) cake pans	5 12 × 3 in. (30 cm × 7.6 cm) cake pans or 10 10 × 2 in. (25.4 × 5.1 cm) cake pans or 13 9 × 2 in. (22.9 × 5.1 cm) cake pans or 18 8 × 2 in. (20.3 × 5.1 cm) cake pans	
	1 lb (16 oz or 454 g)	5 lb (80 oz or 2.27 kg)	Cake flour
	1 lb (16 oz or 454 g)	5 lb (80 oz or 2.27 kg)	Granulated sugar
	1 tsp (5 g)	5 tsp (25 g)	Salt
	1½ Tbsp (18 g)	7½ Tbsp (90 g)	Baking powder
	10 oz (283 g)	3.125 lb (50 oz or 1.40 kg)	Unsalted butter, softened
	6 oz (170 g)	30 oz (851 g)	Almond paste
	2 oz (59 ml or 57 g)	10 fl oz (295.73 ml or 284 g)	Whole milk
	8 oz (240 ml or 228 g)	2.5 lb (1.2 L or 40 oz)	Eggs (shelled)
	8 oz (240 ml or 228 g)	2.5 lb (1.2 L or 40 oz)	Buttermilk
	2 tsp (10 ml or 4 g)	3⅓ Tbsp (50 ml or 94 g)	Almond extract
	6 oz (170 g)	30 oz (851 g)	Chopped walnuts
	As needed	As needed	Vegetable spray

BAKING TIME: 95 to 100 minutes for 12-in. (30 cm) cake pan   TEMPERATURE: 350°F (176.68°C)
                      60 to 65 minutes for 10-in. (25.4 cm) cake pans
                      55 to 60 minutes for 9-in. (22.9 cm) cake pans
                      45 to 50 minutes for 8-in. (20.3 cm) cake pans

- Preheat the oven to 350°F (176.68°C). Vegetable spray and parchment line the cake pans.

- Mix together the flour, sugar, baking powder, and salt with the paddle attachment for 3 minutes on stir speed.

- Add the butter, almond paste, and whole milk. Beat on low speed for 2 minutes and then on medium speed for another 3 minutes.

- Whisk together the eggs, buttermilk, and almond extract. Add to the batter in 3 stages on low speed. Beat on medium-high speed for 2 minutes. Fold in the walnuts.

- Pour the batter into the prepared cake pans. Bake according to the chart or until a toothpick inserted in the center comes out clean. Cool cake layers in pan.

This pound cake would be an excellent complement to a stately and formal design.

Lemon Coconut Cake

5 OR 6-QT MIXER	20-QT MIXER	Ingredients
YIELD: 2 8-in. (20.3 cm) round cake pans or 1 10 × 3 in. (25.4 × 7.6 cm) round cake pan	10 8-in. (20.3 cm) round cake pans or 5 10 × 3 in. (25.4 × 7.6 cm) round cake pans	
8 oz (228 g)	2.5 lb (40 oz or 1.13 kg)	Unsalted butter, softened
1 lb (16 oz or 454 g)	5 lb (80 oz or 2.27 kg)	Granulated sugar
2.7 oz (77 g)	13.5 oz (383 g)	Lemon curd
2 Tbsp (30 ml or 28.35 g)	5 fl oz (148 ml or 142 g)	Fresh lemon juice
Zest of 3	Zest of 15	Lemons
12 oz (240 g)	3.75 lb (60 oz or 1.70 kg)	Cake flour
1 Tbsp (12 g)	5 Tbsp (60 g)	Baking powder
½ tsp (2.5 g)	2½ tsp (12.5 g)	Salt
8 oz (228 g)	2½ lb (40 oz or 1.13 kg)	Shredded coconut
5 large	25 large (about 1.3L or 43.75 oz)	Eggs (shelled)
8 fl oz (236.58 ml or 227 g)	2.5 lb (1.2 L or 40 oz)	Whole milk
2 tsp (10 ml or 4 g)	3⅓ Tbsp (50 ml or 94 g)	Vanilla extract
As needed	As needed	Vegetable spray

BAKING TIME: 40 to 45 minutes for 8-in. (20.3 cm) cake pans
60 to 70 minutes for 10-in. (25.4 cm) cake pans
55 to 60 minutes for 9-in. (22.9 cm) cake pans
45 to 50 minutes for 8-in. (20.3 cm) cake pans

TEMPERATURE: 350°F (176.68°C)

- Preheat the oven to 350°F (176.68°C). Vegetable spray and parchment line the cake pans.

- Cream together the butter, sugar, lemon curd, lemon juice, and zest for 5 minutes. Stop and scrape the bowl. Cream the mixture for an additional 60 seconds.

- Sift together the flour, baking powder, and salt. Stir in the shredded coconut. Set aside.

- In a separate bowl, whisk together the eggs, milk, and vanilla extract.

- Alternately, add the flour and the milk mixtures to the creamed butter mixture in 3 stages. Mix until the batter is smooth.

- Pour the batter into the prepared pans and bake according to the chart or until a toothpick inserted into the center comes out clean. Cool inside cake pan.

This textured cake in blue and white would beautifully accentuate this light, delicious, and fruity lemon coconut cake.

Spackle Paste

YIELD:	29 oz or 822 g	Ingredients
	20 oz (567 g)	Cake crumbs
	4 oz (114 g)	Citrus curd or preserves
	12 to 14 oz (340 to 397 g)	Decorator's Buttercream Icing (page 260), Swiss Meringue Buttercream (page 262), Italian Meringue Buttercream (page 265), or French Vanilla Buttercream (page 261)

Note: This recipe may be doubled or tripled.

- Mix the cake crumbs and citrus curd or preserves and 6 oz (170 g) of the icing together to form a thick paste. If the spackle paste is too stiff to ice with, add more buttercream to soften the paste. The paste should not be too soft, however. It should look like bread stuffing.

- Place 8 to 10 oz (228 to 283 g) of the paste on a medium-size round or square cake board and about 6 oz (170 g) buttercream icing to the side of the paste. Use the buttercream to adjust the thickness of the paste, or use water to help smooth the paste onto the cake.

Lemon, Lime, Or Orange Curd

YIELD:	40.5 oz (2.53 lb or 1.14 kg)	Ingredients
	8 large	Eggs
	2 large	Egg yolks
	1½ lb (680 g or 0.68 kg)	Granulated sugar
	Zest of 10	Lemons, limes, or medium-size oranges
	12 fl oz (355 ml or 340 g)	Fresh lemon, lime, or orange juice
	12 oz (340 g)	Unsalted butter, cut into ½-in. (1.3 cm) pieces

Note: This recipe can be doubled or tripled.

- In a stainless-steel bowl, beat the eggs, egg yolks, and sugar together until well combined. Add the zest, juice, and butter.

- Cook over simmering water in a double boiler, stirring constantly, until the curd thickens, about 20 minutes. The curd is ready when it coats the back of the spoon. Strain the curd using a chinoise or china hat into a metal bowl. Cool curd in a metal bowl over an ice bath.

- Store the curd in a plastic container with plastic wrap placed directly on the surface to prevent a skin from forming. Cover the container with a tight-fitting lid. Refrigerate until ready to use. The curd lasts up to 2 weeks in the refrigerator and up to 2 months in the freezer.

Note: Commercial orange juice may be used instead of freshly squeezed juice.

Pineapple Curd

YIELD: 39 oz (2.7 lb or 1.22 kg)	Ingredients
8 large	Eggs
2 large	Egg yolks
1½ lb (680 g or 0.68 k)	Granulated sugar
10 fl oz (296 ml or 283 g)	Unsweetened pineapple juice
4 oz (114 g)	Chopped pineapple, fresh or canned
2 fl oz (59 ml or 57 g)	Fresh lemon juice
12 oz (340 g)	Unsalted butter, cut into ½-in. (1.3 cm) pieces

Note: This recipe may be double or tripled.

- Beat the eggs, egg yolks, and sugar together in a large bowl until well combined. Add the pineapple juice, chopped pineapple, lemon juice, and butter.

- Cook in a double boiler over simmering water, stirring constantly, until the curd thickens, 15 to 20 minutes. The curd is ready when it coats the back of the spoon or has a pudding consistency.

- Strain immediately using a chinoise or china hat in a metal bowl. Cool curd in metal bowl over an ice bath. Store in a plastic container with lid and plastic wrap placed directly on the surface of the curd to prevent a skin from forming. Refrigerate until ready to use. The curd lasts up to 2 weeks in the refrigerator and up to 2 months in the freezer.

Sieved Apricot Jam

YIELD: 10 oz (283 g)	Ingredients
8 oz (224 g)	Apricot preserves
4 fl oz (120 ml or 113 g)	Cold water

Note: This recipe may be doubled or tripled.

- In a saucepan, cook the preserves and water until they begin to simmer.

- Strain the preserve using a chinoise or china hat into a metal bowl and allow the mixture to cool. Place the jam in a jar with a tight-fitting lid. Refrigerate until ready to use. The jam lasts in the refrigerator for 2 months.

Butter Cookies

5 OR 6-QT MIXER	
YIELD: 3½ to 4 dozen cookies	Ingredients
8 oz (228 g)	Unsalted butter
8 oz (230 g)	Granulated sugar
1 large	Egg
1 tsp (5 ml or 2 g)	Vanilla extract
1 tsp (3.5 g)	Baking powder
12 oz (340 g)	All-purpose flour, plus extra for rolling out

- Preheat the oven to 350°F (176.68°C). In a large bowl, cream the butter and sugar with the paddle whip attachment for 2 minutes. Stop and scrape the bowl. Cream the mixture for an additional 60 seconds.

- Beat in the egg and vanilla until the mixture is well combined, 30 to 45 seconds.

- Sift together the baking powder and 12 oz (340 g) flour. Add the flour mixture in three turns—about 4 oz (114 g) at a time to the creamed butter mixture. Mix thoroughly after each addition. Sprinkle the last 4 oz (114 g) flour mixture on the work surface. Knead the dough onto the flour mixture until all of the flour mixture disappears into the dough, but don't overwork it. The dough should be stiff.

- Divide the dough into 2 parts. Wrap half in plastic wrap until ready to use. On a floured surface, divide the unwrapped dough into 2 parts. Roll out 1 part onto the floured surface to ⅛- to ¼-in. thick (3 to 6 mm). Run a large offset metal spatula under the dough to prevent it from sticking. Cut out cookies with cookie cutters, dipping the cutters into flour before each use.

- Carefully place the cookies on an ungreased nonstick cookie sheet or a parchment-lined half-sheet pan. Bake for 6 to 8 minutes or until the edges of the cookies begin to brown lightly. Let the cookies rest on the cookie sheet until ready to use. The cookies do not require refrigeration if stored in a cool, dry place.

Note: Once the cookies are cut out, gather the scraps and knead fresh dough into them. The wrapped dough can be refrigerated for up to 2 weeks or frozen for up to 3 months.

PATTERNS

This generous selection of patterns is designed to reproduce the techniques in this book. Some of the patterns can be enlarged or reduced to fit your own designs.

Nautical Cake Ring Designs for 10-in. (25.4 cm) cake

Nautical Cake Ring Designs for 7-in. (17.8 cm) cake

Bottom Collars for Nautical Cake

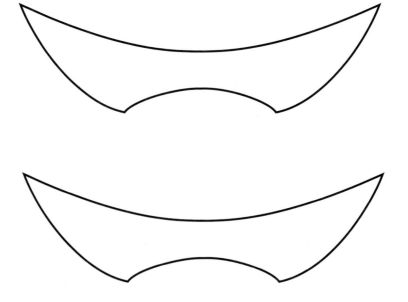

Lace Patterns

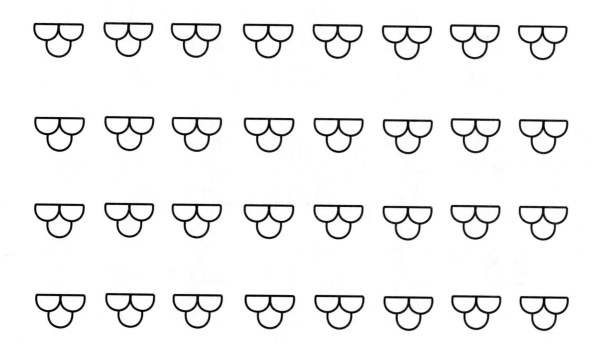

Lace Patterns

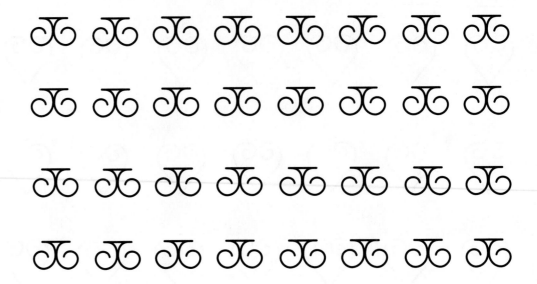

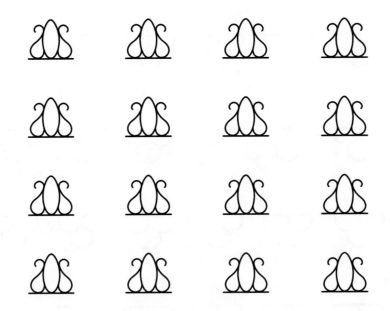

Lace Patterns

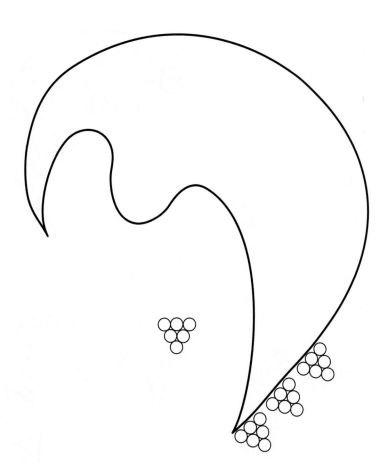

Embroidery Piping

Half-moon Scroll

Cornelli Lace Oval

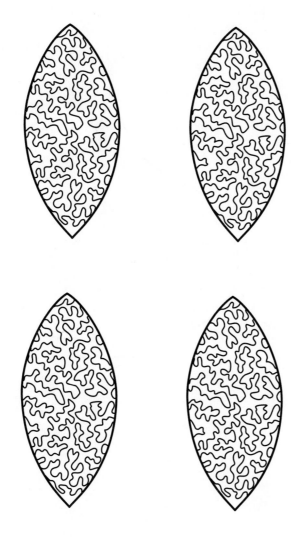

SPADIX

SPATHE

Anthurium Lily

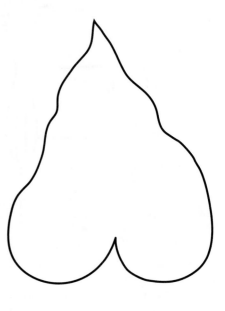

Arum or Calla Lily

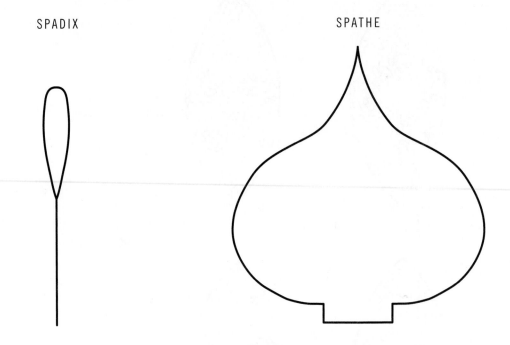

SPADIX

SPATHE

Hibiscus

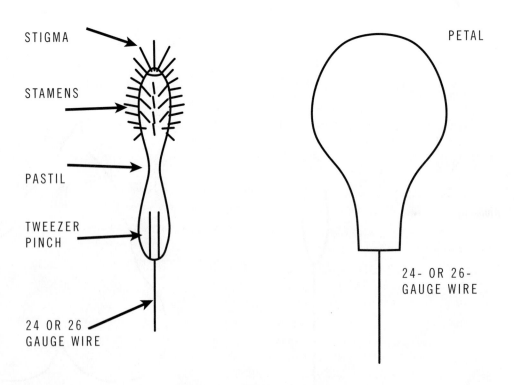

STIGMA

STAMENS

PASTIL

TWEEZER
PINCH

24 OR 26
GAUGE WIRE

PETAL

24- OR 26-
GAUGE WIRE

Tiger Lily

LILY STAMENS

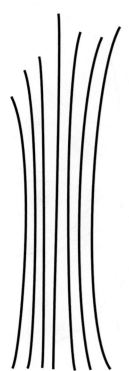

PISTIL

LEAF

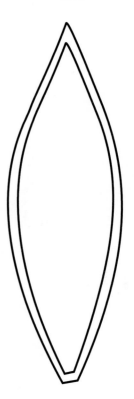

Scalloped Tulip Pattern

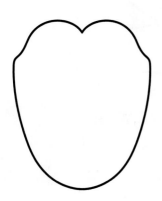

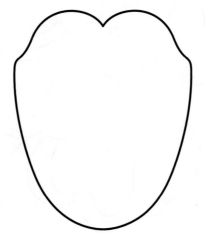

Oval Tulip Pattern

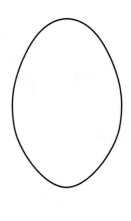

Brush Embroidery Floral Patterns

Brush Embroidery Floral Patterns

Large Pansy Spray (for painting)

Small Pansy Spray (for painting)

Small Leaf Spray (for painting)

Assorted Piped Embroidery Sprays

Barrel of Fruit Panel Pattern

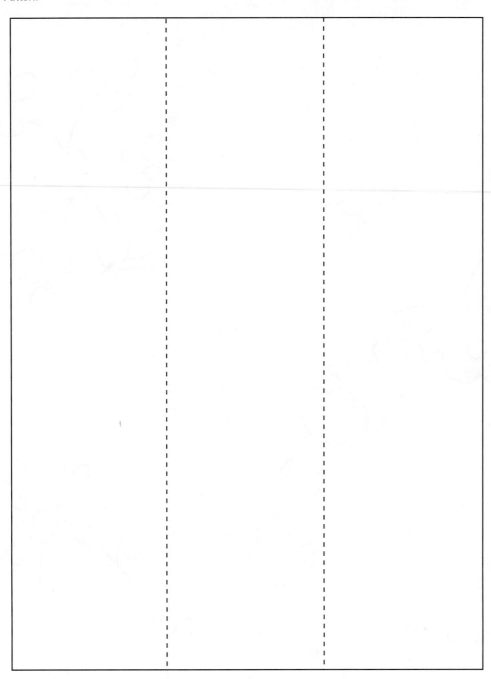

Barrel Lock Pattern

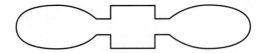

Sailboat Pattern for Nautical Cake

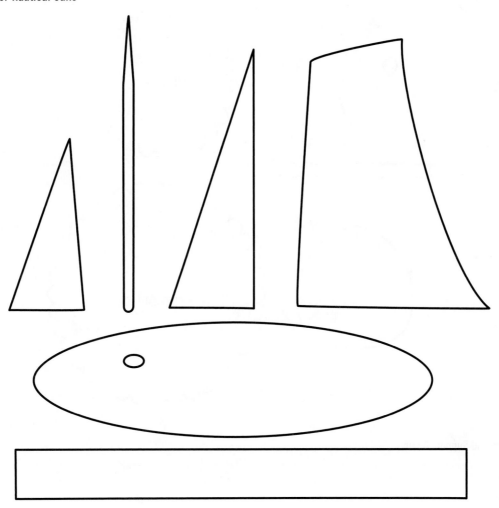

Baby Mouse Patterns

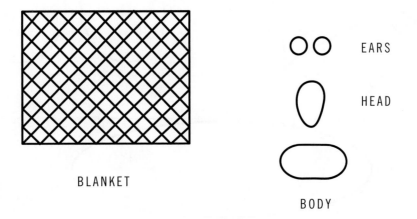

BLANKET

EARS

HEAD

BODY

Party Girl Mouse Patterns

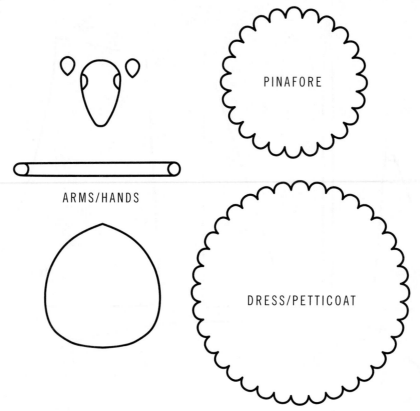

PINAFORE

ARMS/HANDS

DRESS/PETTICOAT

Butterfly Patterns and Support Beam

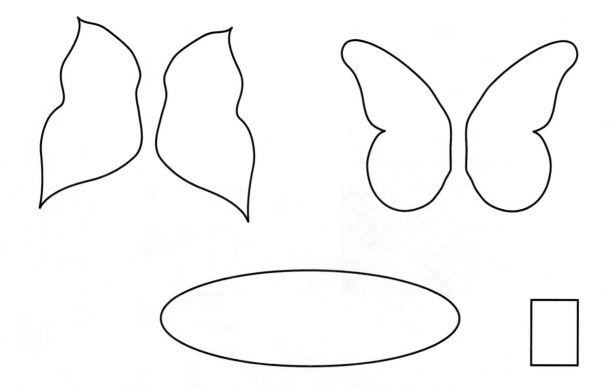

Kiddy Bear Patterns

EARS

SUSPENDERS

BUTTONS

BODY/HANDS
IN POCKET

HEAD/FACE

SHIRT

Bear Chef Patterns

WHITE CIRCLE
BLACK/BROWN NOSE
RED OR BROWN LIPS

PAWS

HAT TOP

WHITE
APRON

WHITE

WHITE

POCKET—ANY COLOR

HAT SIDE

Father Penguin Patterns

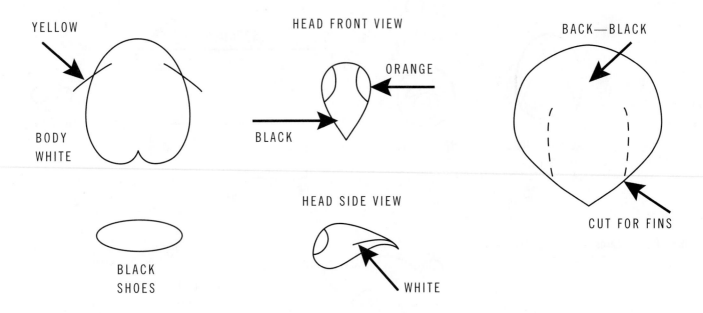

YELLOW

HEAD FRONT VIEW

BACK—BLACK

BODY
WHITE

ORANGE

BLACK

CUT FOR FINS

BLACK
SHOES

HEAD SIDE VIEW

WHITE

Swan Pattern

Pastillage Cart Patterns

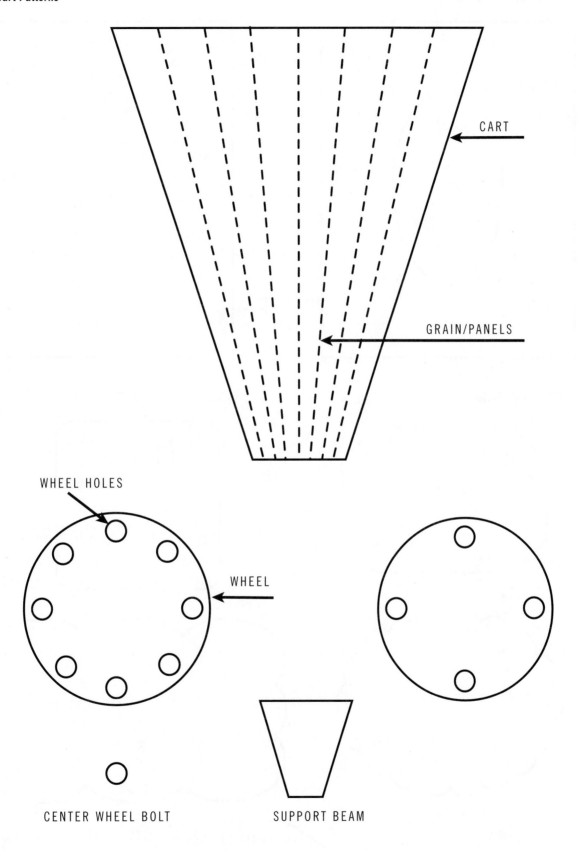

Pastillage Greeting Card Patterns

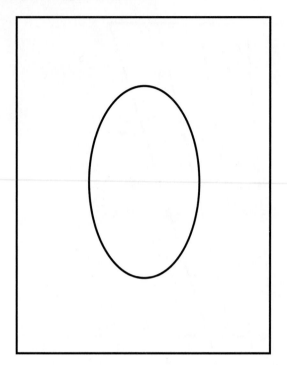

Pastillage Place Card Patterns

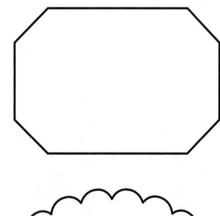

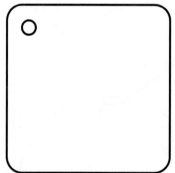

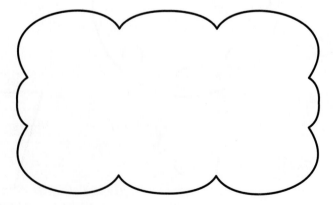

PASTILLAGE
SUPPORT BEAM

6 to 9 in. (15.2 to 22.9 cm) Round Cake Cutting Guide

ROUND CAKE
6-9"

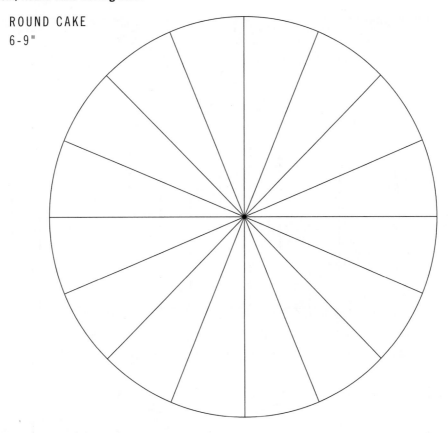

10 to 11 in. (25.4 to 27.9 cm) Round Cake Cutting Guide

ROUND CAKE
10-11"

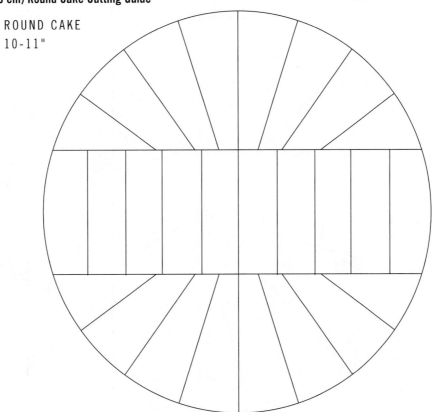

12 to 14 in. (30 to 35.6 cm) Round Cake Cutting Guide

ROUND CAKE
12-14"

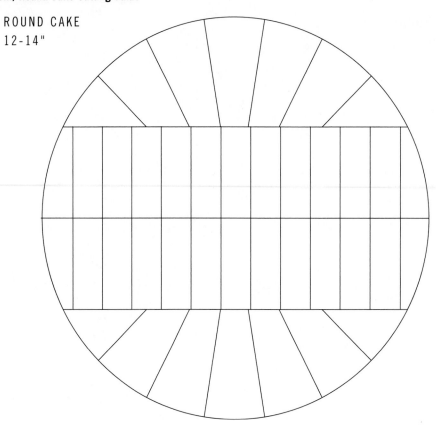

16 to 18 in. (40.6 cm to 45.72 cm) Round Cake Cutting Guide

ROUND CAKE
16-18"

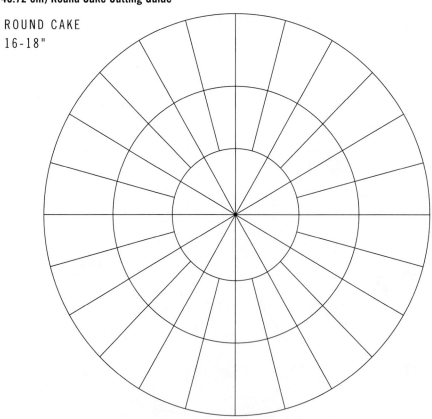

Round Cake / Square Cut Cutting Guide

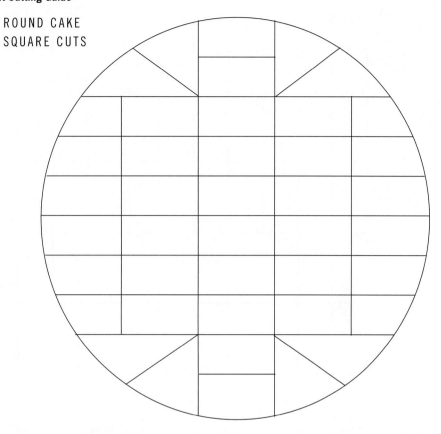

ROUND CAKE
SQUARE CUTS

8 to 10 in. (20.3 to 25.4 cm) Square Cutting Guide

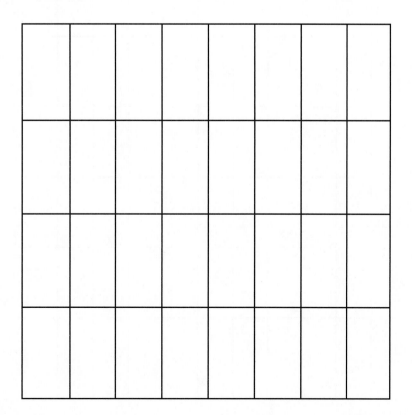

10 to 12 in. (25.4 to 30 cm)
Square Cutting Guide

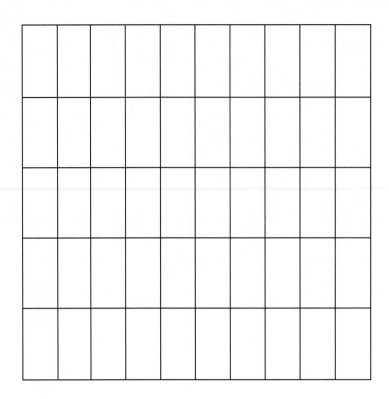

14 to 16 in. (35.6 to 40.6 cm)
Square Cutting Guide

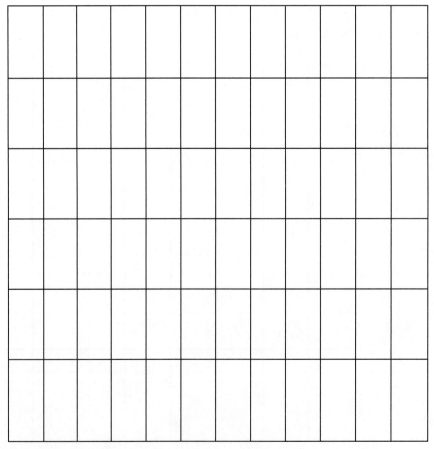

16 to 18 in.
(40.6 to 45.72 cm)
Square Cutting Guide
(98 servings)

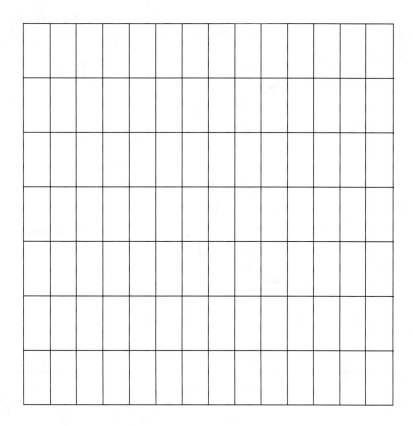

16 to 18 in.
(40.6 to 45.72 cm)
Square Cutting Guide
(96 servings)

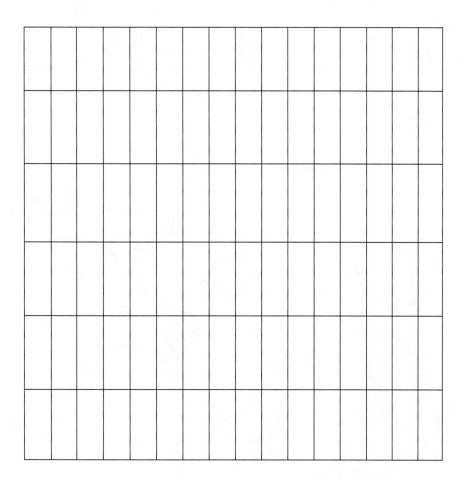

**Monogram Pattern for
Purple Lace Monogram Cake**

Monogram Pattern

**Monogram Pattern
for Extension Work Cake**

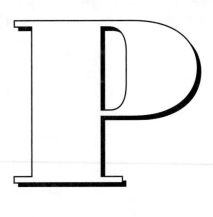

Flooded and Satin-Stitch Pattern

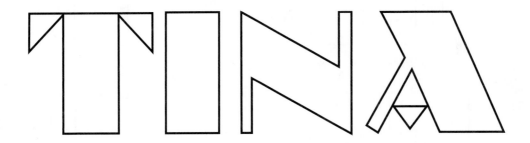

Monogram Flooded and Satin-Stitch Pattern

Rose Pattern

Bow Pattern

Writing Exercise Pattern A

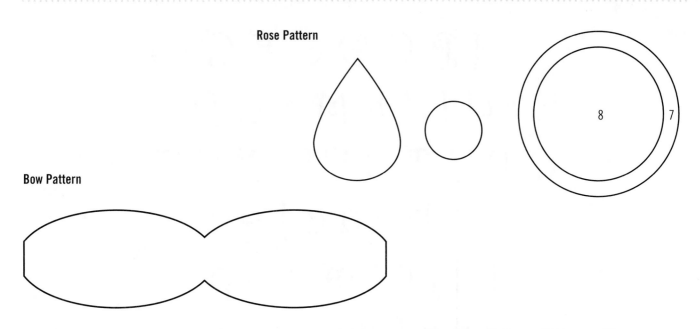

Writing Exercise Pattern B

A B C D E F G
H I J K L M N O P
Q R S T U V W X Y Z
a b c d e f g
h i j k l m n o p
q r s t u v w x y z
1 2 3 4 5 6 7
8 9 0 &

Writing Exercise Pattern C

A B C D E F G
H I J K L M N
O P Q R S T U
V W X Y Z
a b c d e f g h i j k l m
n o p q r s t u v w x y z
1 2 3 4 5 6 7 8 9 0

Writing Exercise Pattern

*A B C D E F
G H I J K L M
N O P Q R S T
U V W X Y Z
1 2 3 4 5 6
7 8 9 0 &*

Writing Exercise Pattern

A B C D E F G H I
J K L M N O P Q
R S T U V W X Y Z
a b c d e f g h i j
k l m n o p q r s
t u v w x y z
1 2 3 4 5 6
7 8 9 0 &

Writing Exercise Pattern

A B C D E F
G H I J K L
M N O P Q
R S T U V
W X Y Z
a b c d e f g h i j k l m
n o p q r s t u v w x y z
1 2 3 4 5 6 7 8
9 0 &

Writing Announcement Patterns

Bon Voyage

BON VOYAGE

Bon Voyage

BON VOYAGE

Bon Voyage

BON VOYAGE

Writing Announcement Patterns

WEDDING

BLISS

Wedding Bliss

HAPPY

BIRTHDAY

Writing Announcement Patterns

Glorious Divorce

Glorious Divorce

Glorious Divorce

GLORIOUS DIVORCE

With Sympathy

Monogram Patterns

HAUTE COUTURE

Haute Couture

SEASON'S

GREETINGS

Season's

Greetings

Monogram Patterns

A B C D E
F G H I J K
L M N O P
Q R S T U
V W X Y Z

Monogram Patterns

a b c d e

f g h i j k

l m n o p

q r s t u

v w x y z

Monogram Patterns

Monogram Patterns

a b c d e

f g h i j k

l m n o p

q r s t u

v w x y z

Monogram Patterns

A B C D E
F G H I J K
L M N O P
Q R S T U
V W X Y Z

Monogram Patterns

a b c d e
f g h i j k
l m n o p
q r s t u
v w x y z

Buttercream Transfer Pattern (Bell in Circle)

Victorian Scalloped Pattern

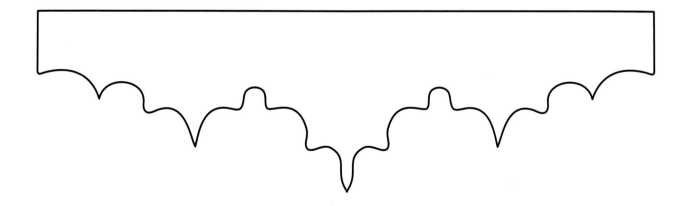

Pastillage Screen Panel Pattern

Panel for Blue and White Cake

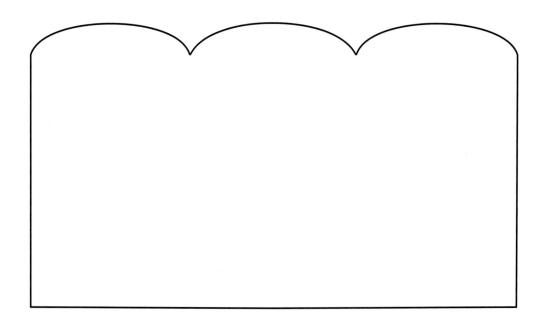

MEASUREMENTS

To achieve predictable outcomes, it is important for the professional cake decorator, pastry chef, or baker to measure ingredients carefully, preferably with an electronic scale or a weight scale. Weighing your ingredients is the most precise method. A less precise method would be to measure your ingredients by volume, using cups and teaspoons.

All the recipe measurements in this book are given in both U.S. standard and metric amounts. In the professional baking world, measurements are generally given in ounces or grams. Some institutions use pints, quarts, and pounds, which can be easily converted to ounces, grams, kilograms, and liters. Use one system consistently to assure accuracy. When converting from U.S. to Metric, rounding numbers up or down can disturb the formulas.

Ingredients

Eggs—In this book, *egg* means large egg. A large egg in the shell weighs about 2 oz (57 g); without the shell, the egg weighs 1¾ oz (50 g).

Flour—All-purpose flour or cake flour should be aerated before measurement, if measuring in volume. Flour weighed in ounces, grams, pounds, and kilograms do not need to be aerated.

10x Confectioner's Sugar— Always weigh and sieve confectioner's sugar before using. This sugar can be weighed in ounces, grams, pounds, and kilograms. Confectioner's sugar is granulated sugar that has been ground into a fine powder. To prevent clumping, a small amount of cornstarch (3 percent) is added. 10x sugar has a 3 percent ratio of cornstarch, however, confectioner's sugar comes in 2x, 4x, 6x, and 8x. In these cases, there is more cornstarch added to the sugar.

Granulated Sugar, Butter, and Vegetable Shortening—These should be weighed in ounces, grams, and kilograms.

Salt and Spices—Measure in volume, using teaspoons, tablespoons, and milliliters. For precise weight, measure in grams or ounces.

Meringue Powder and Cocoa Powder—Measure in teaspoon or tablespoon for volume weight. Measure in grams and ounces for precise weight.

Liquids (milk, water, alcohol, and liqueurs)—Measure in ounces, grams, pints, quarts, gallons, milliliters, or liters.

Corn Syrup, Molasses, Glucose—Measured in volume, ounces, grams, and milliliters. To convert from fluid ounces to ounces, multiply by 1.5.

Inches to Centimeters

Use this chart when measuring the length and width of cake designs or when measuring cake pans or finished cake boards.

To convert inches to centimeters, multiply by 2.54. To convert centimeters to inches, multiply by 0.39.

INCHES	CENTIMETERS (CM)	INCHES	CENTIMETERS (CM)
⅛	3 (mm)	1½	3.81
¼	6 (mm)	1¾	4.45
⅜	1	2	5.08
½	1.3	2¼	5.72
⅝	1.6	2½	6.35
¾	1.9	2¾	7.00
⅞	2.2	3	7.62
1	2.54	3¼	8.26
1¼	3.18	3½	9.00

INCHES	CENTIMETERS (CM)
3¾	9.53
4	10.16
4½	11.43
5	12.70
5½	14.00
6	15.24
6½	16.51
7	17.78
7½	19.05
8	20.32
8½	21.59
9	22.86
9½	24.13
10	25.40

INCHES	CENTIMETERS (CM)
11	28.00
12	30.48
13	33.02
14	35.56
15	38.10
16	40.64
17	43.18
18	46.00
19	48.26
20	50.80
22	56.00
24	61.00
26	66.04

Ounces to Grams

Use this chart when measuring solid masses like sugar, butter, and shortening. To convert ounces to grams, multiply by 28.35. To convert grams to ounces, divide by 28.35.

OUNCES	GRAMS (G)
¼	7
½	14
¾	21
1	28.35
1¼	35.4
1½	42.5
1¾	50
2	57
2¼	64
2½	71
2¾	78
3	85
3½	99
4	114
4½	128
5	140
5½	156
6	170

OUNCES	GRAMS (G)
7	198
8 or ½ lb	228
9	255
10	283
11	312
12	340
13	367
14	397
15	425
16 or 1 lb	454
18	510
20	567
22	624
24	680
26	737
30	851
32 or 2 lbs	907

Pounds to Kilograms

Use this scale for larger weight masses. To convert pounds to kilograms, multiply by 0.454. To convert kilograms to pounds, divide by 0.454.

POUNDS (LBS)	KILOGRAMS (KG)	POUNDS (LBS)	KILOGRAMS (KG)
½	0.23	9	4.08
1	0.45	9½	4.31
1½	0.68	10	4.54
2	0.91	12	5.44
2½	1.13	14	6.35
3	1.36	16	7.26
3½	1.59	18	8.16
4	1.81	20	9.07
4½	2.04	22	9.98
5	2.27	24	10.89
5½	2.49	26	11.79
6	2.72	30	13.61
6½	2.95	35	16.10
7	3.18	40	18.14
7½	3.40	45	20.41
8	3.63	50	22.68
8½	3.86		

Teaspoons/Tablespoons to Milliliters—Volume Measurement

Use this scale when converting teaspoons and tablespoons to milliliters. Also use it to convert fluid ounces to milliliters.

To convert ounces to milliliters, multiply by 29.57. To convert milliliters to ounces, divide the number of milliliters by 29.57.

TEASPOONS (TSP)/TABLESPOONS (TBSP)	MILLILITERS (ML)
½ tsp	2.5
1 tsp	5
2 tsp	10
1 Tbsp (3 tsp)	15
2 Tbsp (1 fl oz)	30
4 Tbsp	60
6 Tbsp	90
8 Tbsp (4 fl oz)	120
10 Tbsp	160
16 Tbsp (8 fl oz)	240

FLUID OUNCES (FL OZ)	MILLILITERS (ML)
½	15
1	30
1½	44
2	59
2½	74
3	89
3½	104
4	118 (120)
4½	133
5	148
5½	163
6	177
6½	192
7	207
7½	222
8	237 (240)
8½	251
9	266
10	296

FLUID OUNCES (FL OZ)	MILLILITERS (ML)
12	355
14	414
16	473
18	532
20	591
22	651
24	710
26	769
28	828
30	887
32	946
36	1,065
40	1,183
45	1,346
50	1,479
55	1,627
60	1,789
64	1,893

Fluid Ounces to Liters

Use this table when converting large amounts of fluid ounces to liters. To convert fluid ounces to liters, multiply by 0.03. To convert liters to fluid ounces, divide by 0.03.

FLUID OUNCES (FL OZ)	LITERS (L)
8	0.24
16	0.48
24	0.72
32	0.96
40	1.2
50	1.5
60	1.8
64	1.92
70	2.1

FLUID OUNCES (FL OZ)	LITERS (L)
80	2.4
90	2.7
100	3
125	3.75
140	4.2
160	4.8
175	5.25
200	6
300	9

Quarts to Liters

Use this table when converting quarts to liters. To convert quarts to liters, multiply by 0.946. To convert liters to quarts, divide by 0.946.

QUARTS (QT)	LITERS (L)	QUARTS (QT)	LITERS (L)
1	0.946	9	8.51
1½	1.41	10	9.46
2	1.82	15	14.1
2½	2.36	20	18.9
3	2.83	30	28.3
3½	3.31	40	37.8
4	3.78	50	47.3
5	4.73	60	56.7
6	5.67	80	75.6
7	6.62	100	94.6
8	7.56	120	113.5

Gallons to Liters

Use this table when converting gallons to liters. To convert gallons to liters, multiply by 3.79. To convert liters to gallons, divide by 3.79.

GALLONS (GAL)	LITERS (L)	GALLONS (GAL)	LITERS (L)
1	3.79	15	56.7
1½	5.68	20	75.8
2	7.5	30	113.7
2½	9.46	40	151.6
3	11.3	50	189.5
4	15.1	75	284
5	18.9	100	379
10	37.8		

Measurement Equivalency

8 oz	=	½ pt
16 oz	=	1 pt
24 oz	=	1½ pt
32 oz	=	1 qt
64 oz	=	2 qt
4 qt	=	1 gal or 8 pt
1 gal	=	4 qt, 8 pt, or 128 fl oz

Ounces/Volume to Weight

Use this table when measuring corn syrup, molasses, glucose, and other heavy liquids. Multiply the number of ounces by 1.5 to convert volume measurement into weight measurement.

OUNCES/ VOLUME	WEIGHT (CONVERTED)	OUNCES/ VOLUME	WEIGHT (CONVERTED)
1	1.5	13	19.5
2	3	14	21
3	4.5	15	22.5
4	6	16	24
5	7.5	20	30
6	9	24	36
7	10.5	30	45
8	12	32	48
9	13.5	40	50
10	15	48	72
11	16.5	60	90
12	18		

Temperature

To convert Fahrenheit to Celsius, subtract 32 and multiply by 0.5556. To convert Celsius to Fahrenheit, multiply by 1.8 and then add 32.

FAHRENHEIT	CELSIUS
125	51.67
150	65.56
175	79.45
200	93.34
225	107.23
250	121.12
275	135
300	148.90

FAHRENHEIT	CELSIUS
325	162.79
350	176.68
375	190.57
400	204.46
425	218.35
450	232.24
475	246.13
500	260.02

Commonly Used Products in Gram Weight

ITEM	GRAMS/TEASPOON	GRAMS/TABLESPOON
baking powder	3.5	12
baking soda	4	12
ground cinnamon	1.5	5
cocoa powder	2.5	8
cornstarch	2.5	8
cream of tartar	2	6
granulated sugar	5	15
ground spices (except cinnamon)	2	6
powdered gelatin	3	9
powdered sugar	3	9
salt	5	15

Bibliography

Beginners Guide to Cake Decorating (Merehurst), 2003, UK.

Charsley, Simon R., *Wedding Cakes and Cultural History* (Routledge), 1992, UK.

Deacon, Carol, *The Complete Step-by-Step Guide to Cake Decorating* (Creative Publishing International), 2003, UK.

The Essential Guide to Cake Decorating (Merehurst), 2003, UK.

Florendo, Avelina Carbungco, *Cake Tops with Philippine Flair* (Manila, Philippines), 1995.

Friberg, Bo, *The Professional Pastry Chef*, fourth edition. (John Wiley & Sons, Inc.), 2006, USA.

Garrett, Toba, *Creative Cookies: Delicious Decorating for Any Occasion* (Sterling), 2001, USA.

———, *The Well-Decorated Cake* (Sterling), 2003, USA.

Holding, Audrey, *The Practice of Royal Icing* (Elsevier Applied Science), 1987, UK.

Lambeth, Joseph A., *Lambeth Method of Cake Decoration and Practical Pastries* (Continental Publications), 1980, USA. Originally published in 1934 by Joseph A. Lambeth.

Lodge, Nicholas, *Sugar Flowers from Around the World* (Merehurst), 1990, UK.

Lodge, Nicholas et al., *The International School of Sugarcraft, Book Two* (Merehurst), 1988, UK.

MacGregor, Elaine, *Cake Decorating: A Step-by-Step Guide to Making Traditional and Fantasy Cakes* (New Burlington Books), 1986, UK.

Maytham, Jill, *Sugar Flowers* (Jem), 1987, South Africa.

Nilsen, Angela, and Sarah Maxwell, *Complete Cake Decorating: Techniques, Basic Recipes, and Beautiful Cake Projects for all Occasions* (Lorenz Books), 2002, UK.

Peck, Tombi, *Decorative Touches* (Murdock Books), 1995, UK.

Peck, Tombi, and Pat Ashley, *The Art of Cake Decorating: Finishing Touches* (First Glance Books), 1986, UK.

Randlesome, Geraldine, *Techniques in Cake Design* (Cupress Ltd.), 1986, Canada.

Vercoe, Bernice J. *Australian Book of Cake Decorating* (P. Hamlyn), 1973, Australia.

Index

for rolling marzipan, 120
Connecting hearts cookies, 230
Cookies:
    Butter, *288*
    connecting hearts, 230
    decorated, 226, 228–231, 254
    Glacé Icing for, *268*
    iced, 226, 228–231
    rolled iced, 230–231
Cornelli lace:
    filigree with, 166
    pattern for, 295
    piping, 92
    purple lace monogram cake, 250
    techniques for, 97–98
    two-tier blue lace chocolate cake,
      248
Cornets, *see* Paper cones
Cornstarch:
    with rolled fondant, 113
    and rolling marzipan, 120
    for ruffling, 177
Corn syrup, measuring, 268, 332
Corsage sprays, 204–205
Covering cake boards, 234–235
Cream Cheese Buttercream, *267*
Crescents, *see* Garlands
Crimping, 239
Crumb-coating cakes, 108
C-shaped ropes, 19, 20
Curd:
    Lemon, Lime, or Orange, *286*
    Pineapple, *287*
Curved lines, piping, 11
Curved shells with shell accents,
  39–40
Cushion lattice, 161, 172–173
Cutting guides:
    for round cakes, 309–311
    for square cakes, 311–313
Cymbidium orchids, 218, 221–223

D

Daisies, piping, 81, 85
Damming cakes, 106–107
Decorated cookies, 226, 228–231,
  254
Decorator's Buttercream Icing, 26,
  260
    coloring, 37
    for roses, 26
Demi-sec, 226

Design transfer, 90, 93–95
    bell in circle pattern, 329
    blue and white cake panel, 330
    buttercream/gel transfer method,
      90, 94–95
    carbon copy method, 90, 94
    pastillage screen panel pattern,
      330
    pinprick method, 90, 93
    Victorian scalloped pattern, 329
Double ruffles, 40
Double strings:
    garlands with drop strings and,
      63–64
Double swags, 41–42
Double webbing (cookies), 229
Doweling cakes, 124–126, 128
Drapery:
    classical, 177–178
    classical, cake with floral spray
      and, 251
    freehand, 178–179
Drop strings:
    with fleur-de-lis, 18
    fleur-de-lis with overpiping and,
      65–66
    garlands with double strings and,
      63–64
    ring design with trellis or, 161,
      167–170
    rosettes with, 66–67
Dryness (on iced cake), 116

E

Eggs, 332
Egg White Royal Icing, 48
    pastry bag for, 172
    recipe, *273*
Elegant writings, 75–77
Embossed leaves, 202, 203
Embroidery piping, 90–101
    brush embroidery, 91, 95–96
    cornelli lace, 92, 97–99
    design transfer, 90, 93–95
    eyelet, 92, 99–101
    flooded pattern, 314, 315
    floral spray patterns, 301
    freehand embroidery, 91, 96–97
    lilies-of-the-valley, 97
    patterns for, 294, 314, 315
    satin stitch, 92, 99–100, 314,
      315

H

I

R

Raspberries, marzipan, 137, 138
Red delicious apples, 134, 135
Reverse scallops:
    overpiped, 56–58
    overpiped garland with ruffles
        and, 58–59
    zigzags with large shells and,
        61–62
Reverse shells:
    creating, 16, 17
    with scalloped strings, 60–61
Rings, with trellis or drop string
    work, 161, 167–170
Rolled fondant:
    applying, 113–118
    calculating size of, 117
    carbon copy transfer with, 94
    Chocolate, 272
    commercial, 176
    Modeling Paste, 176, 276
    recipe, 275
    rolling out, 230
    on round cake, 113–116
    ruffles in, 176
    on square cake, 116–118
    sugar plaques made from, 71
Rolled iced cookies, 230–231
Rolled icing, 176
    appliqué, 179, 180
    braiding, 179, 181–182
    classical drapery, 177–178
    freehand drapery, 178–179
    ruffling, 176–177
    smocking, 182–184
Ropes, 20–21
    C-shaped, 19, 20
    half-C, 20–21
    S-shaped, 19, 21
Roses:
    buttercreams for, 26
    chocolate, three-dimensional,
        153–156
    classic, 208–210
    closed, 28–29
    full-blown, 29–32, 155, 208,
        210–211
    gumpaste, 208–211
    half-, 28–29
    modeling chocolate, Swiss dot
        cake with, 243
    Piped, Buttercream Icing for, 26,
        27, 266

piped on candies, 31
Royal Icing piping for, 30
white chocolate, and ribbon
    cake, 244, 245
white chocolate, chocolate basket
    cake with, 248–249
Rosebuds:
    in modeling chocolate, 154
    piped, 27–28
Rosettes:
    creating, 16–17
    with drop strings, 66–67
Round cakes:
    cake boards for, 235
    cutting guides for, 309–311
    rolled fondant on, 113–116
Royal Icing, 48
    coloring, 48
    condensation on, 14
    Egg White, 48, 172, 273
    food colors for, 48
    and Marzipan Cake, 119–123
    Meringue Powder, 48, 52, 172,
        273
Royal Icing piping, 160
    bridge, 160, 162–163
    cushion lattice, 161, 172–173
    embroidery, 90–101
    extension, 160, 162–164
    filigree lace, 160–161, 166–167
    flooding, 160, 162
    for flowers, 80–86
    hailspotting, 162–164
    lattice, 161, 170–171
    pastry bag for, 80
    ring with trellis or drop string
        work, 161, 167–170
    for roses, 30
    runouts, 160, 162
    simple lace, 160, 165
Ruffles:
    double, 40
    overpiped garland with reverse
        scallops and, 58–59
    with overpiped scallops, 53–54
    piped, 40–41
    in rolled fondant, 176
    in rolled icing, 176–177
    single, 64
Runouts, in Royal Icing, 160, 162

S